The Upper Room

# Disciplines
## 2008

UPPER
ROOM BOOKS®
NASHVILLE

# An Outline for Small-Group Use of Disciplines

Here is a simple plan for a one-hour, weekly group meeting based on reading *Disciplines*. One person may act as convener every week, or the role can rotate among group members. You may want to light a white Christ candle each week to signal the beginning of your time together.

## OPENING

Convener: Let us come into the presence of God.
Others: Lord Jesus Christ, thank you for being with us. Let us hear your word to us as we speak to one another.

## SCRIPTURE

Convener reads the scripture suggested for that day in *Disciplines*. After a one- or two-minute silence, convener asks: What did you hear God saying to you in this passage? What response does this call for? (*Group members respond in turn or as led.*)

## REFLECTION

- What scripture passage(s) and meditation(s) from this week was (were) particularly meaningful for you? Why? (*Group members respond in turn or as led.*)
- What actions were you nudged to take in response to the week's meditations? (*Group members respond in turn or as led.*)
- Where were you challenged in your discipleship this week? How did you respond to the challenge? (*Group members respond in turn or as led.*)

## PRAYING TOGETHER

Convener says: Based on today's discussion, what people and situations do you want us to pray for now and in the coming week?
Convener or other volunteer then prays about the concerns named.

## DEPARTING

Convener says: Let us go in peace to serve God and our neighbors in all that we do.

Adapted from *The Upper Room Daily Devotional Guide*, January–February 2001.
© 2000 The Upper Room. Used by permission.

THE UPPER ROOM DISCIPLINES 2008
© 2007 by Upper Room Books®. All rights reserved.

UPPER ROOM®, UPPER ROOM BOOKS® and design logos are trademarks owned by THE
UPPER ROOM®, a ministry of GBOD® Nashville, Tennessee. All rights reserved.

The Upper Room Web site: http://www.upperroom.org

Cover design: Ed Maksimowicz
Cover photo: Jonathan A. Meyers
First Printing: 2007

Lectionary texts from *The Revised Common Lectionary*. Copyright © 1992 The Consul-
tation on Common Texts (CCT), P. O. Box 340003, Room 381, Nashville, TN 37203-
0003 USA. All rights reserved. Reprinted with permission.

Scripture quotations not otherwise identified are from the *New Revised Standard Version
Bible* © 1989, Division of Christian Education of the National Council of the Churches
of Christ in the United States of America. Used by permission. All rights reserved.

Scripture quotations marked CEV are taken from the Contemporary English Version. ©
1995 American Bible Society. Used by permission.

Scripture quotations marked THE MESSAGE by Eugene H. Peterson, Copyright © 1993,
1994, 1995, 1996, 2000. Used by permission of NavPress Publishing Group. All rights
reserved.

Scripture quotations designated RSV are from the *Revised Standard Version Bible*, copyright
1952 (2nd edition, 1971) by the Division of Christian Education of the National Council of the Churches of Christ in the United States of America. Used by permission. All
rights reserved.

Scripture quotations designated NIV are from the HOLY BIBLE, NEW INTER-
NATIONAL VERSION. NIV®. Copyright © 1973, 1978, 1984 by International Bible
Society. Used by permission of Zondervan. All rights reserved.

Scripture quotations marked (NLT) are taken from the Holy Bible, New Living Translation, copyright ©1996. Used by permission of Tyndale House Publishers, Inc. Wheaton,
Illinois 60189. All rights reserved.

Scripture quotations designated KJV are from the King James Version of the Bible.

Scripture quotations designated ASV are from the American Standard Version of the Bible.

Scripture quotations designated AP are the author's paraphrase.

The week of July 21-27 was first published in *Disciplines 1996*.

ISBN: 978-0-8358-9900-0
Printed in the United States of America

# Contents

# Foreword

Many years ago I led a prayer retreat before the beginning of Lent. The participants were sharing their proposed Lenten practices when one woman confessed her difficulty in past years with her commitment to daily biblical reflection. "Every year I decide to read the *Upper Room Disciplines* for Lent," she said. "I begin on Ash Wednesday and continue for many days, sometimes weeks. Then I forget and miss a day or two or three. So I give up my practice and feel once again that I've failed Lent!"

The group members expressed their sympathy, many of them identifying with her dilemma. As we pondered the situation a statement from Father Thomas Keating, Trappist monk and teacher of Centering Prayer, came to mind. He said: "Faithfulness in prayer is the willingness to always start over." When I shared his wisdom, the whole group sighed in relief.

As you begin this year of Bible study, reflection, and prayer, remember this discussion and be gentle and compassionate with yourself. You will begin, and you will forget. You may delight in the Word one week and ignore it the next. At that point, remind yourself that you have not failed and you are not unfaithful. Be grateful that you have recognized what has happened, open the book, and begin again. Rejoice that you have started over.

Decide for yourself the best time of day for your prayer and reflection time. Be attentive to your own schedule and life patterns to find the time best for you.

I like to begin my prayer time by lighting a candle before I open the Bible. This simple act reminds me that I am presenting myself in love and trust for an encounter with the Holy. Then I read the scripture passage out loud. Giving voice to the Word involves more of ourselves in the reading process. Instead of using only our eyes, we include our ears and our vocal cords. Of necessity we slow down and rather than skimming over the words as we might do silently, we find ourselves chewing on and savoring them, allowing them to nurture us.

Reading scripture aloud and alone may be a new experience for you. Most of us, after we learned to read, were encouraged to shift from reading out loud to reading silently, not even moving our lips or following along with our fingers. We were praised for reading quickly and gathering as much information as possible from the words on the page. But reading scripture has a different purpose. Now we do not read for information but for formation. We read to allow the Word of God to form us and reform us as beloved children of God and disciples of Jesus Christ. In the process of spiritual formation, the Word acts *on* us and *in* us as we surrender to the Spirit's movement in our lives.

The meditative thoughts, closing prayers, and suggestions for meditation offered after the Bible passage are gifts from a variety of people who, like you, long to deepen their relationship with God and Christ through scripture. You will connect to some of the ideas more than others. You may be led to an "aha" moment when the reading serves as a light and you see the words you have read in a completely new way. Other times you might be affirmed by knowing that another person understands the passage the same way you do. You will encounter a few meditations that seem to make no sense at all. Whatever your response, see if you can receive each experience as gift.

The mystics tell us that the immediate experience of prayer is not what is important. What matters is that faithful prayer transforms our hearts and our lives. Although you may hope for a deeply moving experience each day, you cannot expect to be touched by every reading and reflection. In fact, some days you may find yourself being distracted or bored or critical of what is written. Other times you might wonder why in the world you are spending your time this way. But if you stay with your commitment, returning to it when you stray, you will discover your life is slowly and gently being healed and transformed by your willingness to spend regular time with your loving God.

—JANE E. VENNARD

# Sing a New Song

*January 1–6, 2008  •  Roland Rink[‡]*

### TUESDAY, JANUARY 1  •  **Read Psalm 8**

Welcome to this first day of 2008! The early morning air seems so vibrantly alive with the possibility and promise of a new day, a new week, a new year, a new beginning. It is yet another opportunity to serve God and all those whom God places in our path this new year.

Certainly this year will be one of change. New presidents, new regimes, new committees formed by gatherings and meetings of Christians around the globe. Profoundly and mysteriously, God will be in every facet of these changes. We as Christians subconsciously breathe a prayer of deep longing: that during 2008 the entire world will at long last set aside differences and join in singing new songs of joy, hope, and peace.

Psalm 8 clearly depicts the fact that God, our loving parent, supports us, has confidence in us, and has entrusted us with the care of this earth. Yes, even now; though we continue to display our inherent weakness, ignorance, sinfulness, and vulnerability to disruptive and persuasive temporal influences, God continues to show confidence in us. "What are human beings that you are mindful of them?"

As we begin this year, can we determine to show more care for all living things, ourselves included? Dare we, in our sinfulness, hope that God will continue to support and sustain us? The good news is that God longs for our total reliance. If God is for us, who can be against us? Truly, our only hope is in the Lord and no other.

**PRAYER: Lord God, in your infinite mercy empower us to sing a new song among all the nations of the earth. May your name be glorified in all we do, think, and say. Amen.**

---

[‡]Coordinator of publishing for The Upper Room on the African continent; living in Johannesburg, South Africa.

A popular poster many years back proclaimed, "Today is the first day of the rest of your life." I suspect that today's reading from Revelation may have inspired those words. As Christians, we commit to remain faithful to Christ. The road of the disciple—a road we choose to travel with Christ as guide, mentor, and friend—is not for the fainthearted. It has been and will continue to be a difficult road. Oftentimes we have stumbled and fallen. How surprising to discover that we are profoundly human!

Despite our best intentions we still seem adept at clinging to destructive old habits, old ways, and old ideas. Yet Christ, with infinite patience and wisdom, continues to pick us up, dust us off, and persevere with us on our personal journey of life on earth. It is God who chooses and furthers this journey, desiring to be in relationship. It is God who tells us that the home of the divine is among mortals, among those of us who still mourn, cry, and suffer; who fall down and get up.

We find it hard to fathom that this God who created the wonders of the universe, the earth and everything in it, is the same one who promises to bring about a radical new heaven and a new earth. What profoundly consoling thoughts and words these are for us at the beginning of a new year! God says, "I am making all things new."

Today, no matter how challenging our circumstances, with God's help, we may seize the new possibilities that lie before us. Now is the time to discover new songs of hope, joy, and peace and bring them to a world that is in such desperate need of that music. God empowers us to achieve our dreams.

**PRAYER: God of the universe, creator of all, look with compassion upon our feeble efforts to serve you. We acknowledge that we have not loved you; we have not listened to your voice; we have ignored your promptings. Have mercy on us, we pray. Set us free from the constraints of sin that threaten to drag us down. Give us open minds, responsive hearts, and courage to follow where you lead us this day. Amen.**

Loving God, I am writing to ask a question that has challenged me ever since I gave my life to Jesus. Can you help me understand why you gave human beings freedom of choice? Would it not have been easier if we were born with no choice but to help, support, and stand in unity with the hungry, the thirsty, the sick, and the needy? The world would be a completely different place.

O God, it is especially difficult to know what to do when confronted with people who have seemingly lost everything—even hope. These people make me feel uncomfortable! I am never sure if what I offer is a help or a hindrance or too little too late. Lord, the poor, the lonely, the disenfranchised, the lost, the needy seem to appear each day of my life. There are so many of them! Why do you continue to send these people to plague my conscience? Are they you in disguise? Somehow it always feels that way.

Father, make me more sensitive and aware of poor people in all kinds of disguises. I think of those who dress in fine clothes and designer labels. They often drive the latest motor vehicles; they eat at the best restaurants. They always seem to be shopping for something. Yet, despite their frenetic activity, they display a deep hunger for you. They unconsciously show every sign of thirsting for your healing word in their lives. They will not find you in the shops and malls that they visit so regularly. Empower me to be relevant in their world of individualism and consumerism. May I sing your song of love to all I meet this day. Thank you for listening, Lord. Someday I know you will provide the answers to all my questions.

**PRAYER: God of all, make us sensitive to the needs, the hungers, and the thirsts of all we meet this day—whatever they may look like. Give us the gift of discernment in our every interaction with people this day. Amen.**

## FRIDAY, JANUARY 4 • **Read Isaiah 60:1-6**

It's the fourth day of the new year. The old cliché "reality bites" once again takes on meaning. The world, it would appear, is still the same as ever. The arrival of the new year has seemingly not changed anything. Regional conflicts continue to fester on almost every continent. People are dying, many innocent civilians, in conflict created by people who will not listen to opposing points of view. There seems to be no middle road to dialogue and reconciliation.

Unrelenting globalization continues to shred the cultures and languages of less powerful nations. People seem lost and distracted in busyness, chasing personal goals of wealth, honor, and prestige. There seems to be little sensitivity for "the other."

But then the words of Isaiah 60 offer a faint glimmer of light; hope begins to shine through the surrounding gloom. There is wonderful news for all! God intends to bless every nation on earth. It comes like a breath of fresh air gently gusting into our immediate situation. The light will overcome the darkness! The glory of the Lord will rise above us, and nations will come to understand the light of the world. Every nation will display and rejoice in its heritage and culture. The whole world will appreciate each nation's unique God-giftedness.

What will we do this day to hasten and promote the coming of this time on earth? How will we thrill and make glad the heart or life of another? How can we learn to sing a new song of encouragement and hope to those less fortunate? Today, may the tune be in our hearts before our lips form the words.

**PRAYER: Lord, I hear your voice calling. Empower me to be your representative this day. May all I meet receive the gift of hope through the power of the Holy Spirit working in and through me. Let me remember that the light of a single candle defies the darkness of the world. It is time for me to arise and shine. Amen.**

## SATURDAY, JANUARY 5 • Read Psalm 72:1-7, 10-14

Jews and Christians throughout the ages have claimed the Psalms for their own. The words of the Psalms accurately reflect the spectrum of human emotion, speaking a universal language to our hearts.

Clearly today's psalm is a prayer for the king. The psalm gives voice to those virtues found in the reign of a "perfect" leader. Perhaps the Israelites themselves wondered about the disparity between the ideal and the real. And yet this psalm continued in use long after the monarchy fell, perhaps because it articulated the best hope of God for the world and for the governance of people. For Christians, the righteous rule and teachings of Jesus are reflective of these words in Psalm 72. Only through him does the promised ideal become fulfilled in time and space.

The psalm's words resound with the song of justice and hope for all, "for precious is their blood in his sight." God deems justice as far more important than personal wealth and riches.

Is it too far a stretch to demand that the politicians of every government on earth read this psalm every day before beginning work? If they enacted and enshrined this psalm in all their policies, we could rightfully expect a different political, economic, and social landscape for all the world's people. Especially affected would be the poor, the disenfranchised, the needy, and the marginalized who constitute the majority of the world's population.

As you move through the day, in whatever situation you find yourself, remember some of the words of Psalm 72. A new song will begin to form within your heart, a song richly resonant with the triumphant call that demands justice for all God's creation.

PRAYER: **Lord God, grant us the courage to dream *big* dreams. Soften our hearts to make space for your people. Give us the energy to make those dreams reality. Amen.**

## EPIPHANY

According to Eastern Orthodox tradition, Epiphany is the most important festival in the Christian year because it reminds the Christian community that Jesus came *especially* for the foreigner, the stranger, and the poor—all vividly depicted by the visits of the Magi (in Matthew's Gospel) and the shepherds (in Luke's Gospel) to Jesus' birthplace.

Every other day, my family provides gifts of seed and fruit to the bird-feeding table outside our kitchen window. It is amazing to see the variety of bird life that congregates around the table. We expect and receive no payment from these birds. Our payment is to glory in the wonder of God's incredibly diverse creation in nature. We are always thrilled when a stranger appears; we are excited when a foreigner comes to visit the table.

Like the bird-feeding table, so it is with Epiphany. We have an opportunity each day to offer our own God-given gifts to hungry strangers, foreigners, and the needy. If we truly believe that God resides within every human being, if we believe that all our gifts are from God, if we believe that our personal giftedness flows from our loving Parent, then surely the very least we can do, without any thought of recompense, is to present those gifts to God in the form of others we meet on the journey.

Perhaps the Eastern Orthodox faith communities are correct. At the start of each year, it is good to remind ourselves of our ability, in fact our Christian obligation, to bring our own personal gifts, skills, and giftedness to the ones whom God will continue to place in our path every day.

**PRAYER: Loving God, be close to us every minute of every day. We need you, for every breath we take is a gift from you. At the start of this new year, help us discover a new song that will bring us closer to you, a song that will unite us with fellow Christians around the world, and that will empower and energize us to be in service to all the world. Amen.**

# I Baptize You

*January 7–13, 2008 • Jennifer E. Copeland*‡

## MONDAY, JANUARY 7 • Read Acts 10:34–43

"You know the message," Peter begins, and so we do. We know it so well at times that it ceases to impress us as the epic that it is. Peter tells Cornelius, his relatives, and his close friends, about Jesus who came "preaching peace" as "Lord of all" and inaugurated the era of "forgiveness of sins." God "anointed" him and he "went about doing good." "They put him to death," but "God raised him." That might be the end of the story.

As with most great epics, the hero triumphs, his words and deeds vindicated even though he suffered greatly. We can almost hear Peter saying, "He ascended into heaven and lived there happily ever after. . . . " That might be the end of the story except for the command "to preach to the people and to testify that [Jesus] is the one ordained by God." Such a command allows none of us to breathe a sigh of contentment over a story well told and then go back to living as we did before we heard the story. "Happily ever after" is not how it ends precisely because we are now incorporated into the story and offered the gift of becoming part of the body of Christ. In the very next scene after our verses for today, Cornelius and all those with him were "baptized in the name of Jesus." Their job is to pick up where Peter leaves off, just as it is the job of each one of us baptized in the name of Jesus to show and tell the message of peace God proclaims through the life, death, and resurrection of Jesus Christ—Lord of all.

**SUGGESTION FOR MEDITATION: Through the sacrament of baptism we are initiated into Christ's holy Church. We are incorporated into God's mighty acts of salvation and given new birth through water and the Spirit. All this is God's gift, offered to us without price. (*United Methodist Book of Worship*, Baptismal Covenant I)**

‡United Methodist chaplain, Duke University, Durham, North Carolina; member of the South Carolina Annual Conference.

## TUESDAY, JANUARY 8 • Read Isaiah 42:1-4

When we hear the word *justice*, what comes to mind? Is it Lady Justice standing on the steps of the Supreme Court building, blindfolded to symbolize fairness? Do we think of the courtroom itself where attorneys, witnesses, judges, and juries are guided by carefully scripted legalities? Do our thoughts move beyond the trial to the place where justice insures that malefactors are censured? Most of us have preconceived notions when we hear *justice*, and we expect echoes and reflections of those definitions to be embodied by God's servant. Instead, this Servant Song transforms the typical justice expectations of power, verdict, and punishment. Rather than a repetitive cycle of rules, violations, and penalties, God's justice insures lasting results because it seeks restitution rather than retribution. The difference is magnificent, almost miraculous, but the Servant displays the transformation through ordinary, concrete actions that any of us might perform.

Rather than shouting to assert power, the servant does "not cry or lift up his voice" yet is all the more powerful as a result. Rather than following legalistic prescriptions to impose verdicts regardless of the circumstances, the servant does not break the "bruised reed" or quench the "dimly burning wick"; the verdicts are more reasonable as a result. Rather than equating justice with punishment, the servant establishes justice through "his teaching," and the justice is everlasting as a result. We are invited into the servant's activity of subverting power, verdict, and punishment by recognizing ourselves as recipients and not arbiters of justice. Such justice is not wrought through a cataclysmic event but patiently and painstakingly as we listen to quiet power, accept reasonable verdicts, and study the servant's teachings.

SUGGESTION FOR MEDITATION: **Do you renounce the spiritual forces of wickedness, reject the evil powers of this world, and repent of your sin? Do you accept the freedom and power God gives you to resist evil, injustice, and oppression in whatever forms they present themselves?** (*United Methodist Book of Worship*, **Baptismal Covenant I**)

In the fourth century a great debate arose among Christians around the identity of Jesus. If Jesus was indeed God's son, was he conceived or adopted, begotten or made? Was he human or just a divine spirit encased by a fleshy shell? Let's be honest as we struggle to wrap our minds around the mystery of the Incarnation; these questions still plague our need to explain it all through some rationally constructed principle. Our forefathers (there were no foremothers at the Council of Nicaea) settled upon the formula "begotten not made," asserting through this claim that Jesus was conceived and not adopted, was real flesh and not merely a divine spirit. Good for them, but I still meet lots of devout Christians who struggle to understand how the esoteric Latin term *homoousios*—of the same substance—explains the Incarnation. It is, finally, one more rationally constructed principle offered in the face of the greatest mystery of the universe: God loves humanity enough to become one of us.

All the great mythological classics document humans striving after divinity; in these narratives "success" is becoming one of the gods. But we worship a God who becomes human. No wonder Christianity is "a stumbling block to Jews and foolishness to Gentiles" (1 Cor. 1:23). Yet here is the simple truth, echoed in the words heard by Jesus and those around him while he stood knee-deep in the river Jordan on the day of his baptism: "This is my Son, the Beloved, with whom I am well pleased."

Like all great truths, it is open-ended, leaving space for us to tap into the mystery and expand our own feeble imaginations through the gift of God's presence. Such open-ended gifts belie rational explanation.

SUGGESTION FOR MEDITATION: **For us and for our salvation he came down from heaven, was incarnate of the Holy Spirit and the Virgin Mary and became truly human (The Creed of Nicaea, 325 BCE).**

Hurricane season annually presents a new fascination for us, though in January we may have relaxed a bit from our vigils with The Weather Channel. The famously revered storms of days gone by—Hazel, Camille, Hugo—have been dwarfed by a cadre of spectacularly destructive and more frequently occurring phenomena. While conservationists and environmentalists debate the reasons for such prominent meteorology—development encroaching on natural wetlands or greenhouse emissions altering atmospheric conditions—we continue to be obsessed by the storm itself.

The psalmist is no less obsessed, seeing in the storm a manifestation of God's majesty. The "voice of the LORD" sounds through the peals of thunder like the refrain of a hymn bellowed forth by the entire congregation without once glancing at the hymnal. Broken cedars and whirling oaks evoke reverent awe, and the flood defines the boundaries of God's throne. Lebanon and Sirion (home of strong, towering cedar trees) exult in God's tempestuous embrace like a calf and a young wild ox dancing in the meadow without a care in the world. Flooded fields do not become federal disaster areas. Felled trees do not translate into insurance adjustments. Overly given to privatization, we are not prone to see our flooded property as divine real estate, nor are we likely to consider uprooted trees as instruments of glory. The Song of the Storm, however, captures the clear difference between the temporal and the eternal. Here is glory and strength; here is holy splendor; here is full majesty, all on display for no other reason than the wonder of it. And when it all comes to an end, in the end, there is peace, just peace. . . .

SUGGESTION FOR MEDITATION: **Eternal God, when nothing existed but chaos, you swept across the dark waters and brought forth light. . . . In the fullness of time you sent Jesus, nurtured in the water of a womb. . . . Pour out your Holy Spirit, to bless this gift of water. (*United Methodist Book of Worship*, Baptismal Covenant I)**

A casual stroll through the neighborhood solidifies the fact that agricultural knowledge is fading fast. Walking through my neighborhood in the early evening past finely manicured lawns and exquisitely blooming rosebushes, we might be fooled into thinking that these "land" owners know something about agriculture or at least something about growing ornamental plants. Walking through the neighborhood while everyone else is at work reveals a street lined with lawn maintenance service trucks. Just before these lawn care mercenaries arrived, the automatic sprinkler systems were operating at peak performance, insuring green grass regardless of what the clouds might acquiesce to provide. Water is one more commodity that we control by pumping it across our yards in measured amounts at prescribed times.

To satisfy our bodily needs for water, we purchase it in neatly wrapped six-packs at the grocery store. Contrast this carefully regulated water with the wild, unpredictability of water from the storm. What may appear as water out of control is water unleashed in extravagant opulence by a God who knows no boundaries. God's abundance travels as far as the water can spread, which we have learned from Noah's story means the entire face of the earth. The water washing through our lives is never more or less than it was when "the earth was a formless void and darkness covered the face of the deep" (Gen. 1:2). After the storm, gathered back into the banks of the rivers and drawn up into the clouds, it is the same water that has sustained life since the dawn of creation, the same water that has initiated Christians into the body of Christ since the days of the Resurrection, the same water that fills my cup each day that I rise again to say, "Glory!"

**SUGGESTION FOR MEDITATION: Pour out your Holy Spirit, to bless this gift of water and all who receive it, to wash away their sin and clothe them in righteousness throughout their lives, that, dying and being raised with Christ, they may share in Christ's final victory. (*United Methodist Book of Worship*, Baptismal Covenant I)**

The baptism of Jesus is like a coronation ceremony. In fact, the words from heaven echo the coronation liturgy for a king found in Psalm 2: "You are my son; today I have begotten you" (v. 7). So, baptism is a magnificent event, a majestic occasion, a sovereign affair—not just for Jesus but for us as well. In the early church, those coming for baptism, after an entire night of prayer and fasting, were baptized by the first light of Easter morning—a magnificent, majestic, sovereign occasion.

Such symbolic acts remind us that baptism is the great equalizer, not in the sense of reducing us all to the least common denominator but rather by raising us all up to the level of royalty. In a world increasingly described as multicultural but habitually proscribed by immigration laws, the waters of baptism stream across the world forming the body of Christ. Christian relationships are established not on the basis of common background, ethnic similarity, or socioeconomic status. Our relationships are established through baptism—whether we live next door to one another or halfway around the world, whether we see each other everyday or have never met face-to-face.

The implications of such a far-reaching family tree reconfigure the typical markers for international relationships. Would you withhold food from your first cousin? Would you authorize dropping bombs on your grandparents? Would you dam a river that causes your sibling's crops to wither and die? Just as baptism was the first public act in which Jesus committed himself to God's work, so too is our baptism the first public act in which our lives are committed to the reign of God. The work begins by taking care of the family.

SUGGESTION FOR MEDITATION: **Through baptism we are incorporated by the Holy Spirit into God's new creation and made to share in Christ's royal priesthood. We are all one in Christ Jesus. (*United Methodist Book of Worship*, Baptismal Covenant I)**

## BAPTISM OF THE LORD

Who is this miraculous servant able to coax God's justice from a world consumed by competitive tactics and calculating ideologies? Penned by the author of Isaiah near the end of the Babylonian Exile (ca. 538), the likely referent is Israel itself. Israel, however, is never less than God's chosen people, a designation that has little to do with nationalism and more to do with selectiveness. It's an interesting selection process: God chooses a people and then gives them the choice of choosing God. Incidentally, God has never practiced exclusivity, readily including among the chosen people Rahab the Canaanite and Ruth the Moabite, to say nothing of Gentile Christians grafted onto the root of Jesse.

The choice seems straightforward enough, but the Servant's Song implies an element of trust: "Before they [the new things] spring forth, I tell you of them." We must choose between light and darkness while it is still dark, between imprisonment and glory while still imprisoned. We do not choose God from a lineup of equally reliable options. We choose between God and nothingness, a choice with life-and-death implications. In choosing God, we choose God's obligations that require us to hold firmly to the One who has "taken you by the hand and kept you."

Hand holding indicates support and guidance, familiarity and trust. We practice holding the hands of our children until they can cross the street alone without harm. We practice holding the hands of our lovers until we can trust their love without touching their presence. We practice holding the hand of God—who first took us by the hand—as we embody the qualities of God's chosen Servant, choosing to be God's chosen servants.

**SUGGESTION FOR MEDITATION: As members in the body of Christ, we renew our covenant faithfully to participate in the ministries of the Church by our prayers, our presence, our gifts, and our service, that in everything God may be glorified through Jesus Christ. (*United Methodist Book of Worship*, Baptismal Covenant I)**

# Servants in the World

*January 14–20, 2008* • *Young Eun Choi*[‡]

**MONDAY, JANUARY 14** • **Read Isaiah 49:1-7**

God calls Israel as a servant. The first reading of this passage seems to indicate that God is addressing a single individual. "The LORD called me before I was born,/ while I was in my mother's womb he named me" seems to speak of one person; however, we know that this, the Second Servant Song, speaks to the nation in exile. Here Isaiah extends an invitation and a promise to people who live in the Babylonian captivity.

Life in captivity—whether that in Babylon or the captivities experienced closer to our own time—remains difficult and full of longing. The Israelites had to follow and keep the law, customs, and religion of Babylon. Even when the captors respect a conquered people and allow relative freedom, oppression weighs upon those in bondage. They dream of the land of their ancestors. They envision what might have been and long for home.

To that longing for home, God speaks a word of freedom. The vision given to Isaiah is one in which Israel will be glorified. Imagine the response to these words in Isaiah 49. We know from history that the Babylonian captivity ended, and Israel experienced restoration.

Do you know someone who is oppressed? Is that oppression an economic one? religious? cultural? Who today lives in a form of captivity that may seem as harsh as that experienced by Israel in Babylon? Whom will God use to save these people? Through whom will God work? God wants to use us. As Isaiah spoke of God's glory made known through those in captivity, so God will be glorified through our servanthood.

**PRAYER: Dear God, we believe that you give us a mission. Help us to speak your word of salvation to those who are spiritually, physically, politically, and economically in captivity. Amen.**

---

[‡]Pastor, Dayton Korean United Methodist Church, Dayton, Ohio.

John the Baptist refers to Jesus as "the Lamb of God, who takes away the sin of the world!" Here the Gospel testifies to Jesus' purpose. Here we begin to see the unfolding drama of salvation. Ancient promises move toward fulfillment. Again in verse 36, John says of Jesus, "Look, here is the Lamb of God!" John points to Jesus, drawing a mystical analogy to the sacrificial lambs of Israel. Notice that Jesus, the one called the Lamb of God, invites two of John's disciples to follow him. Not only do they follow, they invite others to follow Jesus, the Lamb of God. Each disciple invited another disciple.

Are these disciples clear about Jesus' mission? They see him both as sacrifice and as servant. Do they follow Jesus because his teachings about servanthood and his vision of God's reign speak to their hearts and call them to purposeful living? They become followers, but they will also become servants. As Jesus gave himself for all humanity, so the apostles give themselves in ministry and mission—even martyrdom because of their understanding of Jesus' mission and purpose.

Take time to consider why you follow Jesus. Is it because he is the Lamb of God? Is it because he is the Suffering Servant? Is it because his life models God's love for all humanity? Or do you follow Jesus because someone invited you to "come and see" and you remain attracted to the vision of sacrifice and servanthood? Will you go out in servanthood to reach another?

**PRAYER: Dear Jesus, we thank you for your love made known to Andrew and Peter and made known to us. Because you have given yourself for us, help us to give ourselves in your love to others. Amen.**

Imagine the hardship endured by those in the Babylonian captivity. The Israelites had been captured and taken away from home to a strange land. The people remember their former life through tears of bitterness. This period of captivity brought Israel to sing the lament that we know as Psalm 137: "By the rivers of Babylon—there we sat down and there we wept/when we remembered Zion" (v. 1). To those in captivity, the words of the prophet thunder: "Surely my cause is with the LORD, /and my reward with my God."

People still experience such captivity. Today look at the difference between the Republic of Korea (South Korea) and the Democratic People's Republic of Korea (North Korea). Families are divided on either side of a zone patrolled by the military. It is not a stretch of the imagination to say that by the "demilitarized zone there we also sat down and wept." While this situation does not exactly parallel the Babylonian captivity of Israel, we also live in a godly hope that by God's grace we may reach through the military barriers to proclaim God's love and to serve new brothers and sisters in Christ.

Into the world we go. We feed on the mercy and love of God and reach out as servants to others who do not yet know the good news of God's redeeming love.

Let yourself first feed on the love of God by reading Isaiah 49:4-5 several times. Read it aloud. Read it silently. Read it as if addressed to Israel during the Babylonian captivity and imagine the response of Israel to these words. Read it as if it were addressed to oppressed people today. Now read it as a deeply personal word addressed intimately to you. How will you serve God today, knowing that your reward is in God?

**PRAYER: Dear God, our reward is in you. As we move into a new day, keep us mindful that you are our strength and our cause. Amen.**

Psalm 40 is designated as a psalm of thanksgiving. Actually verses 1-11 are words of thanksgiving, while verses 12-17 are a lament. Psalm 40 contains a richness that gives us a sense of spiritual practice and of servanthood.

"I waited patiently for the LORD" describes our devotional life. We read scripture, sit in silence, and wait. We may cry aloud to God, repeating words that sound as if they came from the lips of Israel during the Babylonian captivity. We wait. Sometimes silence is our friend. Sometimes silence scares us. Still we wait patiently for the Lord. In the midst of the waiting, God surprises us. We hear the word of grace, the word that we need. That word may not be what we seek, but it is God's gift. In that moment God also puts a new song in our mouths.

Recall the pain of Israel during that period of exile. Recall your own pain as you waited for a word of grace from God. Now the psalmist offers a new song: "You have multiplied . . . your wondrous deeds and your thoughts toward us. . . . I have told the glad news of deliverance/in the great congregation." Take time now to think about the multiplication of God's wondrous deeds. Think about Israel's history, starting with the Babylonian captivity and moving forward to the time of Jesus. Continue through the apostolic era and on through church history to this moment. How do you tell the glad news of deliverance to others? How do you remember God's great deeds in your life? What will you say that will invite others to come and see and taste and learn about the goodness of God?

Put yourself in the place of the psalmist, and read again Psalm 40:1-11.

**PRAYER: Gracious God, help us learn to testify to others of what you have done in our lives. Grant that others may look for you and meet you in their difficult times as well. Amen.**

Andrew brings his brother Simon to Jesus right after he meets Jesus. We may wonder why Andrew brought Simon to Jesus. We can uncover aspects of this event that inform our servanthood and ministry.

In his earlier encounter with Jesus, Andrew experienced a life change. Andrew recognized Jesus as the long-expected Messiah. Because of this awareness, Andrew can only proclaim his finding; he needs to tell others. He begins with his brother. We do not know whom Andrew brought to Jesus after Simon. Perhaps he brought a friend or another relative, an associate or a neighbor.

Notice the change in perspective that occurs after Andrew meets Jesus. We do not know Andrew's lifestyle prior to this encounter. We know little about the lives of the first disciples, and much of that knowledge is insignificant. The Gospels say little about these few fishermen and the others. Their *past* lives are less important than their present lives after meeting Jesus. They now focus on Christ. Is that not the way it is with each of us? Our past no longer matters; we live Christ-centered lives that rest upon the Bible as the source of inspiration and knowledge.

Focusing upon Christ, as did Andrew, calls us also to witness to the love of God that we know through Jesus Christ. We invite others to come to Jesus. The Gospels record stories of those who came into contact with Jesus and experienced God's love; many of those stories do not end with the encounter. People go and tell others about the good news of Christ. Despite many changes in culture and technology, this model of inviting others to come and meet Jesus is still part of our Christian living. Like Andrew, we can say to our brothers and sisters and friends and neighbors, "We have met the Christ! Come and see."

**PRAYER: Gracious God, thank you for the gift we have received in Jesus. As I serve you today, encourage me to invite another to come and see the Christ. Amen.**

First Corinthians 1:2 contains two important statements about the church. The first is the phrase "those sanctified in Christ." The second is the phrase "called to be holy." When I read this verse, I think of the Holiness movement, which is part of the Wesleyan movement and emphasizes sanctification.

John Wesley experienced a conversion during and following a reading of Luther's preface to Romans on Aldersgate Street on May 24, 1738. He began to lead a disciplined devotional life. He awoke at 4:00 each morning to read the Bible, meditate on it, pray, and write in his journal. His devotional life bore fruit in the thousands of individuals who came to know Jesus Christ and in the social holiness movement spawned by Wesley and the early members of the Methodist movement. Through his disciplined practice, John Wesley lived a deeply spiritual life that demonstrated the fruits of sanctification.

Jesus habitually prayed each day and went off by himself, even when the crowds who followed him in his ministry threatened to overwhelm his disciples. More often than not, Jesus prayed early in the morning. The fact that he prayed regularly shows a pattern of discipline that we can also imitate as we strive for holiness. To pray and to meditate on scripture is one of the best ways to grow in holiness. Through prayer and Bible reading we can experience a deepening of our spirituality as we open ourselves and sense God's presence.

The deepening of my relationship and intimacy with God helps me live a sanctified life that affects me spiritually, morally, and physically. I can serve others as Jesus wants me to serve. I can be the light and salt of the world.

**PRAYER: Gracious God, help us to pray and meditate on the Bible regularly so that we may live as sanctified servants. Fill us with your love, and let it overflow from us to others. Amen.**

In 1 Corinthians 1:4, Paul thanks God for the people of the Corinthian church "because of the grace of God that has been given you in Christ Jesus." Consider the situation of the church in Corinth. The city is an important Greek seaport, a somewhat cosmopolitan city. Like any seaport, Corinth contains vices and temptations. We do not have a record of the former lives of the Christian converts in Corinth, but many of them were probably once considered outcasts and unclean; they experienced a life turned around by God's grace.

The grace of God is given to us today, helping us to draw nearer to God and to feel God's never-ending love. I used to ask myself this question: "If I did not believe in Jesus Christ, what kind of person would I have become?" I might have become a person who pursued worldly desires and thoughts based on secular values. Or religiously, I might have become a Buddhist, a Confucian, or a Shamanist. But I thank God for the grace of knowing Christ since childhood.

Paul knew choices and options, and he chose a more excellent way—that of self-giving love. Paul demonstrated a life of servanthood. He did not consider power or position in life. Paul tirelessly and passionately reached out to all people in gratitude to God for the grace he had received on the journey begun on the road to Damascus.

As a pastor, I am also obligated to reach out to all people and to give thanks for the grace of God that has been given to them and to me. For this I am grateful, and I pray that I may continue to grow in gratitude.

**PRAYER: Dear God, thank you for your grace that assures us of your never-ending love. Guide our service to you in the world through Jesus Christ. Amen.**

# A Cure for the Crisis

*January 21–27, 2008* • *Kenneth L. Waters Sr.*[‡]

## MONDAY, JANUARY 21 • Read Isaiah 9:1-4

The territory of Israel, the kingdom in the north, included Galilee. Judah, the kingdom in the south, numbered among its inhabitants Isaiah the prophet. Isaiah was less than a hundred miles away when Galilee was devastated by the Assyrians and its people taken into captivity. Twelve years later in 721 BCE the Assyrians complete their destruction of the northern kingdom (2 Kings 16:5-6). Isaiah draws upon the tragedy of the northern kingdom as a lesson and warning for disobedient Judah. Yet Galilee becomes Isaiah's illustration that the story of the northern kingdom will not end on this note of tragedy: "But in the latter time he will make glorious the way of the sea, the land beyond the Jordan, Galilee of the nations. The people who walked in darkness have seen a great light."

Isaiah not only proclaims that those once devastated will be restored; he invites both Israel and Judah to become partners with God in their own recovery. In our own era we have witnessed widespread destruction around the globe as the result of war and nature's fury, but we have also witnessed creaturely resilience in its wake. Isaiah's message is that our resilience has a divine sponsor.

When we allow God's spirit to shape our perspective and response, the healing of both humanity and land will accelerate. Our personal and communal lives become microcosms of the healing miracle that can occur on a global scale when we corporately and positively respond to the prophet's call.

**PRAYER: God, you alone have the power to heal our lives, communities, and lands. Yet you invite us to share with you in the work of restoration. Receive us as your partners. Amen.**

---

[‡]Associate Professor of New Testament, Haggard School of Theology, Azusa Pacific University, Azusa, California.

TUESDAY, JANUARY 22 • **Read Psalm 27:1, 4–9**

One source is sufficient for all the psalmist's needs. His testimony makes it clear. He speaks only of the Lord as light, salvation, and stronghold. He remembers how the Lord alone sheltered and uplifted him. His words are not pious rhetoric. Neither are they fanciful flight nor wishful thinking. On the contrary, his testimony is born out of the crucible of fiery trial. The psalmist has faced fearful times. He has been assailed by enemies and besieged by armies. Others have warred against him to take his life. He therefore speaks out of the experience of heavenly deliverance from real danger. "Though an army encamp against me, my heart shall not fear; though war rise up against me, yet I will be confident" (27:3). Small wonder then that the psalmist implores the Lord not to cast him away. Small wonder that his only desire is to live out his days in the house of the Lord.

Still, we must not allow surface appearances to mislead us. These words are not merely the expressions of an individual worshiper; they are the song of an entire community, the community of the Temple. It is not merely an individual but the entire community that has experienced God's saving grace and now expresses confidence in the Lord.

Perhaps we go astray in modern times when we individually seek God's grace while neglecting the building of community. Does not God dwell in community? Perhaps greater community is the means of more grace, more healing, more light, and more peace in our troubled world. Deliverance is a communal experience for the psalmist. When we achieve community, the door opens to the same divine blessing.

**PRAYER: Lord, your grace and salvation is greatly manifested in the midst of community. Help us to build community locally and globally. When we have more community, we have more of you. Amen.**

Factionalism may have been a greater threat to the church of Corinth than the well-attested immorality and idolatry of the Corinthian environment. Immorality and idolatry are the evils that threaten from without, but factionalism is the evil that threatens from within. Moreover, factionalism is easier to justify on supposedly moral or spiritual grounds. Some who follow the moral and spiritual example of a heroic personality feel obliged to pull away from those who follow supposedly lesser examples. Paul, however, will have no part of such division. He will not even tolerate the existence of a "Paul faction."

Paul expresses thanks that he limited his ministry of baptism in Corinth, for that would only have fed the Corinthian appetite for division. Paul pursues salvation not division for the Corinthian congregation, and he does so by proclaiming the cross of Christ. Later, when Paul speaks of the manifold gifts and ministries of the Holy Spirit, he will still emphasize the unity of the body of Christ (1 Cor. 12:4–31). Spiritual vitality and healing ministry in all their various forms are nevertheless grounded in this very unity. Salvation for both the church and the world depends on our oneness in Christ.

Paul therefore makes his plea, "Be united in the same mind and the same purpose," for as he later says, "We were all baptized into one body" (1 Cor. 12:13). As we near the end of the first decade of the twenty-first century—a tumultuous decade indeed—Paul's summons to oneness in Christ is more critical than ever before. It is nothing less than a summons to vocational revitalization and spiritual empowerment, the attainments that will make us the kind of church the world is literally dying to see.

**PRAYER: Lord God, unite us in the same mind and purpose so that we may be the channel for your Spirit and its manifold ministries and so that our broken world may be healed. Amen.**

## Thursday, January 24 • Read 1 Corinthians 1:10-18

Paul interprets the crucifixion of Christ from two perspectives. From the perspective of Jewish believers in his congregations, the crucifixion is an atoning sacrifice, a means of removing the barrier of sin that separates human beings from God (1 Cor 15:3). From the perspective of Gentile believers, the crucifixion serves as prelude to a cosmic victory; that is to say, a victory over the cosmic forces of sin, death, and the devil (1 Cor 15:57). Paul's pagan detractors, whom he describes as "the perishing," would dismiss as foolishness either interpretation. They would ask, "How can death by crucifixion, the most shameful death of all, have any saving significance for an individual or the world?"

Paul replies that only those who are being saved can understand the message of the cross as the power of God for salvation because only they have come to know the crucified Jesus as the resurrected Lord. When they hear about Christ crucified, they hear a summons to repentance and forgiveness of sins; they hear the promise of new life in Christ. Paul's message of the cross is therefore a word of life, not death. Only those who receive Paul's preaching with faith will discover the salvation hidden in this paradox.

What might this mean for an individual, family or community that has suffered catastrophic loss, as many have this past decade? If they have hope that their livelihoods and community will be restored and, further, that the loved ones they have lost will rise again to life, then the cross is their sign—a God-given sign—that such hope is not without foundation.

**PRAYER: O God, our creator, whose power raised Jesus from the dead, who transformed the cross from a sign of death to a sign of death defeated, make this same power available to us, our communities, and our loved ones in the wake of catastrophe and terrible loss. Amen.**

Isaiah prophesied restoration for Galilee after the Assyrian military deportation of the Israelite population in that mostly Gentile region. History reports various events that could be understood as fulfillment of this prophecy: the reestablishment of Jewish rule in Galilee in the days of the Jewish priest-king Alexander Janneus (104–76 BC), the emergence of Galilee as the new center of Judaism after the Romans destroy Jerusalem in 70 BCE, and the creation of the modern state of Israel inclusive of Galilee in 1948.

However, for the Gospel writer Matthew, Isaiah's prophecy involved more than the mere recovery of land and the reestablishment of political autonomy. Matthew saw the preeminent fulfillment of Isaiah's prophecy in the beginning of Jesus' ministry. "Galilee of the Gentiles—the people who sat in darkness have seen a great light." Jesus was that light. Yet, in this case, more is still to come. Even after subsequent events that could also be taken as fulfillment of Isaiah's prophecy, clearly the truth of these words has yet to be fully realized.

Prophecy tends to have multiple levels of meaning and, therefore, multiple levels of fulfillment. History shows there is always more to anticipate when it comes to the fulfillment of prophecy at any point in time. A prophecy perceived as fulfilled does not indicate a prophecy exhausted of all its meaning; that is to say, not until the kingdom of God comes in its fullness. We can expect then that God's promise of restoration and healing will continue to be fulfilled in surprising ways, and the greatest surprise of all will come when the promise is fulfilled in the kingdom of God. This conviction of more to come keeps us from capitulating to despair when crisis and catastrophe loom over us.

**PRAYER: Gracious God, we wait upon your promise. Train us in the ways of patience, and teach us to be open to the manifold ways that your promise will come to pass. We will not despair, knowing that regardless of what we face, there is more to come from your promise of restoration and healing. Amen.**

Before his arrest, John the Baptist proclaimed, "Repent, for the kingdom of heaven has come near" (Matt 3:1). Strikingly enough, at the beginning of his ministry, Jesus proclaims this same message. What does it mean to proclaim the nearness of the kingdom of heaven when in the centuries to follow the world will see unspeakable evils perpetrated by human beings against other human beings? What does this proclamation mean in advance of immeasurable suffering and calamity attributed to natural causes or human negligence? What does it mean to proclaim and hear this message today?

We still tend to meet the message of the nearness of the kingdom with a passive response. We often suppose that the final coming of the kingdom is entirely God's doing while we need only make the passive response of repentance—as if repentance were entirely passive. Consequently, while we are waiting for the kingdom, the kingdom is waiting for us.

So near is the kingdom of heaven that its culture and beauty frequently spill over into our earthly realm despite our passivity. Yet we would experience more of the kingdom of heaven if, on the one hand, we were not so adept at shutting it out, and if, on the other, we would take more initiative to seize upon kingdom culture and actively draw it into our world. God has brought it near; the least we can do is seize and draw upon it.

Pockets of people all over the world consciously seize and draw upon the culture of the kingdom of heaven—the kingdom is not only near; it is among them. We can only imagine the wondrous transformation in global affairs if large-scale initiatives attempted to incorporate kingdom culture with all its beauty and love. Until this happens, our mandate is to continue proclaiming, "Repent, for the kingdom of heaven has come near."

**PRAYER: Eternal God, you have made the beauty of your kingdom accessible to us. Strengthen our will so that we can make the culture of your kingdom our very own. Amen.**

Jesus calls his first disciples, Peter, Andrew, James, and John at the beginning of his Galilean-Decapolis ministry, a phase that would last about two and one-half years and end with the Transfiguration. Jesus' chief purpose during this time is to establish his identity as Son of God, to signify the in-breaking of the kingdom of heaven, and to train his disciples. He especially pursues this purpose through his teachings and miracles. Naturally, it is to this period that the Gospel of Matthew assigns the greatest number of Jesus' teachings and miracles.

As "fishers of people" the first disciples will be both recipients and ministers of good news and healing. As successors of Jesus they are also predecessors of a Christ-centered community that will model the kingdom of heaven on earth. Through them, the kingdom of heaven will not only be near; it will break into the human realm. This Christ-centered community holds the cure for a world in crisis.

We continue the task the early disciples began: building the Christ-centered community as the embodiment of the kingdom of heaven on earth. It involves bringing the healing resources of food, medicine, education, technology, and faith to a world ravaged by hunger, disease, ignorance, poverty, war, and despair. Our models, Jesus and the first disciples, met the physical needs of people first and then called them to saving faith.

Therefore. the Christ-centered community remains the best hope for global healing whether or not everyone identifies with this community. As members of the community, we are called to serve the whole world—not just those who identify with us.

**PRAYER: Loving God, you have entrusted us with healing resources of heavenly origin for a world in crisis. Guide us in being good stewards of these resources as we lay aside personal agendas and self-serving political programs in order to fulfill the mandate of a Christ-centered community. Amen.**

# Mountaintop Faith

*January 28–February 3, 2008 • P. Joel Snider[‡]*

**MONDAY, JANUARY 28 • Read Psalm 99:1-5**

Throughout the Bible, worship seems to call for a mountain. Abraham took Isaac to Mount Moriah. Elijah's deity challenge with the prophets of Baal took place on Mount Carmel. And, of course, Yahweh revealed the law to Moses at Mount Sinai. Mountains seem a natural place for an altar, a temple, or a religious experience.

No wonder David follows God's lead to make Jerusalem the political and worship center of the Israelite nation. Jerusalem is "up" from almost everywhere in Palestine. The city sits at twenty-five hundred feet above the nearby sea. Atop Mount Zion, at the pinnacle of Jerusalem, David's son Solomon built the Temple dedicated to the nation's worship of God. Pilgrims making the journey to worship at the Temple are always climbing, ascending, going up. Where else could God be enthroned?

Psalm 99, which leads us to toward Transfiguration Sunday, reminds us that God is above us—a symbolic way of saying that God is holy, worthy of praise. Using multiple images, the opening verses create a strong impression that Yahweh is higher than all those who worship: Yahweh is seated among cherubim, exalted over the nations, and enthroned in (Mount) Zion. No matter how high worshipers might climb, we still find ourselves offering praise and prayers from God's "footstool."

Today we do not find God on a particular mountain, but mountains lead us to worship because they point heavenward, toward God. Church steeples were originally designed for the same purpose. They draw our eyes from common surroundings toward the throne of God, who is "up" from wherever we are.

**PRAYER: God above us all, dare we lift our eyes toward heaven and your holiness? Grant us a glimpse of your glory today. Amen.**

---

[‡]Pastor, First Baptist Church, Rome, Georgia.

Psalm 99 offers a glimpse of two facets of our unknowable and multifaceted God. Believers in every generation tend to make God either too chummy or too fearful. Choosing one facet of God's personality over another, we may portray God either as too much a friend to be feared or as too fearful to love. It is hard to find the right balance in our theology or in our worship. The psalmist, however, manages to portray both sides of God's nature quite well.

Yesterday's portion of Psalm 99 creates distance between God and those who worship. God is "up" from wherever we are; the refrain of the psalm reminds us God is holy. Today's reading holds us in the tension of worshiping a God who is removed from us by holiness but who is also loving and forgiving.

The God who is "up" is not too distant to care and not too removed from believers to hear and to respond to our praise. The psalmist mentions the experiences of Moses, Aaron, and Samuel as examples. Despite the fact that God spoke from a pillar of cloud (to Moses and Aaron, at least), these priests called on the Lord, and God answered. Verse 8 repeats the tension when it reminds us that God chides but also forgives. The Holy One of Israel is both a consuming fire (Exod. 13:21) and a God who listens to prayers and responds to believers.

Were God merely close, touchable, and familiar, could God be trusted to have power to save us from our sin? Or, if God were so distant from us in holiness that we feared to approach, could we have a relationship with God that calms the soul, brings peace to our hearts, or forgives us of sin? We need God to be both above us and present with us. And God is.

**PRAYER: Dear God, may we not fear you so much that we avoid approaching you. May we never think you so common as to forget you are holy. Be both to us today. Amen.**

Many people love the mountains as a recreational site—so much so that today's culture often confuses recreation with spiritual hunger. Skiers, hikers, and cabin owners speak of worshiping during their activities: a moment of silence while overlooking a vista is believed to be prayer; a cup of coffee sipped while sitting on the deck is described as an offering. Possibly they are.

Yet these reflections do not approach the same level of reverence as do the mountain experiences of Moses, Joshua, and the elders of Israel. Waiting on Sinai for the bidding of God, these believers have no casual experience. None of them would have considered it simply a nice weekend on the mountain. For six days Moses waits, preparing himself to receive the word. Then, upon God's summons, Moses enters the cloud. To those watching from below, the scene looks as if the mountain is burning.

The outdoor experiences that we describe as worship require little personal preparation, little invitation from the Holy, little devouring fire. It takes more than nature to worship the God revealed in the Christian scriptures. It takes more than a weekend at the lake to wait on the one who may be experienced as a pillar of smoke by day and a column of fire by night.

God calls Moses into the cloud for a task. The next time we are tempted to think of recreation as worship, perhaps we might review a few questions: Has this experience called me to action? Has this worship asked anything of me—any offering, any sacrifice, any service? Our positive response may indicate a God-given moment.

**PRAYER: O God, may my worship never be about me but solely about you and your greatness. May I not focus my praise on what I prefer; rather, let my worship center on what I owe you for the gift of everlasting life, through Jesus Christ our Lord. Amen.**

Matthew begins the story of the Transfiguration with the words, "After six days . . . " (NIV), reminiscent of Moses' waiting period before he entered the holy cloud on Sinai (see yesterday's devotion). Matthew's "after" refers to the confession of Peter at Caesarea Philippi, and Jesus' revelation of his full identity. During the six days that have passed, the disciples have been soaking it in, trying to understand completely what Jesus has told them about himself. For six days they try to make their preconceived conceptions about the Messiah fit what Jesus has told them. For six days they ponder the ramifications for their own lives.

The philosopher Nietzsche said, "If we knew the whole truth at once it would kill us." After six days of contemplating, maybe now the three disciples who accompany Jesus up the mountain are ready to understand more about Jesus. Perhaps they can learn from the object lesson that will visibly demonstrate what Jesus has tried to tell them at Caesarea Philippi. Suddenly Moses and Elijah appear as a way of confirming the scripture (representing the law and the prophets) that affirms who Jesus is.

Yet, Moses, Elijah, and the brightness of the moment are not enough. Peter, who confessed Jesus as the Christ, still does not quite understand. His desire to build a booth for Jesus, Moses, and Elijah indicates that he puts Jesus in elite company. Yet, he does not place Jesus on a plane higher than the other two. So, as Jesus shines like the sun, God's voice booms from heaven, restating what Jesus has told the disciples before.

The divine interruption finally breaks through to Peter and the other disciples. In reverence, awe, and fear they fall down before Jesus. This is holy ground; Jesus is worthy of worship, devotion, and obedience.

**PRAYER: O God, may we listen to Jesus today. May we put aside our preconceived ideas of what he might ask of us or teach us. May we listen and be open to his word. Amen.**

"Don't tell anyone" (NIV). Jesus gives this order time and again. Those who receive healing must keep it to themselves (Matt. 12:16). Jesus not only casts out evil spirits, but he also commands them to keep quiet (Mark 3:12). He tells cleansed lepers to make an offering with the priest, but they are to tell no one (Matt. 8:4). As he has instructed the disciples to keep silent before, after this great affirmation of his role in God's plan, Jesus does so again. Why not tell everyone?

During the most grueling parts of practice, a high school football coach told his players, "No guts—no glory." The message was clear: only those who paid the price during practice and conditioning drills could hope to succeed in the game. Only those willing to suffer when no one was watching could hope to excel in front of the crowd. The hard work comes before the praise.

That illustration runs parallel to the experience of Jesus. His full glory was reserved until after the suffering. Jesus must climb the Mount of the Skull (Golgotha) before the disciples may tell about the mount of Transfiguration. Thus, Jesus charges the disciples to keep silent about the shining brilliance they have witnessed until after the cross.

How would our witness to Jesus change if we could not tell about the Resurrection and eternal life until we had clearly communicated his death? What if we could not speak of the risen Lord, the glorified One, until we had described his suffering and death? What if we made no promises about what Jesus can do for a person until we have described what he has already done? Such a witness would be the model of Jesus.

**PRAYER: Thank you, God, for the suffering and death of Jesus. May I not give in to the temptation to seek his benefits before I have understood his sacrifice. Amen.**

Faith looks forward and backward. We are aware of faith's forward look when faith is tested. "Will I trust God for the unknown? Can I believe in God's word, God's way, God's plan when I cannot see where belief will take me?" I remember a poster on the wall of a minister's office: *Faith is walking to the edge of all the light you have—and taking one more step.* Faith looks forward when tested.

But faith also looks backward. We find faith's foundation in the past. Prior moments when God has proven trustworthy serve as our basis for believing God will be trustworthy again. The memory of God's presence in the past buoys our belief that God will not leave us in the future.

The early church experienced turmoil as it moved further and further away in time from the Resurrection. False teachers and their heresies increased in number. In this moment, confronted by defections from the church, the writer of Second Peter recalls a past moment that gives him confidence and that serves as a credential for others to believe in his teaching. He recalls the Transfiguration as an event he witnessed. This event shaped his understanding of Jesus there on the mountain and his teaching about Jesus in the present. He looked backward in order to look forward. His conviction about Jesus is not based on speculation or upon clever teaching; rather, it is based on his memory of the Transfiguration.

The Hebrew Bible is replete with admonitions to remember. Remember and tell. . . . remember and tell. Keep the stories alive to encourage faith in the present moment. Faith finds its roots in past experiences with God.

PRAYER: O God of past, present, and future, help me remember the times you have worked in my life. May these remembrances strengthen me and give me confidence for this day. Amen.

## THE TRANSFIGURATION

Our culture highly regards personal experience. Truth and morality possess an unusual flexibility. "What is true for you," the saying goes, "may not be true for me." If we debate theology or ideology, and someone argues that his or her experience differs from ours, we do not know how to overcome that objection.

The transition between verses 18 and 19 is confusing. How does the writer go from remembering the Transfiguration to "the word of the prophets" and scripture? As he advocates his position for the church's integrity of belief, the author starts with his personal experience but does not stop there. The word of the prophets and scripture judge even his own experience—even the experience of witnessing the Transfiguration.

I participated in a Bible study several years ago where a man was confronted by a passage of scripture that ran contrary to his own belief. "I don't care what the Bible says," he stated emphatically. Perhaps he was simply more honest than most of us. If you do not believe it, ask yourself this question: "When was the last time I read a passage of scripture and changed my mind about something I believed?"

Influenced by our culture more than we care to admit, we often judge scripture by our own experience. In this passage, the writer reminds us that when we try to decide what's good, what's bad, what's right, what's wrong, our own experience is judged by scripture—not the other way around. Personal experience is not the highest judge of our beliefs. Conscience is too easily domesticated in order to let us off the hook. Our opinions are too easily swayed by factors that benefit us personally. But scripture judges our decisions by God's standards.

**PRAYER: Dear God, may I yield my opinions to your word. May I judge my experiences by scripture and not the other way around. Amen.**

# God's Gracious Boundaries

*February 4–10, 2008 • David M. Griebner*[‡]

### MONDAY, FEBRUARY 4 • Read Genesis 2:15-17; 3:1-7

Our readings this week include the lessons for Ash Wednesday and the first Sunday of Lent. What are we supposed to do for the next forty days? Is Lent a season we keep or something we need to learn to do every day? Is this the season *of* Lent? Or is it a season *to* Lent?

In other words, what kind of life questions does Lent ask of us? What does it mean to be more authentic with God? What does it mean to engage God in a way that honors not just this season, not just tradition, not just habit but opens us to the real gift God wants to give us through the life, death, and resurrection of Jesus? What does it mean to Lent?

First, to Lent means to accept boundaries. God said no. Adam and Eve chose to ignore that boundary. As a consequence they lost the privilege of living in Eden; intimacy with God was all but destroyed; sin entered the world, and events were set in motion that would one day require a cross.

To Lent is to wrestle with where we have allowed appropriate boundaries to break down and inappropriate boundaries to creep in. Some of the areas to look at include work, sexuality, food, relationships, and emotions such as anger and resentment. Where are you living outside God's boundaries in any of these areas of life? When have you been tempted to Google something illicit? Where in your life is anger a problem? What relationships have broken down? What commitment has become too hard to honor? To Lent is to think about God's wise boundaries.

**PRAYER: Holy God, open my eyes to the perfect boundaries you have set for my life out of your infinite love and understanding. Amen.**

---

[‡]Pastor of Riverside United Methodist Church, Columbus, Ohio; author of *The Carpenter and the Unbuilder* and contributor to *Weavings*.

This week we are asking what it means to Lent. What happens if we treat Lent as something we need to do every day instead of a season we keep once a year? Today the psalmist beautifully describes what we need to do about sin. At first he expresses resistance: "While I kept silence, my body wasted away through my groaning all day long." Next comes release and an acceptance of the truth: "Then I acknowledged my sin to you, and I did not hide my iniquity; I said, 'I will confess my transgressions to the LORD,' and you forgave the guilt of my sin." Finally, the psalmist experiences a new sense of home: "You are a hiding place for me; you preserve me from trouble; you surround me with glad cries of deliverance."

To Lent is to acknowledge our offense in a way that can truly make a difference. All too often even genuine repentance stops with a sense of regret or sorrow for what we have done. We have all had the experience of asking God or someone else to forgive the same thing over and over again. But what if we acknowledged our sin in a deeper way? What if instead of simply asking God to forgive us, we asked God to change the *source* of that sin in us? What if we asked God to reform our desire or will to sin in that way?

For example, if you have just hurt someone you love by something you said, don't just say you are sorry. Don't just ask for forgiveness; ask God to change the part of your personality or experience that produced those hurtful words. "Steadfast love surrounds those who trust in the LORD."

**PRAYER: God, show me my sin, and send your grace to the place, the thought, the desire in me that is responsible; change me there. Amen.**

What does it mean to Lent? Are you getting used to the question? Yesterday we talked about asking God to change the source of our sin, not just repair the damage caused by it. Our task today is to consider what it means to accept the breathtaking heart of God's plan to change everything about us, to restore everything in us to an "Edenlike" righteousness. To Lent means to accept God's solution and, conversely, not to make up our own.

Some argue today that Paul's classic language in Romans 5:12-19 is outdated. It does not make sense to the modern mind. We need to substitute something more relevant for the concepts of *sin*, *atonement*, *salvation*, *judgment*, and the like. While these words may need some refreshing, it seems foolish to abandon them because they don't square with today's thinking.

Consider Paul's subject here, the Atonement. I will never be able to explain how "the free gift in the grace of the one man, Jesus Christ" took away our sin and opened up a path "that leads to justification and life for all." But I don't think God asks me to understand it fully. I believe God invites me simply to accept that this is what God knew needed to happen so that we could be forgiven and reconciled. Only God in God's infinite glory can fully understand or explain it.

To Lent means we are not only coming to terms with what has led us astray but are turning to the clear path that God has established to lead us home. After all, there is the little matter of Good Friday between here and Easter.

**PRAYER: God, open my mind and heart to receive what you know I need from you. Amen.**

What does it mean to Lent? One of the things it means is to acknowledge just how easy it is to forget to Lent. Got it? Part of the purpose of Lent is to remind us that the invitation to choose against God is as real today as it was in Eden. The evil one still hates what God loves and is still earnestly dedicated to finding any and all means to trip us up.

Here we read about the classic confrontation between Jesus and Satan. On one side, Satan has an arsenal of exquisite temptations. On the other side, Jesus has intentionally allowed himself to be led to an extreme position of vulnerability. This battle will continue on the cross. Yet here, at the beginning of his ministry, Jesus wants to reassure us that, at least for now, he has stood the test. He has resisted the evil one, remained faithful even as one fully human, and begun to reverse the damage done in Eden.

On a personal level I think Jesus wants to encourage us to deal with the side of ourselves that sometimes wants to believe the tempter's lies; the part of us that still wants to believe there is another way, a simpler way, a compromise. To Lent is to challenge all the ways we want to have our cake and eat it too.

So what do we need to do to Lent? Shall we give up something knowing that we can take it up again after Easter? Shall we stop doing something, only to spend Lent dreaming about the day when we can resume the activity? Why waste Lent on such options? A better alternative might be to go after something that needs going after, something we want to change in our life permanently. Better to fail at something important than to succeed at something far less meaningful.

**PRAYER: Lord, show me where my battle is this Lent. Amen.**

BATTLE : OUR HOME

What does it mean to Lent? Part of what it means to Lent is to accept the truth that until a time of God's choosing, we will always need another Lent. As long as we reside in the body, there will still be times when we cry out, "Restore to me the joy of your salvation, and sustain in me a willing spirit." We will still need someone to remind us it is not too late. "Who knows whether he will not turn and relent, and leave a blessing behind him, a grain offering and a drink offering for the LORD, your God?"

For a period of about five years I watched helplessly as a dear friend became depressed and started drinking heavily. Finally, when the choice was almost life or death, he accepted the help of a Christ-centered treatment ministry our church supports. The men live in community on a farm a couple hours away.

One Sunday morning the leader of this ministry was to speak at our church. He did not tell me that he was bringing my friend with him. Oddly, earlier that morning I had been over-whelmed by a strong urge to rewrite my message. I had cobbled something together, but I wasn't really thrilled with it. The moment I saw my friend I realized that God had created this new message with just the place for him to testify. He talked to our church, his church, about what God had done for him; and we were all blessed.

How will my friend's story come out? God knows. My friend may stumble and need to cry out for forgiveness again. As long as we are in the body, there will always be another Lent.

PRAYER: **God, show me where I need to cry out, and help me appreciate that it is never too late. Amen.**

ROBERT GLENN BUSSINGER

What does it mean to Lent? To Lent means we don't just think about what we need to let go of; we think about what we need to take up. To Lent means we don't just let go of what doesn't work; we pick up what *does* work. To Lent means we don't just stop pursuing what isn't God's dream for our life; we start pursuing what *is* God's dream for our life. Reconciliation is about what we need to let go of and what we need to take up. As we are reconciled to God, our life, our ordinary life, can become an invitation to others to join us on this road. Paul says, "So we are ambassadors for Christ, since God is making his appeal through us" (2 Cor. 5:20*a*).

To Lent is to learn to be an ambassador for Christ, to point away from ourselves to what God has done for us in Jesus. Paul has not led an easy life. Most people would say he had a lot to complain about. But he will not let anything come between him and what it means to point to Jesus. Read the description of his life again. Paul's attitude toward his life is such that even his suffering points to Jesus. No matter what he has gone through, he has gone through it as an ambassador for Christ, reaching the place where his whole life, no matter what, still points to Jesus.

I wish I could say the same about my life. I can't right now. But that's what Lent is about. Lent isn't just looking for what *isn't* pointing to God; it's looking to see how everything can be transformed into something that *does* point to God. What does it mean to go through every experience of life as an "ambassador for Christ"?

**PRAYER: God, as I learn to Lent, let my life, my whole life, point to you. Amen.**

## FIRST SUNDAY IN LENT

What does it mean to Lent? For our final day, what it means to Lent is to discover what it means to Easter. Jesus did not come so that we would spend our whole life lamenting our sin and focusing on what we are not. He came to give us life, life in abundance (John 10:10). What it means to Lent and what it means to Easter are both present in Matthew 6.

In this passage Jesus is determined to point out what needs to change in our lives. He warns us that we can seek God and care for one another with impure motives. God knows why we do everything we do. God knows why we do something good for someone else and why we put our offering in the plate. God knows why we pray and fast and work. And God knows that we sometimes do good things for the wrong reasons.

But look deeper. Why would Jesus point out what we do wrong if he didn't believe we could get it right? Jesus doesn't just describe how we can get prayer or giving wrong; he says we can get them right. There is a way to give and a way to pray that pleases God. God believes we can begin to treasure those things that cannot be stored up on earth but only in heaven.

Will we ever get there? Will we ever leave Lent behind forever and live only in the light of Easter? My experience of faith so far tells me that the answer is probably no, not in this life. However, if we will take seriously what it means to Lent, we will discover that in marvelous and amazing ways we can begin to Easter here and now.

**PRAYER: Lord, may I begin every day knowing that you believe in me. Amen.**

# Keeper of Promises

February 11–17, 2008 • Karla M. Kincannon[‡]

## MONDAY, FEBRUARY 11 • Read Genesis 12:1-4*a*

All of us long to be accepted; we are born with an innate desire to belong. This longing serves as a driving force in life, guiding us to seek its fulfillment through human relationships. As children we look to our parents or guardians for acceptance. As teenagers we desire to "fit in" with our peers; we want to be a member of the pack. By the time we reach adulthood, if we have not received a blessing from a significant adult figure, we can spend our entire lives feeling as if we don't belong.

Blessings have power to create; they can shape our future. A blessing holds the promise and the power of what we shall become. Though critically important, parental blessings do not have the ultimate power to satisfy our need to belong. Only divine blessings completely quench our thirst for acceptance. God's blessings confer a sense of well-being, purposefulness, and belonging; they reveal our rightful place in the universe.

Our task in life is not so much to get God to bless us, as to realize the divine blessing God has already bestowed upon us. Divine blessings, like the one Abram received, root us deeply in God. God's blessing of Abram included a promise that enabled him to become his very best self and thereby bless all the families of the earth. Through the blessing, Abram became Abraham, the person God intended him to be all along.

**SUGGESTION FOR MEDITATION: How has God blessed you? How might you grow into a deeper awareness of that blessing? Imagine the words God would use to bless you into becoming the person you are intended to be. Allow those words to sink into your soul. How is God inviting you to share this blessing with others?**

---

[‡]United Methodist minister, artist, and author of *Creativity and Divine Surprise: Finding the Place of Your Resurrection.*

Native American tribes make communal decisions based on the benefit of the decision for the seventh generation to come. The tribe's future is more important than the gratification of a single generation. I wonder if Abram had a similar perspective as he abandoned his pagan way of life to follow God's call to an unidentified destination. On a promise Abram left everything familiar and journeyed into an unknown future. He never saw God's promise fulfilled. He died without knowing how God would bless all the families of the earth through him; yet, his response to God shaped the future for the seventh generation and beyond.

How many other people did God ask before Abram said yes to the divine call? We will never know. We do know that Abram's faithfulness contributed to God's purpose for creation because we are part of the "families of the earth." God has blessed us through Abram. Blessing the earth and all its inhabitants is part of our Creator's intention for the world.

The God who was committed to Abram's future is committed to our future. Yet, today, Siberian permafrost melts at an alarming rate. Alaskan trees that once stood tall and straight now lean drunkenly from the defrosting tundra. Monster storms wreck coastlines and lives. Worldwide climate change is occurring in our lifetime, and scientists agree the speed of these changes corresponds directly to the human imprint on our earth home.

God remains committed to our future. Like Abram, our job is to align our actions with God's purposes. How can we live as a blessing for the seventh generation to come? How will our decisions about energy consumption and stewardship of earth's resources cooperate with God's plans? Will our lives be a blessing or a curse for our great-grandchildren's grandchildren?

**PRAYER: Keeper of promises, grant us the wisdom and courage we need to be a blessing to others. Amen.**

Thousands of Christians on pilgrimage to Jerusalem have recited or sung today's psalm. A pilgrimage is an outward journey with an inward component. The central purpose of a pilgrimage is to seek a closer relationship with the living God, just as Abraham did by leaving his homeland.

Christians began as early as the fourth and fifth centuries to make pilgrimages to Jerusalem to deepen their relationship with the living Christ by walking where Jesus walked. Today persons of faith understand that life itself is a pilgrimage, a journey from birth to death and beyond. We do not have to travel to distant lands in order to seek God's presence; we only have to travel inward to our deep center.

Since my family's pilgrimage (and move) to the hills of East Tennessee I've gained insight into this psalm. Having never spent much time near mountains, I didn't realize how comforting they are. The purple and blue hills I see from my bedroom window have come to represent a quiet strength. As I open the curtains each morning, they greet me with their calm, steadfast beauty, and I am filled with awe.

Even as glorious as are the hills, the psalmist proclaims that our help comes from *the maker* of the hills! The One who made such exquisite beauty is even more majestic than creation itself. The psalmist promises that the maker of hills is also the keeper of our pilgrimage through life. Though powerful enough to make the lofty mountains, God cares enough to guard us by day and by night. The God of the distant mountains intimately watches our steps and protects us from evil. In our going out and our coming into this life, God hovers over us like the eagles I see soaring over the mountains.

Greeting the mountains each morning, I know my help comes from the Lord.

**PRAYER: Go before me this day, O God. Prepare my path. Amen.**

## Thursday, February 14 • Read Romans 4:1-5, 13-17

Who is in? Who is out? Who belongs to the family of faith? Christians have been trying to answer these questions since the birth of the church. Denominations and religious sects have emerged in response to the question of belonging. Wars have been fought over these questions. Individuals and groups of people have been denied membership in churches because someone determined they did not belong. What is it about human nature that needs to build walls of inclusion and exclusion?

In today's passage, Paul addresses an audience that wants to build walls. He wrestles with what it means to belong to the Christian family. Members of the church at Rome thought a person needed to be part of the ethnic family of Abraham in order to become a Christian. Gentiles didn't meet that requirement. Paul argues that inclusion is quite simply a matter of faith in the God who raised Jesus Christ from the dead; nothing more, nothing less.

The apostle uses the analogy of earning wages to demonstrate that the saving grace of God is a free gift to everyone, not something we earn through heritage or right living. Paul slips in a phrase about justifying the "ungodly" to remind the Roman audience that before Abram became Abraham, he was a pagan from the land of Ur. Abraham had as much in common with the Gentiles (considered ungodly by law-abiding Jews), as he did with those of Jewish ancestry. The covenant God made with Abraham was a gift.

Christians of Jewish ancestry could no longer boast that ethnicity opened the doors to membership, neither did their willingness to obey Jewish law. Paul makes it clear that faith in the God who resurrected Jesus was and is the only thing necessary to be a Christian.

SUGGESTION FOR MEDITATION: **What does it mean to belong to the family of God? What's the criterion for being a Christian? Are your church's doors open to all persons?**

At first glance this passage seems to be only about Abraham and his faithfulness—but the main character is actually God. These verses wonderfully describe God's nature. Paul paints a glorious portrait of God whose grace extends to the ungodly or the unsavory elements of society, even before they come to believe in God. The apostle tells us that divine grace reaches into our lives as a free gift, impossible to earn. God loves us too much to use our worth or our works as the condition for relationship with the divine!

With detailed brushstrokes, Paul shows that God has fulfilled the covenant and kept the divine promise to create a family not through human effort but through faith. God intended that this covenant rectify what was wrong with the world. It was an outpouring of God's grace. The God of whom Paul writes is shown as generous beyond measure, faithful beyond steadfastness, and so desirous of being in relationship with us that any unworthiness on our part is not an obstacle.

Furthermore, Paul describes a God who miraculously gives life to the dead. The first audience to hear these words would have heard a double entendre. Through the birth of offspring, God gave life to Abraham when he was as good as dead; and, God raised Jesus Christ from the dead. The apostle declares the God who made covenant with Abraham is the God of Jesus Christ. Christ is the one who shows us most clearly the nature of God who keeps promises and makes all things new. In Christ, humanity is set right with God, and the ungodly find welcome in the family.

SUGGESTION FOR MEDITATION: **What is your image of God? List all the names and descriptors for God that come to mind. What new ways of knowing God might the Spirit want to show you?**

Nicodemus reminds me of many on the Christian journey. We think highly enough of Jesus to call him "teacher" and are impressed with the stories of his miracles and healings. We go to church and try to do the right things. We desire a deeper relationship with the Holy, but we have yet to experience the life-giving power of God to which Jesus invites us. We do not know the joy of the Lord.

Jesus doesn't judge or condemn Nicodemus but issues an invitation, saying, "Come on in, Nicodemus, the water's fine! There is more to life than what meets the eye. If you want to see the kingdom of God, jump in the pool." Jesus invites Nicodemus to go deeper on the faith journey, but Nicodemus wants to know how deep the water is before getting his feet wet. He desires proof of God's presence in his life before taking the next step; however, the faith journey is a matter of trust not proof. Without trust in God's love, Nicodemus can't understand Jesus' invitation. He cannot hear with the ears of faith.

Until we make a leap of faith, the joy of the Lord remains beyond reach. Christ invites us to surrender to God's intention for our lives and move into greater intimacy with our Creator. Without the trust that enables us to let go into God's love, we only see the surface of the pool. We miss the depth of God's love and the joy found in an intimate life with our Creator. Faith in God gives us eyes to see and ears to hear; it opens a new realm of life to us.

SUGGESTION FOR MEDITATION: Think about the birth process. A baby does not know what awaits its arrival or the quality of life it will experience after its first cries of life. How is your life with God similar to the birth of a baby?

SUNDAY, FEBRUARY 17 • **Read John 3:1-17**

## SECOND SUNDAY IN LENT

Poetry and metaphor are the language of faith. Given the limitations of human language in talking about God, poetry and metaphor come closest to articulating the truth. They best describe what is indescribable on the spiritual journey.

Today's scripture is full of metaphors, each one building on the others. To be "born from above" also means to be "born again." If taken literally, we wonder with Nicodemus about the physical possibility of entering the womb for the second time, but the author is speaking metaphorically. He's talking about conversion. The phrase "born of water" could refer to the water of a womb or the water of baptism, and the use of the word *wind* to explain birth can mean "wind" or "spirit." Each metaphor has a meaning deeper than the surface understanding, revealing a hidden aspect of the spiritual life.

As we reach verse 15, hopefully the double meanings are growing clear. The climax of the text resides in the Hebrew verb meaning to "lift up," which can also mean "to exalt." Jesus physically lifted up on the cross is an act of exaltation.

In this verse the Gospel writer proclaims that Jesus' crucifixion mysteriously and miraculously makes eternal life possible for those who believe. We are so used to hearing the words "eternal life" that we do not hear them as metaphor. This is Nicodemus's problem too. The Gospel of John uses "eternal life" to mean not just the endless duration of life but a life lived in the unremitting presence of God. Eternal life is a here-and-now life, a life lived on earth as a forgiven and beloved child of God. Eternal life begins with our leap of faith and our decision to follow Jesus in worshiping the God of love.

**SUGGESTION FOR MEDITATION: How does the understanding of eternal life as beginning in the present moment change the way you look at your life? What difference does it make in how you live?**

# Hearts Drenched with Love

*February 18–24, 2008* • *David Davies*[‡]

## MONDAY, FEBRUARY 18 • Read Exodus 17:1-4

Two chapters earlier, the Hebrews were dancing about and singing Miriam's song of victory, boasting of god Yahweh's victory over god Pharaoh and probably eating and drinking too much of the provision they had brought with them out of Egypt. By Exodus 17, water, or rather the lack of it, continues a chain of afflictions, and the mood turns as sour as the water at Marah. My heart beats with the Hebrews here. They are the mail-order bride of this god Yahweh. Forty generations after they last heard anything, they have to be introduced by Moses. A promise of freedom from the slavery imposed by Pharaoh is given, along with a promise of their own land. But now it appears that this god Yahweh is going to neglect them—first bad water, then no food, now no water and a trackless waste of a desert looming before them.

What have they gotten themselves into? The good old-time religion of god Pharaoh included their degradation and slavery, but at least they had food and water. You can hear the Hebrews revising the memory of Pharaoh's production society, as Walter Brueggemann calls it, into something positive: "Yes, the work was hard, but it built character. You could see what you had done at the end of the day. You were part of something big and the cities and monuments you built would stand for generations." This god Yahweh expects them to follow blindly day to day a pillar of smoke that seems blown by the wind to the edge of calamity and to trust in an abundance that defies all their ability to search or strive for it. Often we too get lost in our relationships when our imaginations come between us and one another.

**PRAYER: God who frees the captive, free us from expectations of you that keep us from entering into a relationship of trust in you with all our heart and mind and strength. Amen.**

---

[‡]Computer programmer, owner of Soul Desires bookstore in Omaha, Nebraska.

The rock/mountain of Horeb appears in so many different places in the Exodus story that one of the traditions in rabbinic literature is that Horeb actually moved with the Hebrews like the pillar of smoke and fire. It makes no more sense to me to try to explain Yahweh's standing on the rock Horeb or what kind of rock formations in the Sinai peninsula might contain water that would be released if they were broken open. Have you ever tried to break any kind of rock with a stick?

This is not a story about hydrology or mineralogy or geography. It is a story about trust and the building of relationship between the Hebrews and Moses, between Moses and God, between the Hebrews and God. Moses' poll ratings are so bad he feels his life is threatened. A pragmatic leader would have figured out the quickest way back to the seventy-palm oasis in chapter 15. A pragmatic leader would not have taken the members of the press corps and leaders of the opposition further into the wilderness to watch him whack away at a rock with a stick. But Moses' experience with Yahweh has built a relationship of trust.

And what is this god Yahweh like who is being revealed? What god but the God of all creation and all the surprises creation holds would choose the unlikely combination of rock and water? In the desert you might seek a rock for shelter in a sandstorm or from the noonday heat. You would not cling to these rocks or expect them to provide you with water. A relationship with this God will be filled with surprises: pleasant surprises, life-giving surprises that can break open hard, barren situations to give refreshment and hope to travel on. This God of the rock that becomes a spring calls the Hebrews into relationship. Surprises can frighten us, frustrate us, or amuse us; but always they call us to change. We may respond by defending against surprises or by embracing the change.

PRAYER: God, who cannot be limited by my imagination, help me open my heart to your abundant providence from the places I least expect to find it. Amen.

This is a singularly disconcerting psalm. The psalms often change tone from the beginning to the end. Sometimes they change voice as to who is speaking. Usually, however, there is a flow of emotion or a connection of experience from the one to the other. This psalm starts out like a pure praise psalm such as 93 or 96, but in the middle takes a radical turn when the psalmist suggests that we hear what God is saying to us today. The psalmist then hands the microphone over to God who encourages us not to harden our hearts as the Hebrews did in Exodus 17. In a remarkable revelation, God admits that God finds this mail-order marriage with the Hebrews as vexing as do the Hebrews. God just doesn't like them.

One of the homeless people who orbits our bookstore I will call Doug. Doug is a paranoid schizophrenic who has many demons that visit him. He is a vocal bigot of every group you can imagine, including poor people of whom he does not consider himself a member. Though he will tame his tongue when reminded and can have a certain charm when he chooses to exercise it, I find very little to like about Doug. Nevertheless, I help Doug with whatever I judge to be of assistance. Though I was once his Social Security guardian and signed a lease on an apartment, my help now comes in the form of a beverage or lunch from the cooler and occasional paid odd-jobs that fit his rather limited skill set.

I don't like Doug, but I have a covenant with him that will not let me abandon him to his desert. Psalm 95 seemingly acknowledges the same for God and the Hebrews of Exodus 17. God does not like them but has a covenant with them. The good news is that God does not expect us to be more than God is and to have warm feelings toward everyone. It is easy to serve those we are fond of; our struggle may come in our commitment to be in community with those we dislike.

PRAYER: God, help me acknowledge all my feelings and remain constant in my service. Amen.

Paul as Saul was an aggressive and angry man. Like most angry people his image of God was probably angry and wrathful. After his Damascus experience, Paul retained an aggressive edge despite his experience with a God of love and compassion. He still tends to expect and fear God's wrath (he apparently anticipated the end of the world before his death) and to describe human relationships in terms of power, aggression, and anger.

Here Paul not only describes humans as being in a position of weakness to God ("helpless" in one translation) but also as being enemies of God. My dictionary defines an enemy as "one who opposes the purposes or interests of another." Now Paul, who generally qualifies the observations he makes about human nature—case in point, what kind of person might one die for— makes no qualification here. He considers all humans, even the strictly observant Jews of which he once counted himself a member, to be enemies of God, bent on opposing God's purpose.

Even those most dedicated to God oppose God's intention. How does he know this? Because despite human powerlessness, God allowed Jesus, God's son, to be killed by weak humans. No action more surely would require vengeance from an angry god, a god who was as much against humans as humans were against God. Instead, people are being changed by the touch of the living Christ, changed to live out God's purpose. And what has Paul found to be God's purpose? To love us (v. 8), to be at peace with us (v. 1), to share the glory of God (v. 2), to have our hearts drenched with God's love through the Holy Spirit (v. 5). In our striving to be faithful followers of Christ, we too can be opponents of God's purpose. Only through Christ do we receive reconciliation.

**PRAYER: God, whose presence can change an enemy into a friend, be present to me that I may be at peace with you and overflow with your love for the world. Amen.**

Paul being the person he is, skilled and trained in logical and legal ways of thinking, struggles to make sense of his experience of the living Christ, the glorified Jesus. How can this be? The man Jesus was executed by the state. Jesus, when alive, had spoken with authority, as one touched by God. But he did not fight for his beliefs. If he were not going to fight, at least he could have said what they wanted, gotten off with a lashing, and lived to use his resentment and frustration to strengthen his faithfulness and the faithfulness of others to the religious traditions. He could have used that angry faithfulness to fuel his active subversion of the occupying pagan forces. One or the other: argue and fight with them or gain glory through a demonstration of the strength of your faith—or say what you need to live and fight another day, another way to gain your glory. Those were the choices that Saul might have considered.

But Saul experienced the living Christ, Jesus raised in glory as the Son of God. The unimaginable, unexpected experience that out of his death—this submission to execution, this relinquishment of power, this exercise of humility—could come glorification and new life, a life that filled others with love and peace and joy. This was the rock that Paul had to beat with his stick again and again to explain how living water had come forth.

One spiritually formative event of my childhood came when I was working on a project that involved a hammer and nails. I struck poorly and brought the hammer down on my finger. As I paced the garage, I cried out asking God what I had done to deserve this. My mother, hearing my cry, came out from the house. Though concerned with my finger, she also told me that this was not how God worked in the world, that God loved us and would not cause us to suffer. How natural it seems to look for God's vengeance in the events of our lives and how hard to let God's love overflow in our lives.

PRAYER: **God, whose love far exceeds my ability to offend, help me give up my human measurements of your love. Amen.**

The story of the Samaritan woman at the well encapsulates all the elements of the Johannine Gospel for me: Jesus speaking with a person who is not his follower in a conversation in which they talk past each other. Jesus speaks in spiritual metaphor; the other person speaks in terms of concrete, physical world events.

Perhaps the writer of John's Gospel liked to present Jesus this way because the writer also speaks so much in metaphor. This story involves much more than a conversation between Jesus and one woman. The central image of the story gives us a clue: a well, Jacob's well, and the non-Jewish people who claim the land and its god. In pre-urban society, wells and springs are about divine providence, about a people's claim to the land and relationship with the god of the land.

When the Northern Kingdom of Israel fell and its people were deported to Assyria, Samaritans from five regions were brought into the land by the Assyrian king to replace them. They brought with them a specific god, and the people worshiped Yahweh as well. The Israelites never accepted the Samaritans, and the hostility continued well after Jesus' day. In allegorical language, nations are women who are married to the god they worship: Five gods (five husbands) and the one she currently lives with (Yahweh) is not her husband. This story is not about the relationship between Jesus and a much-married woman but about the relationship between God and non-Jews—the other, the pagan. We are in relationship with God not because of birthright, not because of wells, not because of land or country but because of the Spirit. All who worship in spirit and truth are welcomed by the God of Jesus to drink of the living water. As humans our anxieties and fears about being right with God can cause us to withhold God's love from the other.

**PRAYER: God, whose love knows no bounds, help me when I want to withhold your living water from others because they do not meet my standards—standards that I mistake for yours. Amen.**

SUNDAY, FEBRUARY 24 • Read John 4:27-42

THIRD SUNDAY IN LENT

Once Jesus finally connects with the Samaritan woman at the well, along come the disciples who are every bit as concrete and physical in their thinking as she had been before she "got it." The disciples get confused and bothered when Jesus tells them that in their absence he has been fed. *Has someone been bringing him food?* they wonder, looking suspiciously at one another lest one of them is currying favor with the teacher.

Jesus responds that the members of the body are fed when the work of the one who sent him is being done. And then, mixing metaphors but staying with food, we get an explanation of how this happens. We don't start from scratch, and we don't work alone. If we had nothing to eat from the time we planted the seeds to the harvesting of the wheat (four months, the Gospel says) we would not live long enough to see the grain ripen. What we gather, others have planted. We are fed by the efforts of those who came before us, and we sow what we will not reap. This chain of tending and caring stretches back to the story of God's garden where God fed and cared for our forebears directly.

In such a great chain of sustenance based on God's example and empowered by God's loving providence, there is no room for suspicion or competition or possessiveness. God's work is not about my success. My very life is rooted in the relationships seen and unseen, past and present, human and divine that are part of this chain of abundant sustenance. When that sustenance is shared with others, then they too become part of the chain just as the Samaritans are able to say they believe not because the woman at the well told them but because they have experienced it for themselves. In that sharing, those who worship in spirit and truth are fed.

**PRAYER: God, who has cared for those who sowed what we harvest, who feeds us as we feed others, help us give up our possessiveness, our suspicion, our competitiveness and celebrate your abundant love. Amen.**

# Seeing More Deeply

*February 25–March 2, 2008 • Gina Gilland Campbell[‡]*

## MONDAY, FEBRUARY 25 • Read 1 Samuel 16:1-5

A physician friend has gifts for healing persons with serious brain injuries. Almost always, patients or their families ask this question on first visits: "Doctor, can you help?"

Sometimes my friend tells me that given the severity of a patient's injury, no precedent exists in medical literature for answering yes. "Yet, I always smile and answer yes. And I am telling the truth," he says. "I have learned when it comes to the human brain, it is important to keep asking questions. Questions create an opening in which the way to healing makes itself known." The power of questions can open a way when he can see no way.

When God tells Samuel to go to Bethlehem to anoint Israel's new king, Samuel asks a question: "How can I go?" He has good reason to fear. Why would Saul, reigning king, permit anyone to anoint his successor? Samuel seems willing to go; he simply does not see a way to do as God asks and live.

Samuel places his dilemma squarely before God. "How?" And God respects Samuel's dilemma. God does not chide Samuel for expressing honest fear or suggest that Samuel ignore very real danger. Instead, God steps into the space created by Samuel's openness and offers a strategy for entering Bethlehem and the promise of divine discernment in the task ahead.

How do I forgive? How can I let go? How can I obey God's request? Powerful questions. Yet, when we ask with open minds and hearts in a spirit of yielding and trust, God respects honest seeking. God helps us see a way where we cannot.

**SUGGESTION FOR MEDITATION: Where in my life does the "how" question present itself? Where might God see a way where I cannot?**

---

[‡]United Methodist pastor; adjunct faculty, Center for Family Process, Bethesda, Maryland, and Wesley Theological Seminary, Washington, D.C.

Jesus takes the initiative, heals the man, leaves the scene. Jesus reappears as the story closes, finds the man, and affirms his seeing. Seeing deeply begins with Jesus. The man born blind never sees Jesus' face before the questioning begins. "How were your eyes opened?" neighbors ask. Responding, the man mentions Jesus' use of ordinary things to bestow eyesight. "Jesus made mud, spread it on my eyes, and said . . . 'Go . . . and wash.'"

Using ordinary things, Jesus invites deeper seeing. Can we see in the mud our beginning: God scooping and shaping humanity from earth's clay? Can we see in the Siloam pool baptismal waters and God's ongoing renewal of creation? In the hands of Jesus, ordinary things become extraordinary, sight-bestowing, life-transforming things. Seeing deeply begins with God's love of ordinary things.

The Pharisees then ask how the man received his sight. As the man repeats his story, we notice that receiving sight involves touch and movement. Students of the physiology of seeing say only ten percent of our "seeing" comes through our eyes. Most of what we "see" actually enters our brain through touch and movement, which the brain translates into vision. We know that babies who never crawl struggle with depth perception.

The man's willingness to receive Jesus' touch and to move to the pool creates the possibility of eyesight and insight. Seeing deeply requires eyesight, touch, and motion.

The challenges intensify. The man's family isolates him; his neighbors avoid him; his faith community expels him. Paradoxically, the challenges increase the clarity of his seeing: "One thing I do know. . . . " Times of challenge and loss invite a look into the depths to see grace, to see clear through to the glory of God.

Seeing in this way asks that we hold open a place for surprise. The man touches this place, astonished that the religious authorities miss the glory of God in the opening of his eyes.

**SUGGESTION FOR MEDITATION: How is God opening my eyes through ordinary things: touch, movement, challenge, surprise?**

The parade of Jesse's sons before Samuel begins with Eliab. A strapping young man, Eliab looks like king material to Samuel. God wastes no time in setting Samuel straight. Look again, God instructs. Look beneath the skin. Look until you see as I see—I see the heart.

David's own father sees nothing worth mentioning related to his youngest son. Even when Samuel rejects his other sons, Jesse cannot see his shepherd son as royal raw material. Sometimes even those closest to us cannot see the potential God sees; they cannot see our hearts.

A friend says, "If all we can see is what actually is, we are in trouble." Seeing truly and deeply means looking beyond existing conditions. It means seeing into the heart of people and situations, leaning into our imaginations until we see the reality beyond what is.

Victor Frankl, imprisoned by the Nazis, freed himself to visualize life beyond the barbed wire of the concentration camp. His capacity to look beyond existing conditions preserved life in the midst of death.

God trains Samuel's eyes. Samuel looks at all God does not choose, then waits as the last, remote possibility comes in from tending sheep. God acknowledges that this is the heart that pleases. In the seeing of God's heart, this young shepherd boy becomes shepherd king for all of Israel.

The church gives David's heart a hymnbook. In seventy-three Psalter songs, the heart God chooses seeks wisdom, finds courage, breaks, meditates, stirs, praises, rejoices. According to these songs, God even sees beyond the times that David's heart hardens, closes, and rebels. Israel will grow to love the heart of this king beyond all others.

SUGGESTION FOR MEDITATION: **Where in my life, relationships, prayer, and service is God inviting me to move from looking to seeing? What songs does my heart long to sing?**

What does it mean to be light? Six people, ages fourteen to eighty, gathered for Bible study. For three years they shared a commitment to one another and to looking deeply at scripture.

Mr. Jones, the oldest member, was a retired attorney. He had studied scripture and theology for years. Articulate, forceful, and abrasive, he frequently launched into lengthy, harsh critiques of passages he rejected: stories of animal sacrifice, violent psalms, any text related to sharing generously with the poor.

The youngest member, a quiet fourteen-year-old, wondered along with me about Mr. Jones's tirades. She experienced him as cynical, judgmental, and bitter. She struggled with how to invite him to see the effect of his speech on her.

One particular night, Mr. Jones attacked Jesus' "I am" statements: "I don't believe Jesus said such presumptuous things. Who would follow such a narcissist?"

As he spoke, the young woman reached out and placed her hand on Mr. Jones's arm. He stopped in midsentence. In the gentlest of voices, she said, "Mr. Jones, for two years I have listened to all you reject in the Bible. I know what you *don't* believe. When you talk the way you do, I find it hard to be here. I don't want to come back. It would help me if just for tonight you could tell me what you *do* believe."

A deep stillness settled over our small group. The anger in Mr. Jones melted away before our eyes. Later, his wife would say, "I don't know what you do in that Bible study, but it has changed my husband. He is a different man."

Sometimes being light means seeing darkness and exposing it. It means having the right question and asking it in a moment carefully chosen from a place of authenticity and love. It means making darkness so visible it becomes light.

**SUGGESTION FOR MEDITATION: Where and how is God, through Christ, preparing me to be light? to bear fruit that is good, right, and true?**

Our culture encourages consumption. With overflowing closets and pantries, we continue buying. The psalmist says that those who call the Lord their shepherd will not lack anything, that they will not "want." But as we blur the line between what we need and what we want, the desire for more of everything can blind us to the abundance of God's gracious providing.

Some confirmation class members were invited to create collages to illustrate their wants and needs, yet virtually everything the students included was considered a need. Reflecting on the projects, the teacher said, "I realized that these children lack criteria for making distinctions between wants and needs. If they want it, they need it."

Wanting affects our vision. Without realizing it, we come to ask for the green pastures to be greener, the cup fuller, the anointing oil to be a better brand. Wants can evolve into selfish needs that refuse satisfaction.

"I shall not want," the psalmist wrote. When it comes to looking at our lives, we have a choice. We can want our way into a feeling of deprivation and neediness, or we can step back and focus on all that God has given. Our choice can transform us.

My husband struggled through six months of chemotherapy. Each week in the treatment room, we joined the same group of patients, families, and friends. Certain patients were never satisfied: the nurses were too rough, the physicians dismissive, the side effects of treatment unbearable. In contrast, other patients embodied gratitude for tender nurses, caring physicians, soothing medicines, good friends stepping in for exhausted family.

What we choose to see matters. Do we see with wanting eyes or with eyes attuned to God's gracious provision? Choosing the latter we will discover even in the shadow places God's generously laden table, God's guiding rod and staff, God's very life spilling over into ours.

SUGGESTION FOR MEDITATION: **Where in my life is wanting obscuring my vision? Where do I see the evidence of God's gracious provision?**

SATURDAY, MARCH 1 • Read Psalm 23:5-6

A woman requested prayers for healing. Her son had been mur-
dered in a convenience store robbery gone wrong five years earlier. "For two years," she said, "I could hardly get out of bed.
Then, one day, I heard God tell me to go to the prison and meet
the young man who killed my son. I went against my husband's
wishes. He thinks I dishonor our son's memory by going there.
The prison staff put us together in a windowless room, two cold
metal chairs with an institutional grey table between us. When
our eyes met, he could see I was nervous. I could see his fear. I
asked where he grew up. We talked."

"We talked that way for months. Then one day he asked me
why I came to see him. I said God told me to come. He put his
head in his hands, down on that table, and sobbed. He said he
never thought anyone would get hurt. He was wrong. He asked
my forgiveness. I put my head down on the table close to his and
whispered my forgiveness. Now our visits are deeper somehow."

"And the healing prayer you need?" I asked, marveling at the
healing already taking place.

"For my husband," she said. "He hates that boy and hates me
for going there. His hating makes things worse. It's already breaking our marriage. If he could only see what I see across that table."

What creates an enemy? Enmities rise up in broken, vulnerable, hurting places. We know our enemies so well that when the
shepherd places them across the lovingly prepared table, right in
our sight lines, we recognize them.

Why would God bring us so close to our enemies? Something transformational occurs when the shepherd companions
us, even in the presence of our enemies.

SUGGESTION FOR MEDITATION: **Where does enmity have power
in my life? What table is the shepherd preparing for me for the
healing of enmity?**

## FOURTH SUNDAY IN LENT

Our own truth, even sacred and holy truth, can blind us when it grows hard, closed, arrogant. It never occurs to the Pharisees that claiming special spiritual knowledge makes them blind—more than blind. According to Jesus, it makes them sinful.

Guarding the law against heretical interpretation, the Pharisees fill a legitimate role in Israel's life. Given by God, the law shapes Israel's identity as God's people, contains the patterns for closeness to God and neighbor, guides covenantal living.

Over time, the Pharisees grow smug, so sure of themselves, so sure of everything regarding law and holiness; they squeeze out the space rightfully occupied by God. The Pharisees come to believe themselves in charge of holiness, living so fully in the illumination of their own lesser lights that when the light of the world comes in living form, it proves too much for them. In the presence of Jesus, the Pharisees recede into a darkness of their own choosing, a blindness and sin.

The consequences of the Pharisees' sin spill over into the life of the man born blind. Intensely focused on sniffing out the sin of others, the Pharisees create tensions in the man's relationships. It takes enormous courage on the man's part to hold open a space for holy unknowing in the face of pressure to point out sin. The man's neighbors, family, his fellow worshipers—unable to withstand the Pharisees' mean-spirited persistence—desert him.

In the name of holiness, the Pharisees leave a wake of brokenness they do not see. The Pharisees hold open no space for God's mysterious vitality. Trusting in their own truth, they miss God's truth. Trusting in their own light, they miss God's true light. Trusting in their own vision, they miss God's invitation to see differently.

SUGGESTION FOR MEDITATION: **How is God illuminating brokenness that flows from my certainties? inviting new vision? seeking space in my life?**

# Concerning the God We Serve

*March 3–9, 2008* • *Laurence Hull Stookey*[‡]

## MONDAY, MARCH 3 • Read Ezekiel 37:1-3

As we journey further into Lent, we do well to look closely at the nature of the God whom we serve. Today's lesson reveals a vast disparity between divine and human knowledge. God asks the prophet, "Can these bones live?" Ezekiel knows better than to answer that one. Instead he confesses his own limitations: "O Lord GOD, you know." One temptation to which religious leaders are apt to succumb is presuming to know more about God than mortals are capable of knowing. Because Ezekiel senses the grandeur and greatness of the God whom we serve, he does not fall into the trap.

Yes, Matthew does say of Jesus that "he taught them as one having authority, and not as their scribes" (Matt. 7:28-29). But to contend that we teach with the full authority of Jesus betrays a weak Christology and encourages others to dismiss us quickly and justifiably as being both incorrect and hopelessly arrogant.

Notice that God does not reprimand Ezekiel for refusing to answer the question, "Can these bones live?" God accepts the prophet's meekness; but then, in instructing Ezekiel to speak to the bones, God implies the answer: "Yes, they can live again."

Although we often assume that the scribes to whom Matthew referred taught with indecision or timidity, in fact, it may be that they came across as being authoritarian experts who allowed no dissent or variation in opinion. There is a vast difference between *having* authority and *being* authoritarian. It is the latter that so easily does us in. From this we pray to be delivered.

**PRAYER: Grant, O Lord, that I never presume to know more than mortals can know. Guide me in the path of knowledge, and patiently show me your ways. In Jesus' name. Amen.**

---

[‡]Professor of Preaching and Worship, Wesley Theological Seminary, Washington, DC, for thirty-five years; in retirement, pastor, Asbury United Methodist Church, Allen, Maryland.

Once Ezekiel has acknowledged his limitations, he is ready to receive instruction from God. His obedience in prophesying to the dry bones results in a noise, a rattling, and a connecting of bone to bone. Behind this action lies a clearly stated divine purpose: the enlivening of the bones occurs so that all may know "that I am the LORD."

The Almighty does not do stunts to impress or entertain us. The Almighty is a God who seeks to bring us into covenant in order that we may experience saving grace firsthand. So astounding is this possibility that we meet it with skepticism, as did the whole house of Israel, saying: "Our bones are dried up, and our hope is lost; we are cut off completely."

Much of life is a contest between the promises of God and human incredulity. Even devout believers are caught on the wrong side. We say we believe that "a warrior is not delivered by his great strength. The war horse is a vain hope for victory" (Ps. 33:16–17). But how many "Christian" nations have dared to abolish all standing armies and weapons? We say we believe Jesus' word: "Do not store up for yourselves treasures on earth" (Matt. 6:19). Yet we spend inordinate amounts of time and energy shopping for, buying, and maintaining treasures and fretting about our bank and investment accounts.

We, like the bones in the valley, need to hear again that "I, the LORD, have spoken and will act." The God we serve works to redeem us, transform us, and breathe life into our dead bones. Only that conviction propels us toward Holy Week and moves us beyond the sorrow of Calvary to the joy of an empty tomb.

PRAYER: **Ever-active God, breathe your Spirit into my dry and disconnected bones; enliven them that I may serve you and your creation, according to your word; through Christ who died and lives again. Amen.**

WEDNESDAY, MARCH 5 • Read Psalm 130

Perhaps no passage of such brevity in the Hebrew scriptures anticipates the Gospel message as fully as Psalm 130. The writer cries out of the depths of an unspecified crisis. Perhaps the author's own iniquity calls forth this plea. On the other hand, the psalmist may be in agony because of the sins of those he loves. We could easily imagine this psalm to be the anguished prayer of David over the rebellion and death of Absalom. (See 2 Samuel 18:9-33.)

Having made so loud a cry for help in verses 1-2, the psalmist turns 180 degrees and in verses 3-4 strongly affirms God's goodness. If the Almighty is a heavenly bookkeeper (as even many Christians suppose), who among us can survive the severity of divine judgment? But God is merciful, so instead of cowering in fear, we may bow in awe and wonder.

The second half of the psalm is pure praise. For God we wait more eagerly than a sentry watches for morning's light. The One who has great power will redeem Israel from all iniquity. How wise it is not to wallow in self-pity or to become obsessed by personal guilt or that of others. Self-absorption leads only to a downward spiral of the human spirit. Even in the most distressing times we do well to focus on the incredible love and strength of God, which can draw us up out of the miry pit. For that is the nature of the God whom we serve.

Is not this psalm the gospel in a nutshell? Here are verses to memorize for our use against that time when our anguish seems to make prayer impossible. When we cannot form our own words, can we not recite the words of others with great effect?

**SUGGESTION FOR MEDITATION: Ponder some great anguish with which you are familiar. Then paraphrase Psalm 130 in a way that makes it your own prayer in the situation you call to mind.**

*Concerning the God We Serve*   77

We may readily understand the biblical term "the flesh" to mean the physical body in a very restricted sense. In the history of Christianity this understanding has come to imply that spirituality involves the mortification of the body: a severely restricted diet, sexual abstinence except for purposes of procreation, even forms of self-torture that supposedly restrain or punish physical desire.

But we read that Jesus himself attended festive banquets and weddings, such that his opponents called him a glutton and a drunkard. Far from living in a six-by-nine-foot cell and eating trée roots, he seems to have enjoyed the usual pleasures of the table and social interaction. In this regard, he was quite unlike John the baptizer.

Beyond that acknowledgment about Jesus' indulgences, reside theological questions. If the body is evil, why did God create us with bodies? And how could the Almighty assume a body in the Incarnation? Such questions were raised in the earliest centuries by those whose views came to be considered heretical.

"The flesh" refers not only to the physical body but to our whole disposition toward selfishness and our disregard for God's will and the welfare of creation. Our motives, values, and goals all are part of "the flesh." All forms of self-centeredness comprise the flesh. Even mortifying the body can be a subtle form of self-absorption or a way of seeking admiration from others.

Therefore, the God we serve requires a totally new disposition on our part, a set of values and accompanying acts that seek godliness and the common good. Nothing less is needed than a radical reworking of our being.

**SUGGESTION FOR MEDITATION: Consider any aspects of your being that are centered on you to the exclusion of God and others. Then ask God to restore in you the divine image and likeness intended at creation.**

We closed yesterday by saying that the God we serve requires a totally new disposition on our part, a set of values and accompanying acts that seek godliness and the common good. But who among us is up to that kind of radical transformation? How do we accomplish it? (Unless you are totally unlike me, you have tried many times already and are all too aware of the futility of self-help approaches to this task.)

Honesty compels us to acknowledge that *we* do not accomplish this. We cannot. So the Good News is only bad news? Read on in Paul's letter until you get to verse 11: The very One "who raised Christ from the dead will give life to your mortal bodies also through his Spirit that dwells in you." Here is the true Good News: That what the God we serve requires of us is offered to us as gift by this same God when we truly seek a new disposition.

Lent is no time for espousing a "boot-strap" theology. The season began by sternly notifying us of our limitations: "You are dust. To dust you shall return." That says it all with regard to salvation by *self-help*. But Lent ends in Easter, which says it all with regard to salvation by *grace*. The God we serve is the One "who raised Christ from the dead." This same One bestows on us the Spirit who enlivens us. So even in the midst of the church's season of penitence, there is abounding joy.

**PRAYER: What I cannot do for myself, great God, do for me. What I have failed to accomplish on my own, grant to me as your gracious gift. Re-create me according to your image and likeness, and keep my heart open to give residence to your Spirit now and always; through Christ the Risen One. Amen.**

We discover a clue to the central meaning of this passage in verses 25-27, which use some form of the word *believe* four times. Before that (v. 15) Jesus states he has purposely deferred his visit to Bethany "so that you may believe." Subtle instances of people who believe the wrong things or partial things crop up throughout the entire chapter.

There are, of course, levels of belief. Some settle for believing in what they consider to be "the facts" of Christianity but never quite give themselves over to a personal commitment that results in a covenant of faithful life and work. What Jesus seeks for us is a deeper and more persuasive conviction that issues forth in joyful service.

The occasion of Jesus' visit could thereby have been one of condemnation: "You do not believe rightly, so off to hell with you." Instead the entire tone of the passage is positive. Jesus is eager to help everyone believe—just as later in John's Gospel, after his own resurrection Jesus will help to engender faith within Magdalene, within his disciples in the upper room, within Thomas a week later, within his followers at the seaside, and ultimately within us, the readers of John's Gospel.

Too often in the church there are attempts to intimidate people into belief. To the extent that these attempts succeed, they often result in superficial "faith" that cannot endure the pressures and strains of daily living. Such belief readily collapses into cynicism or into total unbelief. Lent calls for the deepening of faith, not its diminution. The God we serve wills to work such effective faith in each of us.

**PRAYER: Lord, I believe; help my unbelief. Cause my faith to grow more deeply into the soil of grace, that the fruit I bear by your power may become increasingly sweet and nourishing to others; through Christ the vine. Amen.**

## Fifth Sunday in Lent

If it is true that "grown men don't cry," Jesus fails the test miserably. On at least one occasion he wept over the sins of the entire city of Jerusalem—perhaps indeed over the sins of the whole world. Today's reading clearly states that Jesus weeps at the tomb of Lazarus. Earlier, verse 33 reports that "he was greatly disturbed in spirit and deeply moved" and later (v. 38) that "Jesus, again greatly disturbed, came to the tomb." Why such an emotional reaction inasmuch as Lazarus would rise up at his command? Did Jesus not believe his own words to Mary about being the resurrection and the life?

But viewed from a different angle, do we not take comfort in the fact that Jesus does not hide his human emotions behind a fake smiling facade? He was truly human as well as truly divine. To deny him his tears, even in the midst of hope, is also to deny tears to devout Christians who need to weep after a sudden or brutal death. Charles Wesley understood that when he wrote:

> If death my friend and me divide,
> thou dost not, Lord, my sorrow chide,
> or frown my tears to see;
> restrained from passionate excess,
> thou bidst me mourn in calm distress
> for them that rest in thee.[*]

Nor do we cease to be sad on Good Friday, although we know full well how the story will end on Easter morning. In the perspective of Christian faith, joy and sorrow are not opposites but complementary partners. Their opposite is indifference—that incapacity to be moved that some wrongly believe should characterize grown men or devout believers of both genders.

**PRAYER: Blessed Jesus, grant me the capacity to see both your tears and your victory so that I may weep with those who weep and rejoice with those who rejoice. Amen.**

---

[*] "If Death My Friend and Me Divide," by Charles Wesley, 1762.

# Who Will Carry Jesus?

*March 10–16, 2008 • Carol Padgett[‡]*

## MONDAY, MARCH 10 • Read Matthew 21:1-11

Jesus was a walker! He walked into the Jordan to be baptized and into the wilderness to be tested. He strolled beside the sea to call disciples and across fields to instruct them. He walked up hills to teach followers, from home to home to commune with friends, and between villages to heal strangers. He crossed cultures to include the excluded, ascended a mountain to be transfigured, and descended to a city to be betrayed. He walked to a Passover meal to speak of blood in sacrifice, to Gethsemane to sweat blood in submission, to Pilate's court to be tried, and to Golgotha to be crucified. Jesus traveled on his own feet to enter human lives during his time of ministry.

For events, however, that marked his entry into human life across all time, God ordained that Jesus be carried. A young woman delivered him to earth, a donkey's colt bore him into his kingdom, and an Arimathean man lifted him from a cross at death. What powerful portents of God's eventual call upon us to carry Jesus into the world by humbly bearing his likeness!

As the Ash Wednesday service ended, eight-year-old Lucas voiced concern: "Brother Ben, somebody needs to put ashes on your forehead." The departing congregation fell silent in reverent awe as its pastor knelt at the prayer rail and its youngest member marked a cross on his forehead. The light that shone from every face enfolded the visual benediction in a soft glow. We had witnessed the Lenten arrival of the living Lord, carried into our midst by a young "colt" eager to serve and a humble pastor willing to bow in submission to lead us to Easter.

**PRAYER: Lord, give me a humble heart in which to carry your likeness. Amen.**

---

[‡]Health ministry consultant, writer, and speaker; member of New Oregon United Methodist Church, Lookout Mountain, Alabama.

*Daddy Died March 11, 1972*

TUESDAY, MARCH 11 • Read Psalm 118:1-2, 19-29

My family laid gratitude as my cornerstone. Later, as a young-adult life-builder, I rejected this firm stone for rocky self-reliance. As my foundation threatened to crumble under the weight of superficial abundance and distracting allure, persons subsisting on bare necessities in a faraway land assured its restoration.

For several years, our United Methodist conference had hosted "recuperation visits" for children affected by residual effects of the 1986 Chernobyl nuclear accident. Families whose children our group had housed in America now hosted us in the former Soviet country of Belarus. Pouring out their gratitude in joyful waves of sacrificial hospitality, they greeted us in "festal procession with branches, up to the horns of the altar." Welcoming us into steadfast community that survived the plowing under of their irradiated villages, they opened the doors of decrepit "relocation" tenements as if opening the gates of the Lord.

I rubbed my eyes in amazement at the Lord's doing! In opening our hearts and homes to "Children of Chernobyl," we had carried Jesus into the darkness of Belarus. Now, Belarusians with only rudimentary understandings of God, bore the living Christ into our midst! Newly liberated from regimes that had stolen and hidden God for generations, they guided our hearts home on waves of generosity born of gratitude.

Eight years later, from opposite sides of the world, blessed ones who came to one another in the name of the Lord celebrate an Easter of the spirit, certain that neither regimes nor radiation nor abundance nor allure can separate us from God's love! When my congregation sings, "This is the day that the Lord has made," I belt out in broken Belarusian, "*Eh tah deen—Pah dah Reel Gos pod*," and thank God for loving, sustaining, and ordaining even those who don't know God's name to guide my return to my chief cornerstone. "This is the Lord's doing; it is marvelous in our eyes."

**SUGGESTION FOR MEDITATION: Through whom has God answered me and become my salvation?**

*Who Will Carry Jesus?* 83

We can easily read Isaiah's account of the Lord's action in his life as a record of God's role in the Son's ministry. Isaiah's testimony parallels Jesus' certainty of God's presence as he moves from teaching and healing to his final service as sacrificial offering.

For both Isaiah and Jesus, interaction with a deeply involved God is the central fact of life! Each understands and experiences life solely in the context of relationship with God. Each acknowledges God's continual presence and recognizes God's steadfast participation, identifying God as the source of personal power and the nurturing force that assures its fruits.

Each assents to God's defining and ongoing initiative and experiences the Holy One as so personally invested as to open the ear into which the divine call is whispered, so intimately involved that "morning by morning" God wakens the ear with direction. Each confesses God as sole savior and submits to God as sole judge. Each trusts that God stands nearby as advocate and alongside as defender.

Isaiah, a son of God who foreshadowed the Son of God, gives us a primer for living as sons and daughters of our participatory God. The prophet's personal account proclaims that to serve God's people, we must learn at God's knee; to speak to others effectively, we must listen to God constantly; and to sustain the weary, we must allow God to waken us.

To fulfill our missions as faithful servants, we must simultaneously face and turn from the world, obeying God without regard for consequences and looking only to God for support and judgment. In words both confessional and prophetic, Isaiah teaches us that today's sons and daughters of God carry Jesus by carrying ourselves as Jesus did—in relationship to a deeply involved Father.

**PRAYER: Father, morning by morning waken my ear to your words and my heart to your direction! Amen.**

Our community potter discovered her talent and her art form during a season of sighing. When an accident left her unable to resume her career or even familiar household tasks, she lamented her loss in mournful isolation. Mirroring the psalmist's depiction of distress, she "passed out of mind like one who is dead" as she spiraled between deep despair and anxious fearfulness. Then, into days emptied of purpose and hands emptied of work, a friend dropped a lump of clay. The clay found a natural home in hands that found their natural shape around its contours. Sitting at a simple pottery wheel on a riverside bluff, her life bereft of form and function and drained of visible value, the novice artisan found comfort in forming clay and value in creating functional art. Into pottery vessels she released her sorrow, and from them she eventually poured her grief.

As she worked, the potter remembered her home in the Great Potter's hands and returned to its sanctuary. Gradually, the Great Potter's steadfast love repaired her broken heart and re-fashioned her shattered mind. Over time, the shining face of the Holy polished the dullness of her lament into the luster of a new creation. As she moved from brokenness to wholeness, she found inspiration in a traditional practice of Eastern potters who, after perfecting a pot into an item of great value, carefully break it and lovingly seam the pieces with gold, rendering the pot priceless.

"How often," says the potter today, "we whine as we're broken, reshaped, or fired in life's kiln, forgetting that all the while we're in God's hands!" Like the psalmist as he faced sorrow and scorn and Jesus as he faced death on the cross, we find rest in remembering *whose we have always been*. Only then can we release our anxious despair about who we have become and be formed into vessels that carry Christ to others.

**SUGGESTION FOR MEDITATION: What areas of my life loving touch?**

*Who V*

Emptiness fascinates me! I'm drawn to pottery bowls and wooden boxes, deep caves and carved canyons, empty tombs and open hearts—womblike forms that receive, hold, and bring forth new life. How like Jesus to empty himself before coming to us, so he could receive humanity as his own and tenderly hold it while preparing to give birth to a new creation!

Though remaining fully divine, Jesus laid aside the trappings of glory so that we might see our likeness in him and imagine his likeness as our own. Becoming fully human, he shared life with those he served, relating from feelings that unite rather than distinctions that divide. He entered our world as one of us, valuing service over supremacy and preferring identification to idolatry. His self-emptying challenges us to become humble vessels through which his Spirit can flow.

Our mission team members hollowed themselves before going to people stripped of life's trappings by the Chernobyl nuclear accident. We emptied our minds of easy answers formed in our land of ready resources, our hearts of easy truths untested by radioactive disaster, and our pockets of easy altruism with which to avoid the life-crushing reality of the stranger. Except for rituals of arrival, for which we bore coffee and candy for host families, medical supplies for hospitals, and vitamins for orphanages, we related only from the fullness of our hearts.

In make-do apartments and makeshift facilities, Jesus was present in our laughing and crying, giving and receiving, celebrating and grieving with real people in the midst of real-life circumstances. As we shared our common humanity, the Spirit flowed through our mutual emptiness. As we freed our minds of preconceptions, we assumed more of the mind "that was in Christ Jesus." As we humbled our hearts and let one another in, we became more fully human and, perhaps, just a bit divine.

**PRAYER: Lord, make me a "carrying vessel" through which your love can flow! Amen.**

*Will Carry Jesus?*

This week's devotionals focus primarily on carrying Jesus into the world through the way we relate to others. Our Lenten observance calls us also to consider how we carry Jesus to the cross through the way we relate to his Spirit.

When Jesus told his disciples that one of them would betray him, none of the twelve could declare, "It is not I!" One planned to betray him; the others knew that betrayal lurked within, too slippery and sly to deny with certainty. Indeed, the remaining eleven learn that betrayal can take the form of "not looking" as well as that of "looking for" an opportunity.

As today's disciples, we mirror the original twelve. Who among us can declare, "It is not I!" who will betray the one we profess? Though we may not mirror Judas by intentionally looking for an opportunity to betray him, we surely mirror those who help send Jesus to the cross by not looking.

We betray Jesus by not looking to his Spirit for guidance. Like Judas, we too often live with self-interest as our priority and worldly abundance as our goal. Like the other eleven, we debate and even redefine God's kingdom rather than living the kingdom life that Jesus modeled.

We betray Jesus also by not looking for his Spirit in our midst. Like the judge who dismisses Jesus without examination, we deny his Spirit's life-giving power by ignoring evidence of its action.

Our collective Christian history bears witness to the sly means and slippery progression by which we betray Jesus. This Lent, we need look no further than our personal histories for examples of how we kill his Spirit as certainly as if we were to give the verdict "He deserves death."

**PRAYER: Lord, it is I! Keep me ever mindful of my potential to betray your Spirit. Keep me focused on looking to you and looking for you! Amen.**

## PALM/PASSION SUNDAY

For many silent hours during two successive retreat days, I meditated on "longing for God" and "hoping for God." The exercise left me longing for hope! My intense focus on God-in-the-Future set me adrift on the surface of the present with no source of power, no compass to determine my course or rudder to direct it, and no lighthouse to shine as a beacon or beckon me to its shore. I tossed about—at the whim of winds and the mercy of rocks of my own making.

Weary from longing, I drifted off to sleep, to be awakened by an epiphany from the deep that had eluded me earlier: Looking for God is like trying to find myself! With a sense of relief, I recalled a recent insight: *I'm sixty-three years old! Perhaps it would be better to be myself than to keep hoping for my eventual arrival.* Likewise, perhaps it is better for me to notice God's presence than to wander the seas looking for God.

It is difficult for us to imagine the depth of longing and hope with which the people of Israel looked for the messiah. Crying "Hosanna!" and waving branches as Jesus enters Jerusalem, they express ecstasy at the long-awaited arrival. However, even though the prophesied donkey carries Jesus into the city, the people have become so focused on looking for the imagined messiah that they cannot accept the real Messiah.

How can we carry Jesus today so that others recognize him as a manifestation of God in the present? Experiencing his presence may free us from *looking* for him, allowing us to carry Jesus best by seeing with his eyes and responding on his behalf to others adrift on a sea of longing.

**SUGGESTION FOR MEDITATION: Trusting God for light and power, I will set the compass of my attention and the rudder of my intention toward a new way of looking for Jesus!**

# God's New Creation

*March 17–23, 2008 • Timothy Reinhold Eberhart[‡]*

## MONDAY, MARCH 17 • Read Isaiah 42:1-9

As Holy Week begins, it is good to recall where we hope to arrive in the end. God's messianic servant, indwelt by the spirit of life, is sent forth to usher in the universal reign of God's righteousness. In this sense, we can say that the messiah, the servant of the Lord, saves us precisely in establishing the messianic kingdom of God where captives are released from prisons, warring peoples greet one another with the kiss of peace, and the earth is restored to vibrancy and health. The promise of the messiah, then, finds ultimate fulfillment in the manifest appearance of "a new creation" (2 Cor. 5:17), a "new heaven and a new earth" (Rev. 21:1).

Indeed, God's purpose for creation is not a never-ending recurrence of the way things have always been, with nothing new under the sun except for yet another modern convenience, the latest in seasonal fashion, and increasingly advanced instruments of war. "See, the former things have come to pass, and new things I now declare; before they spring forth, I tell you of them." How blessed is this news on the lips of God's messengers!

And yet, as we hope for the flourishing of God's new creation, we simultaneously grow anxious about a tired world scarred by ancient hatreds; imprisoned in addictions to self-improvement, national security, and individual financial well-being; and threatened by an ecological sickness unto death. Who shall save us from the folly we have sown? Who shall show us the way to God's righteousness and peace? Thanks be to God for Jesus Christ, the good and faithful servant who confronts us with the truth, grants to us life, and provides for us the way.

**PRAYER: Servant of God, Lord Jesus Christ, establish in us a longing to seek your reign, and we shall be made anew. Amen.**

---

[‡]Graduate student in Theological Studies and Ethics, Vanderbilt University, Nashville, Tennessee; ordained elder in the Dakotas Conference of The United Methodist Church.

## TUESDAY, MARCH 18 • Read 1 Corinthians 1:18–31

Perhaps the basic question addressed in contemporary theological reflection concerning Jesus is this: Who is Jesus Christ for the world today? Many speak of Jesus as their personal Lord and Savior. Others maintain he is the Liberator of the poor and oppressed. The scriptures themselves offer an abundance of christological titles—Jesus is the Lamb of God, our High Priest, the Bread of life, Emmanuel, Rabbi, Prophet, Master, Shepherd, Prince of Peace.

With the question of *who*, however, belongs the equally decisive matter of *how* Jesus Christ is in and for the world today. Without clarifying just how Jesus is our Lord and Liberator, we might all too easily fuse our worship of Christ the King with allegiance to the rulers, the principalities, and the powers of this present age. Christ on the cross insistently confounds all such confusions. Here is a Master who is stripped and taunted, a Shepherd who is butchered like a lamb, a God who is executed between two criminals. Moreover, we cannot forget that it was the most pious among us who judged this prophet a blasphemer, the most intellectually refined who dismissed this teacher as simplistic and naive, and the most remarkable imperial power the earth has ever known that carried out orders to silence this prince.

Jesus continues to establish his kingdom in and for the world today not by coercion and threats of violence but through the forgiveness of sins and love for enemies. And he continues to be present within and among us, not with dazzling displays of social influence or popular appeal but in the bodies of the weak, in those who are low and despised in the world: the hungry, the sick, and the imprisoned (Matt. 25). Do we still not stumble upon this message and, in truth, consider it absurd?

**PRAYER: Servant of God, our Lord and our Savior, return us to your cross and so destroy our wisdom and make us weak, that we become certain in you alone. Amen.**

We have little difficulty condemning Judas' profoundly distorted sense of value and rightly so. "What will you give me if I betray him to you?" Judas asks the chief priests. He receives thirty silver coins (Matt. 26:15). How utterly absurd that God's beloved servant, the precious Son of God, is handed over because one of his own chooses a bag of coins over his Master and Lord!

Yet Judas's love of money is not an unusual problem among Jesus' followers. Especially for those of us who live and work within the wealthy nations of the world, the temptation to betray our deepest allegiances in exchange for financial prosperity is great. Seeking after wealth, of course, is not necessarily iniquitous. The natural world, given freely as a gift of God, is filled with a luxurious abundance of riches.

The scriptures depict the coming messianic feast with images of an extravagant table overflowing with delectable foods, choice wines, and joyful festivity. God never creates abundance, however, at the expense of life. Rather, God shares with us the wealth of created existence and the riches of salvation out of an overflow of God's gracious love.

All too often, our own wealth depends not upon a trust in God's abundance or love for our neighbors but a fear of scarcity and the exploitation of the poor. And it is here, we must confess, at the very point where our pursuit of wealth leads us to participate in ways that deny life and dignity for all God's creation that we follow Judas in handing over our Lord for a bag of coins.

PRAYER: **Servant of God, Lord of Creation, pour out your mercy on us, your prodigal sons and daughters—we who have squandered your riches on reckless pursuits. Show us how to live seeking after your kingdom, that we shall be made whole. Amen.**

**THURSDAY, MARCH 20 • Read John 13:1-17, 31b-35**

### MAUNDY THURSDAY

In the ancient world, the evening meal not only signified but literally established the relational bonds and obligations, communal boundaries, and social rankings at the heart of society. The host was responsible for issuing invitations, coordinating meal preparations, and determining the specific seating arrangements of the guests, with the guest of honor—judged by age, political eminence, social importance, etc.—seated at the highest position and the other diners placed according to status to his right. As guests arrived at the household of the host, table servants led the guests to the dining room, removed their shoes, washed their feet, and offered a basin of water for hand washing.

On the night he is betrayed, at the last supper he will share with his disciples, Jesus not only acts the part of table host, procuring a furnished room and arranging food preparations (Luke 22:8-13), but because he is their Teacher, Lord, and Master, the disciples accord Jesus the highest status of honored guest. What the disciples do not at all expect—because it is too astonishing to foresee—is that Jesus will also assume the lowliest role of the table servant. Like the parables he tells of the kingdom of God, in which all common sensibilities are inverted, and like the actual tables he overturns at the Temple, Jesus incarnates a very different mode of social existence through his actions at this meal. In the unexpected form of a table servant, Jesus manifests the presence of and the way to God's new social order—the kingdom of God.

**SUGGESTION FOR MEDITATION: Spend time contemplating Jesus' words to his disciples at the last supper. "The kings of the Gentiles lord it over them. . . . But not so with you. . . . For who is greater, the one who is at the table or the one who serves? Is it not the one at the table? But I am among you as one who serves" (Luke 22:25-27).**

## GOOD FRIDAY

Ultimately, it is the propriety of religious leaders, the securing "peace and order" of imperial officials, and the weight of public opinion that combine to convict, humiliate, and execute Jesus, God's beloved Son. Yet here, precisely amidst humanity's most reckless and destructive act, the messianic servant displays the restorative way to God's peaceable kingdom.

Jesus doesn't just point toward a future wholeness but offers us a tangible strategy for making peace with our enemies in the present. And the cross of Good Friday shows us how. He never ceases to love his enemies, even as their guilt is made manifest upon his own body. With his words, "Father, forgive them," Jesus opens up an entirely new way to overcome evil: with good.

By insistently pressing upon the sinner with righteousness and mercy, like black students, arms linked, sitting at a "white-only" lunch counter, whose beaten bodies will not move but whose lips are filled with nothing but words of grace, the violence and enmity that is the sinner's true way in the world is laid bare. The possibility now arises that the guilty party, while gazing upon the visible work of his or her own hands, will come to recognize that, "Truly, this One whom I have condemned is not guilty, but I am." And at that moment, a reconciling peace between the forgiver and the forgiven is actually possible. It isn't necessary or inevitable, but it is possible. By taking the violence, madness, and perversity of humanity upon himself bodily Jesus discloses to us, precisely through his marred appearance, who we truly are: corrupt sinners in desperate need of grace.

**PRAYER: Lord Jesus Christ, suffering servant of God, fixing our eyes upon your broken body hanging on the cross, we behold our transgressions and our iniquities. How utterly astonishing it is to see you gaze back with eyes of love. Amen.**

## SATURDAY, MARCH 22 • Read Isaiah 55:1–11

The period between Good Friday and Easter Sunday, between the crucifixion and the resurrection, is not a time of inactive dormancy, as if God, along with us, is simply waiting for the day to pass. Holy Saturday is the space God makes present for our active transformation in the Spirit in response to Jesus Christ on the cross. God does not coercively force us to change; but rather, in and through Christ's suffering love, presents us with a visible display of both human wickedness and divine grace and, in this way, opens up the possibility that we might be affectively changed.

Jesus was made "to be sin for us" (2 Cor. 5:21), although he was without sin. He was "born under the law" (Gal. 4:4) and subject to its judgment, yet he was not actually guilty. He became a slave to the powers, though the rulers of this age had no true authority over him.

Jesus causes the forces of death to die on the cross by exhibiting their ultimate impotency over him, the Prince of Life. He thereby demonstrates, for good, the end of death's grip on human existence. On the cross, the minions of death—sin, evil, the law—are proved powerless to judge rightly, guide, and determine human life. What remains in their place is Christ's invitation to true life by way of his humble mercy, his pardoning hope for sinners, and his tender love for humanity. Here, in the shadow of the cross, backlit by the dawn of resurrection, the Spirit of Life stirs within the tomb of humanity, beckoning those with eyes to see and ears to hear to forsake their ways and return to the Lord.

**PRAYER: God of the in-between time, as the rain showers down from heaven making the earth to bring forth and sprout, so may your Word, our Lord Jesus Christ, accomplish through your Spirit that which you purpose, that we may rise up and live. Amen.**

## EASTER SUNDAY

On Easter Sunday, the first day of the coming new creation, we give witness to the intimate connection between Christ's resurrection and our being raised into newness of life. Just as Christ, though bound by the grave, arose by the resurrecting Spirit of life, so we too, though entombed in the ways of death, are baptized by the life-giving power of the Holy Spirit into the resurrected body of Christ.

The early church visibly enacted the inseparability of baptism from resurrection in its Easter liturgy. Catechumens were baptized in the first hours of Easter morning. Rising up out of the pool, they received a white robe and a lit candle. As the newly baptized members entered into the still-dark sanctuary, the gathered congregation spoke in unison, "Behold, the Lamb of God."

Freed from the death-serving ways of sin and evil and awakened to new life in the Spirit, we are raised as the resurrected body of Christ in and for the world. Here is the purpose for God's sending the Son, the servant, that humanity might be restored to its true purpose as a harmonious society of love-infused citizens of God.

The true church, through humble servanthood, continues a sacrificial love of enemies and the forgiveness of sins, offering its very life to redeem the world that God so loves. Behold the Lamb: the presence of and the way to God's everlasting kingdom of peace.

**PRAYER: Lord Jesus Christ, you are the Lamb of God, who takes away the sins of the world. In you, we receive new life through the power of the Spirit to manifest your loving-kindness for the salvation of others, till you return and we share in your eternal kingdom, world without end. Amen.**

# No Matter What

*March 24–30, 2008 • Mary A. Avram[‡]*

## MONDAY, MARCH 24 • Read Acts 2:14a, 22–32

This public proclamation of the gospel of Jesus Christ, inspired by the Holy Spirit and spoken by Peter with the eleven standing with him, is the first act of the newborn church. Peter lifts up his voice in testimony to what they know and have witnessed of God in Jesus of Nazareth, raised from the dead. If we tarry a moment in the scriptural memory of this scene and look out of the corner of our eye, we can see the church both then and now standing as one in this witness and proclamation.

I recall a Wednesday evening worship service in a small church in Toledo, Ohio. My family didn't usually attend this service, and as a six-year-old I was a bit restless. I remember Mother gently putting her hand on my knee to remind me not to fidget in church.

After the sermon and before the last hymn, the minister asked if anyone wanted to "speak a word." One by one people stood and spoke, giving testimony, like Peter, about what they personally knew and had witnessed of God in Jesus Christ. Through their earnest words, the Holy Spirit touched me; and the church was born in the heart of a little girl.

On the birthday of the church so long ago when Peter stood with the eleven, the church proclaimed and is always and everywhere proclaiming: "God has raised this Jesus to life, and we are all witnesses to the fact." Thanks be to God!

**SUGGESTION FOR MEDITATION: Think about your life. Ask yourself this question: In what ways does my life witness to and proclaim the resurrected Jesus?**

---

[‡]Spiritual director, School of Theology, University of the South; retreat leader, author, educator; living on St. Simons Island, Georgia.

This psalm, a Song of Trust and Security in God, is titled, "A Miktam of David." *Miktam* is an interesting Hebrew word that may be used as a musical or literary term but basically means "secret" or "gold." Some believe Psalm 16 holds the key to the secret of a rich, full life—a secret more precious than gold. If we listen carefully to these verses of Psalm 16, we hear an insistent echo of Joshua saying to the Israelites with all his powers of faith in the living God, "Choose this day whom you will serve" (Josh. 24:15, RSV). The echoes of Joshua continue as we read about the "portion," "my lot," and "goodly heritage." All these phrases honor promises kept.

From the opening word of the psalm, *protect*, we sense the psalmist's reliance upon God as refuge as he affirms his loyalty to the one true God. The "portion" in Joshua was each Israelite's fair share of the land; God offers a sustainable future to all.

When in our lives have we seen a dead end rather than a thoroughfare? When has the sense of future vanished in despair and fear? How do we claim the faith of the psalmist in the promises of God? Perhaps we can hear these words and each day choose to live out afresh the secret of a rich, full life. The secret, so simple and yet so profound, is to *choose God*.

The psalmist acknowledges that God holds his life—and that's enough. From his heart he blesses the Lord, and in our deepest hearts we too can bless God and affirm divine accessibility "because [God] is at my right hand." The key to a rich, full life is within our grasp; the secret is readily shared.

Many times, today and throughout our lives, we will be called upon by the words we speak, the attitudes we bear, love given or withheld, God blessed or forgotten, to choose whom we will serve.

**PRAYER: You know my deepest heart, Holy One. May I always turn to you for refuge, knowing that I "have no good apart from you." You are the cup of my salvation. Amen.**

The first word in today's reading is *therefore*. Whenever we find a *therefore* in scripture, it is wise to look carefully and see what it's there for.

Some Bible students date this psalm to the time when David (the attributed psalmist) has run away from Saul for fear of his life. Saul, king of Israel, with his army of three thousand, is trying to find David and kill him. David finds himself in an extremely difficult situation, a real mess. Yet he sings from a glad heart, a rejoicing soul, confident that he is secure. His song rings true because of the *therefore*.

David has chosen the Lord; he keeps God at the center of his life ("always before" him). He knows the God who gives him counsel and holds his life. The pleasant places of verse 6 in the present become pleasures to be enjoyed forevermore through his trust in God. Therefore, David's confidence and trust rest in the Lord who shows him the path of life, no matter what.

My mother, close to one hundred years old, lay in her hospital bed with her heart growing weaker each hour. She took my hand and said, "It's OK, Mary. I'm not afraid. God's been with me all these years, and God's not going to leave me now." Therefore, because of God and her own "choosing," she found comfort and peace—and so did I. Now in God's presence, my mother experiences fullness of joy and pleasures forevermore.

God provides the answer to life's difficulties, storms, and even our worst messes. God reminds us again and again, "I am here in your midst, your chosen portion and cup."

**PRAYER: Gracious God, thank you for your presence in all of life, no matter what. All praise and honor and glory is yours. Amen.**

Easter evening. Even though the disciples have heard the resurrection story and some have even seen the empty tomb, they are afraid and gather behind closed doors. They have witnessed Jesus' death by crucifixion, and they have allowed fear to grip them.

And then Jesus stands among them, raised from the dead by the plan and power of God. His first words to them are not words of recrimination because only one of them stood with his mother at the foot of the cross, or words of disappointment because fear has overtaken their faith. Jesus speaks words to assuage their consciences and calm their fears: "Peace be with you!" For the disciples, like us, these words don't bring the calm desired. Simply wishing it does not make it so. The disciples are in hiding for "fear of the Jews." How can such a greeting allay their fear? The medium is the message; Jesus shows them his hands and feet. Their fear turns to joy. Then once more he offers them his peace, which they willingly accept as a gift from their Lord.

One of the most often used phrases throughout the Bible is "fear not" in its many variations. In Luke's Gospel the angel of the Lord greets the shepherds on the night of Jesus' birth, "Do not be afraid. . . . Glory to God in the highest heaven, and on earth peace among those whom he favors" (2:9, 14). Fear and peace do not reside together.

Words *about* him at his birth. Words *from* him at his resurrection.

Through our experience of Christ's presence and the breath of the Holy Spirit, we may know God's peace—no matter what. We remember the nail-scarred feet of Jesus and offer ourselves to God so that wherever we go and whatever we do, we leave footprints of peace.

**PRAYER: In the midst of my fears, Jesus, may I feel your peace, which can overcome any fear I feel now or may ever feel. Amen.**

## FRIDAY, MARCH 28 • Read John 20:24–31

Now enters Thomas, the one absent when Jesus first stood with the ten behind closed doors. Thomas has yet to see the scarred hands and side of Jesus and receive his peace. Just as the disciples earlier failed to believe Mary's story of the resurrection, so now does Thomas have difficulty believing their story. The others tell him and share their joy, but Thomas is not ready to believe.

Eight days have passed. What was going through the mind of Thomas during those eight days? This time when the disciples gather in the house behind closed doors, Thomas is with them.

Again Jesus comes and stands among them saying, "Peace be with you." Abruptly, or so it seems, he turns to Thomas, offering his hands and side to be touched. I sense a great love for Thomas as Jesus says to him (and to us in our unbelieving), "Do not be unbelieving but believe." And Thomas answers, "Lord of me, and God of me!"[*]

Jesus offers the very thing that Thomas needs to believe: his own body and its wounds. We don't know if Thomas put his finger in Jesus' wounds; we do know that Thomas sees Jesus with the eyes of faith. His belief results from Jesus' gracious offer of himself: "Have you believed. . . ?" All of us who follow after Thomas and declare our faith in Jesus are blessed since he continues his response to Thomas by saying, "Blessed are those who have not seen and yet have come to believe."

**PRAYER: Thank you, Holy One, for Thomas and for your blessed presence and saving grace in our moments of unbelief. May we perceive you when you come to us in ways that bolster our believing. Amen.**

---

[*]Green, Jay P., Sr., editor, *Pocket Interlinear New Testament* (Grand Rapids, Mich.: Baker Book House, 1983), 272.

Peter is the impetuous disciple with a large and tender heart; the Galilean fisherman who, by the power of Holy Spirit through the risen Lord Jesus Christ, became Peter the fisher of men's and women's hearts. Today's text bears Peter's name—in part as tribute to the apostle and in part to appeal to the strength of Peter's reputation.

To read this letter calls us to remember the living situation of the first Christians. Once relatively unknown followers of the Way, they are now a persecuted group, blamed for many of the ills within the Roman Empire. These are the martyrs whose blood became the seed of the church.

After the letter's salutation, the writer offers praise to God for the church's redemption. As the early church grows, it faces hostility, false accusations, and slander. In contrast to such hostility, the letter offers a beautiful testimony concerning God's love: God "has given us a new birth into a living hope through the resurrection of Jesus Christ." The epistle writer goes one step further: "In this you rejoice, even if now for a little while you have had to suffer. . . . "

The early church counted its suffering as temporary. Today we seem to live in a time in which misery and suffering are normal. Fear and anxiety can become our driving forces as we face terrorism, live with global warming, and witness genocide and famine. We can no longer perceive or respond to this agony and shrug our shoulders with "compassion fatigue." Fear and anxiety keeps us from seeing the living hope of Jesus Christ. This is the time when we need the new birth spoken of in First Peter. The early Christians knew that when everything was taken away, all that mattered was this living hope that they knew in Jesus Christ. Be strong in your faith in God who is faithful—no matter what.

SUGGESTION FOR PRAYER: **In God our prayers join with the great communion of saints throughout time and space. Rejoice as you pray now with the church saints of the first centuries in the words of Jesus: "Our Father, who art in heaven . . . "**

## SUNDAY, MARCH 30 • Read 1 Peter 1:8-9

This week's Gospel lesson focuses on Jesus' appearance to the disciples. Peter and the other disciples were present when the resurrected Christ said to Thomas, "Blessed are those who have not seen and yet believe." Today's epistle reading echoes the words of the Gospel, repeating them to others who have not seen.

The readers of First Peter did not witness the crucifixion and resurrection of Jesus Christ; however, they rejoiced in the salvation brought by this love of Christ. We remember that these first Christians were downtrodden and persecuted and yet, they believe "with an indescribable and glorious joy." Their joy reflects their experience of God's love and grace. They were not eyewitnesses; nor were we eyewitnesses to Christ's death and resurrection. What religious emotions or affections come from you and your community of faith? How do you express your joy in God's redeeming love?

Many before us and many who will follow are part of that grand crowd of whom Jesus spoke to Thomas. We have not seen, but we believe. Like those who were the first church, we lead profoundly blessed lives, filled with glorious joy in the faith that leads to the salvation of our souls. No matter the circumstances of our life, we hold the hope of Jesus Christ.

It's easy to be swept up in nostalgic longing to have walked the dusty roads and sailed the stormy seas with Jesus and the disciples or to have been with the disciples when our risen Lord appeared. But the writer of First Peter reminds us of who we are in God *right now* in the midst of our daily lives. Our call in the Lord is to sing hallelujah in "unutterable and exalted joy"—just as it was for the early church—no matter what.

SUGGESTION FOR MEDITATION: **How do you express joy concerning the presence of God in your life today? How will joy grow within you?**

PRAYER: **Holy One, may my heart and my life rejoice and sing your praise—no matter what. Hallelujah! Amen.**

# Walking with Christ in the World

*March 31–April 6, 2008 • David Lowes Watson[‡]*

## MONDAY, MARCH 31 • Read Acts 2:14*a*, 36–41

The first step in being a disciple of Jesus Christ is to accept him for who he is. Peter makes this clear at Pentecost, proclaiming to "devout Jews from every nation under heaven" (2:5) that Jesus was the fulfillment of the Hebrew scriptures and confronting them with the scandal that their Messiah, long awaited, had not only been spurned by his own people but tortured and executed. Since God had raised Jesus from the dead and affirmed him as Lord, Peter boldly denounces those who rejected him, convincing thousands to repent, be baptized, and receive the Holy Spirit. The exhortation could not have been clearer: "Save yourselves from this corrupt generation."

Since then, two millennia of Christian witness have shown that we must temper Peter's sharp distinction between those who accept Jesus as the Messiah and those who do not. The early church had to accept that the gospel was not only for Jews but for all people, and while Christian disciples must sometimes repudiate the world in which they live, many other times they encounter the Holy Spirit preparing the world for the promised kingdom. The gospel is not a Christian copyright.

Is Peter's challenge obsolete? Not at all. Christ and Christ alone is Lord and Savior, and his call to discipleship remains a shot toward the heart, just as at Pentecost. But those who have the honor of walking with Messiah Jesus must not assume an identity that excludes the rest of humanity, nor yet planet Earth. God's salvation is bigger than the church, much bigger.

**PRAYER: Lord Jesus Christ, make your disciples open to the fresh winds of your Spirit, that we might glimpse the fullness of your salvation. Amen.**

---

[‡]Retired elder in the Tennessee Conference of The United Methodist Church. Former Director of the Nashville Area Office of Pastoral Formation; living in Murfreesboro, Tennessee.

## TUESDAY, APRIL 1 • Read Acts 2:14a, 36–41

Peter's challenge to the Jews at Pentecost remains a call to repentance for all of us. Precisely because God *does love* planet Earth, God seeks to make it a new creation, inviting us to turn away from the world as it is and toward the world as God intends it to be. This makes Peter's challenge as compelling today as it was two thousand years ago. If we are to know the risen Christ, if we are to receive the Holy Spirit, then we must acknowledge our sinful nature, accept the forgiveness and reconciliation offered us in Christ Jesus, and become new people.

The problem, as we noted yesterday, is that many of us find it awkward or even dishonest to assume this new identity if it means regarding our world, our nation, and, especially, our neighbors as a "corrupt generation." Even as we experience the profound change that comes from the indwelling Spirit of God, we hesitate to dissociate ourselves from the kind and generous people we encounter day by day, who may not share our faith in Christ, who may not even be religious, but who make Peter's words seem abrasive and sectarian.

The answer lies in acknowledging that the grace of God we have experienced is also at work in every human being and throughout the whole of planet Earth. This acknowledgment allows us to view the world through the lens of hope rather than despair. Its present struggles and conflicts are the birth pangs of God's new creation rather than God's condemnation (John 3:17). We rejoice that Christ's saving grace will ultimately prevail against every adversity, including human sin and death (Rom. 8:18–39). As true disciples we will love the world for which he gave his life.

**SUGGESTION FOR MEDITATION: Do I view my salvation in Christ as a rescue from the world or as the privilege of helping Christ fulfill the redemption of the world?**

Once we cross the threshold of repentance and conversion to new life in Christ, we begin to discover what it means to truly depend on God. Our Jewish forebears have much to teach us about this, as we find in today's reading. Here we have a psalm of thanksgiving for deliverance from a crisis sufficiently serious to have been life-threatening, so the psalmist first praises God for heeding his cry of distress. He then gives public thanks through sacrificial offering and vows of faithful service, declaring that God does not welcome the death of the faithful.[*]

This psalm has come to have a prominent place in Christian worship, especially in the Lord's Supper. The contrasting words of suffering and deliverance, of captivity and freedom, of death and new life, express the deep gratitude of those who confess and follow Jesus Christ. The psalmist likewise plumbs the depths of our need for repentance. How can we trust God to save us if we have not experienced the impotence of self-sufficiency? How can we thank God for new life in Christ if we stubbornly refuse to turn away from the old? How can we center our lives on obedience to Christ if we have not surrendered to the prompting of the Holy Spirit?

We do not begin to understand our radical need of grace until we have finally exhausted our own strength, and this comes only through the continual repentance of believers, to use the title of a sermon by John Wesley.

When God comes to our aid, we are overwhelmed with gratitude, praise, and love. But for reasons that often leave us confounded, God allows our cry to come from the depths of our despair (Ps. 22:1).

**PRAYER: O God, my Creator and Redeemer, bring me to repentance and refine me with your fire until my spirit is contrite and I come to trust you at all times and in all things. Amen.**

---

[*]The Hebrew word translated "precious" (v. 15) should be understood in the sense of "costly" (*The New Interpreter's Bible*, 4:1149).

This letter carries the name of Peter, though many scholars now question his authorship. But whoever wrote it, it is clearly a word of encouragement to young communities of Christians coming of age. They are facing the challenge and the persecution of living in a world that is not yet the kingdom Jesus promised, nor is his return as imminent as first expected (1 Thess. 4:13–5:11). How are they to keep faith with the risen Christ and sustain their anticipation of the coming reign of God?

We should be heartened to find ourselves in such close kinship with these early Christian forebears. We too await the coming reign of God, and we too face the challenge of living in a world that does not acknowledge Christ as Lord, much less follow his teachings. Yes, we see signs of the Holy Spirit's preparation for this kingdom. We witness remarkable progress in bringing health and hope to millions of people as we all become better global neighbors, and we can praise God that there are more Christian disciples worldwide than in any previous age.

But the residual signs of the old world, with its injustice, hatred, warfare, famine, disease, and death are still with us. Christians could well be taken to task for a gospel that seems to be such an illusory hope, and well might the world respond with incredulity and cynicism, "You talk of a kingdom of love, peace and justice, on earth as in heaven? Like when? After another two thousand years?"

The question therefore continues to be compelling: How should Christians live in a world they confidently expect to be changed by Christ—but not yet? Our reading gives us two significant compass headings, which we will consider tomorrow.

**Prayer: Most gracious God, help us to live as faithful witnesses to our Lord Jesus Christ, in active expectancy of the coming of your kingdom, on earth as in heaven. Amen.**

The letter urges these early Christians to live in reverent fear during the time of their exile, the time between the breaking in of the kingdom in the person of Jesus Christ and its fulfillment at his return. Since we too live in the tension between the now and the not yet of the coming reign of God, we may take note of the writer's twofold exhortation.

First, we are reminded that the life into which Christians have been born anew cost the Son of God his life. Accordingly, our faith and our hope must center on Christ and Christ alone. The challenge facing these early Christians was to hold fast to their faith as they encountered the hostility and persecution that would increasingly become the cost of their discipleship, as it is for countless Christians around the world today. But those of us with the benefit of religious freedom face a more subtle challenge. If we are not watchful, our new life in Christ can become more of a priority than Christ himself, leading to religious consumerism and thereby cheapening his work of salvation. For example, how many of our church activities are really worth the life of the Son of God?

The letter also cautions our early Christian forebears not to underestimate what happens when we are born into this new life. We are ransomed and purified through the costly blood of Christ, but our ongoing purification lies in obedience to his commandments. This will be shown by a genuine, mutual love for one another. When this love is lacking in the church, we forfeit our friendship with Christ. In the words of another early Christian letter, "Whoever says, 'I have come to know him,' but does not obey his commandments, is a liar" (1 John 2:4).

**PRAYER: Jesus, my mentor and friend, keep me mindful that love for my neighbor will always be the condition of my walk with you. Amen.**

Of all the resurrection appearances of Jesus, this is one of the most intimate. This enthralling narrative holds a special place in the hearts of all who seek to walk with Christ, culminating in what has been described across the centuries as the inward witness of the Holy Spirit.

What strikes us first of all is the nature of this encounter with the risen Christ. He takes the initiative to join these two pilgrims—Jesus always calls people to discipleship—but not with a pressured intrusion. He is open yet courteous, engaging them in conversation and giving them the opportunity to disengage or even dismiss him. When they arrive at the village, he again gives them the option of asking him to stay, or not. As we look back on our own walk with Christ, all of this must surely be familiar. Jesus is a matchless role model for spiritual good manners.

Note also the pastoral skill with which he draws them out. Knowing that they desperately need to talk about the recent happenings in Jerusalem, he asks them a couple of simple but leading questions. And talk they do, about the execution of the prophet in whom they had placed so much hope, about the empty tomb, about the incredible tale from some of the women that he is alive, and much more. Then and only then, come the words of assurance and comfort from Jesus as he unfolds the scriptures and warms their hearts.

Perhaps the most telling and authentic detail of the story is that they fail to recognize him. Consumed by their own bewilderment and despair, they need a further initiative from Jesus to bring their conversation to a moment of amazing grace. As we shall see tomorrow, such moments are the supreme privilege of our walk with Christ.

**Prayer: Lord Jesus, walk with me day by day, even when my cares and concerns prevent me from recognizing you. Amen.**

The disciples invite Jesus to stay with them, and they recognize him in the breaking of the bread. Given the conversation on the road, to say nothing of the recent events in Jerusalem, this moment must have been electric.

Recognition is also the key to the theme of discipleship we have explored all week. When we begin to walk with Christ in earnest, we find we do not know him as well as we thought. In fact, at times we do not recognize him at all. We discover, often to our dismay, that his priority is not to keep us company but rather to seek out his other sisters and brothers, our sisters and brothers, who lack food, clothing, and the love that can bring them home to the family of God. To stay close to this Good Shepherd we must share his passion for the needy and the lost. He expects nothing less.

Thus the moment of amazing grace at Emmaus comes in a simple earthly meal. Like the supper Jesus shared on the night he was betrayed, this has become the dearest token of his life, death, and resurrection. It unites us in communion with the God who became one of us, breathing our air, eating our food, pulsing with our blood, and loving planet Earth with every fiber of his being. To be his disciple is to yearn for the glorious fulfillment of his promised kingdom, when he will hand over to God a world that is a new creation, with the last enemy, death, finally destroyed (1 Cor. 15:20-26). Until then, we recognize him, unexpectedly and irresistibly, in the breaking of the bread.

**PRAYER: Grant us, therefore, gracious Lord, so to partake of this sacrament of thy Son Jesus Christ, that we may walk in newness of life, may grow into his likeness, and may evermore dwell in him, and he in us. Amen. (*The United Methodist Book of Worship* [Nashville, Tenn.: The United Methodist Publishing House, 1992], 49–50.)**

# Together We Stand

*April 7–13, 2008 • Dorothy Watson Tatem[‡]*

## MONDAY, APRIL 7 • Read Acts 2:42–47

The Christian faith is community. The invitation of the community of faith is to learn of Christ and to implement that learning. The believers remember Christ's sacrifice in the breaking of the bread. The Holy Spirit empowers and expands our praying when we engage as followers of Christ. In unison we can witness and hear the testimonies, the stories of the workings of God in the lives of others, and thereby strengthen our collective and individual faith. We attain great heights of celebration in worship when as one body we give praise to God. In the midst of our abundance, we readily share with those in need.

Fellowship offers a strength that the solo state cannot generate. Out of this dynamic of assembly, there arises the desire to care for one another. In the "much time" that Christians spend together, corporate and individual transformations are realized.

In the assembly of the people of God, we discover a superlative endurance and fortitude that is much like a rope comprised of multiple strands of cord. The fellowship cannot be easily torn apart. In community, Christians are sustained in calamity and buoyed up in good fortune. By observing the dynamics of intimacy, learning, caring, and the impossible made possible, others come forward to be enfolded into the beloved community of Christ. Together we exemplify the abundance of life through Jesus Christ.

**PRAYER: Thank you, God, for the abundant relationships that sustain me in the community of Christians. Thank you that in the intimacy of these relationships you are ever-present. Amen.**

[‡]Director of the Office of Urban and Global Ministries, Eastern Pennsylvania Conference of The United Methodist Church; living in Philadelphia, Pennsylvania.

Horns blare. Many voices fill every inch of space. Laughter ripples through all sounds. Hands clap while feet dance. Drums set the rhythm, and a piano tosses out a melody and its improvisations. Folk are celebrating. Something wonderful has happened. Then a sparkling shower descends upon all the acts of joy. Confetti, a signature of celebration, rains down upon hair, clothing, tables, floor—everywhere.

We do not think of confetti in singular terms but in plural. This item of celebration always comes in many pieces. A single fragment of it would be considered litter. In fact, one piece would not grab our attention and direct us in festive activity. The material of confetti is of no consequence unless its many parts come together in the exuberance of a joyous occasion.

As followers of Christ, we are quite like confetti
- when we gather to worship;
- when we lift our voices together in song;
- when we bow in unison to pray;
- when collectively we hear, receive, and live out the preached word of God;
- when we study to enhance our understanding and relationship with God through Christ Jesus;
- when we engage in many other spiritual disciplines (meditation, fasting, etc.).

At these times we celebrate and experience Christ most powerfully. In this union of Christians, we can see beyond ourselves and discern as well as respond to the needs around us. At these times we humbly receive from others.

Like confetti, our collective worship, praise, and service fall upon lives and bear witness to a festive occasion! The fellowship of those in Christ invites all to come and join the celebration and praise. Our collective lives are confetti for God.

**PRAYER: Gracious God, may our life together rain down your love for all. Amen.**

God will not neglect the creation and its human inhabitants. This psalm invites us to stillness even as we rush headlong into agenda after agenda to reach our goals. We seem to define plenty in pitifully narrow terms. God beckons us into an abundance that encompasses mind, spirit, and heart.

What are the characteristics of the One in the midst of those who assemble together under the banner of Christ? Above all, the Holy One is a leader, taking the initiative. We need not beg for divine presence or care. The great Shepherd is attentive, aware of every need, desire, and act of the group as well as those of the individual.

Far beyond generous, the word *magnanimous* best describes our God. We find ourselves blessed with even more than we need—blessings above and beyond the tangible. Plenteous love, patience, kindness, joy, peace, faithfulness, gentleness, self-control, and generosity allow us to give away the bounty.

Our profoundly observant God attends not only to the needs of the group but also to the needs of the individual—a soul finds a quiet space in the midst of turbulence. God sets clearly before the body or the individual the best life direction in which to proceed.

In this Shepherd's fold we become the recipients of more than we could ever ask.

**PRAYER: Lord, I am so inclined to focus on me. Today, help me to focus on you. Amen.**

God our loving, nurturing shepherd is also God our protector. God moves in the vicissitudes of our lives. Humankind urgently needs the power of the divine presence in collective and individual lives—and this psalm reassures us of its reality.

God intimately knows all the creation. Sometimes the "right paths" on which God leads us are not those of quiet and solitude but of work or service. These paths can at times be harsh and demanding, even dangerous. Rather than being sent through these times alone, we are accompanied by our fiercely protective Shepherd. We see an image of this kind of shepherd in the prototypical Old Testament shepherd David. First Samuel 17:31–38 tells about David protecting his sheep valiantly against attacks by wolves and lions, even pursuing the marauders to rescue those for whom he cared. Our Shepherd is even more powerful and protective. In our harsh times, God is present in sovereignty. God's omnipotence can snatch us from the devastations of adversity. God fights on our behalf. (We resist this image, but warfare is a reality of many lives. We need to know that God is ready for the battles that confront us.)

When threatening hosts surround the community of faith, we can experience shelter and peace that defy explanation. Plentiful blessings can abound in the midst of the negative because the Holy Spirit is present with us. When we abide in Christ, enemies observe the goodness of God toward us and, in that moment, are invited into the community of faith.

God is in charge! God moves! The people of God endure with hope and joy because the Lord is our protecting shepherd!

**PRAYER: Lord, you are the shepherd. Help me follow you obediently, that my life may be blessed and that I may be a blessing to those I encounter on my journeys. For your beloved church, I also pray this prayer. Amen.**

First Peter addresses Christians who are suffering persecution. Given its content, the audience seems to include more slaves than masters and believing wives with pagan husbands. The author puts forward a "station" code: relating to others in the household. But clearly implied is how believers relate to the world. Too often household slaves found themselves demeaned by their owners. These slaves were to exemplify Christian behavior in their workplaces despite their circumstances.

Today, slavery of any sort is repugnant to Western culture; yet, many of us find ourselves slaves to our workplace. School, office, church, factory, cyberspace, truck, car, bus, plane, hospital—the workplace demands much of our daily lives. Verse 18 suggests that household workers are to be subject to those in authority—both good and bad. Christian fidelity is tested only in the face of unfair treatment. In our workplaces we may have to deal with envy, strife, anger, gossip. We are often torn apart by a lack of affirmation, defamation, accusation, and frustration.

How might First Peter inform our response to such environments? When we who populate the flock of Christ find that we are misused, overused, or not used at all in the workplace, retaliation is not an option. When our skills, talents, ideas, and efforts are belittled or overlooked, we are to endure patiently without yielding to the urge to fight. Brave the situation; withstand the onslaught. Be patient in the midst of degradation. Those of the flock of Christ do not seek power at all costs. Our right conduct may convince unbelievers, and through it we submit for the sake of God, not earthly authorities.

The body of Christ is not always subdued; sometimes God's approval requires that truth be spoken to power. God's guidance determines our action. May we willingly follow the shepherd and guardian of our souls.

**PRAYER: Help us, Lord, to submit our dreams and aspirations to you for approval, and guide us in ways that you desire for us. Amen.**

Today ask a friend to "covenant" together that the two of you will do your work for God's approval. Wherever your place of employment—home, church, office, school, cyberspace, conferences, seminars, wherever—let all that you do in the workplace this day be subject to God's approval. Your acts as well as your thoughts, feelings, and spiritual state are to be attuned to God.

As you move through the day, note the changes you make in your work area. Observe how you relate to others whatever their temperament. At moments you may have to be direct and uncompromising; will your initiations and responses meet with God's approval? Observe yourself within and without. What would divine approval warrant? You may spend time surfing the Internet; where do you surf when intentionally seeking God's approval? How might the anticipation of God's approval influence how you help others and/or permit them to assist you?

When we seek God's approval, what happens to our manner of accomplishing mundane tasks? How does the seeking after such approval affect our quiet moments in the midst of the work day?

Tell no one beyond your friend or your support group about the search for God's approval of your work this day. (This is indeed an engagement between you and God. It is not at all dependent or to be influenced by arbitrary external criteria of what others may deem pleasing to God.)

Sometime tomorrow or as soon as possible, appoint a time for you and your partner(s) to reflect on the quality of this day in which you sought the approval of God in the workplace.

**PRAYER: O God, develop our sensitivity to your leading, as well our awareness of your approval as you guide us in every area of our work. Amen.**

External issues break into our lives and assault us; we are seemingly caught without defense or shield from the onslaught. Then again, soul and heart implosions appear to be capable of shattering all that we hold dear as the essence of our being. We cannot run from the turbulence within. Yet, in whatever manner the fluctuations of life assail us, there is one whose uttered name leads the soul to shelter. There is one whose presence does not offer escape from life but rather an interval to be still, to regroup, to remember whose we are. *Jesus.*

This Jesus describes himself as both the shepherd who leads the sheep to the sheepfold in the winters of life and also as the gate that secures the sheepfold once the flock has entered. In that place doubts, fears, past and present evils, angers, frustrations, and all other manner of attacks cannot destroy the flock or even a single sheep.

From the sheepfold of prayer, Communion, study, service, fellowship, worship, and collective praise, the destruction that would decimate the flock is kept at bay. The toxicity of the violent is rendered harmless in the intimacy of the fellowship of believers who know the voice of their shepherd Jesus Christ.

Who is the gate of the sheepfold except Jesus? He himself says the shepherd is the one who protects the sheep. Daily for the sake of the flock, the Christ puts himself in the way of ostracism, ridicule, and even existential denial in order to save the flock. Yet today Christ still places himself in harm's way to protect and save those who follow him. Repeatedly in praise, we say the name of the one who saves. *Jesus.*

**PRAYER: All-loving God, you care for us as a good shepherd cares for the flock. Your tender love reaches out to all people, and you invite us to your sheepfold. Sustain us by your shepherd spirit to live in the peace of Christ. Amen.**

# Touched by God

*April 14–20, 2008* • *Deborah E. Suess*[‡]

## MONDAY, APRIL 14 • Read Psalm 31:1-5, 15-16

"Wait a minute!" Kris protested, "you're asking me to start fussin' at God!" I was leading a *Companions in Christ* small-group session in which we were invited to write our own lament—a prayer asking God for help while telling God our actual feelings. Earlier in the week the group had explored a variety of laments found in the book of Psalms, but Kris wasn't convinced he should be "fussin' at God."

I understood his reluctance. Throughout my high school and college years I avoided reading the Psalms because I didn't understand why the psalmists were so eager to curse people, complain about their lot in life, and in general question God's integrity. However, in my early thirties I faced new challenges and desperately needed a new way to pray. I no longer wanted to use pretty phrases or sanitized language, so I turned to psalms of lament. They became my lifeline. And they still are.

Through these ancient lines of poetry, I offer unedited my anger and fear as well as my love and hope. But I don't just read the Psalms quietly to myself. Some days I sing them as my own version of the "blues"; some days with shaking fists I literally stomp the words out in my living room. And occasionally— when driving on an empty freeway in the privacy of my car—I shout my laments, curses, and questions as loudly and as vigorously as I can. In doing so, more often than not I touch the One who touches me.

**SUGGESTION FOR PRAYER: In today's psalm of lament, what word or phrase speaks to you? Let that word or phrase become your prayer today. Experiment by singing, stomping, or shouting your prayer. Then listen for God's response.**

[‡]Pastoral Minister, Greensboro First Friends Meeting (Quaker), Greensboro, North Carolina.

I wonder from whom Jesus first heard Psalm 31. From his mother, Mary, as she sang the lament one night while fixing supper? Or maybe he first heard it being chanted by Joseph at the synagogue. Did Jesus intentionally memorize this psalm because it carried particular meaning for him? Or was it simply part of his growing-up vocabulary?

According to Luke's Gospel, Jesus' final words spoken from the cross come from Psalm 31. While Luke does not offer any details, I imagine that Jesus began that final prayer on the cross as he had so many times before:

> In you, O LORD, I have taken refuge;
>     let me never be put to shame;
>     deliver me in your righteousness. (NIV)

When Jesus came to the words "Into your hands I commit my spirit," might it be that those familiar and comforting words helped release him into death? A death that would culminate in that which is beyond comprehension—resurrection life and Easter hope.

Today when we pray, sing, or recite Psalm 31, we join with saints and sinners throughout the centuries in asking for deliverance and in giving ourselves over to God's care. Or as *The Message* renders verse 5:

> I've put my life in your hands.
>     You won't drop me,
>     you'll never let me down.

**SUGGESTION FOR MEDITATION: Read Psalm 31:1-5 through three times. During your first reading, imagine Jesus as a child singing the song at home with his parents. During your second reading, picture Jesus offering these words with his disciples as they gather for evening prayer. During your third reading, hear Jesus praying these words on the cross. How does such a reading impact your understanding of the text or your understanding of Jesus? How might this prayer of Jesus also become your prayer today?**

I write today's meditation from a lovely retreat center in Massachusetts. Upon my arrival, Carol welcomed me: "Deborah, we have put you in the Merton room. You'll love it." And I do—the sage-green décor is soothing, the quilt on the bed cozy, and the room spacious. I am thankful that such a lovely place has been prepared for me.

Above the desk, Thomas Merton's words are framed: "We are living in a world that is absolutely transparent, and God is shining through it all the time." Merton got it right. But sometimes it is easier to see God shining through than at other times.

During Jesus' final hours with his disciples, he tries to prepare them to see God shining through all that will shortly take place. He breaks the difficult news to them: "I will be with you only a little longer." His friends, confused and distressed, raise questions: "Where are you going? Why can't we go too?" Jesus tries to comfort them by describing a present and future hope using the imagery of home.

> There is plenty of room for you in my Father's home. If that weren't so, would I have told you that I'm on my way to get a room ready for you? And if I'm on my way to get your room ready, I'll come back and get you so you can live where I live. (THE MESSAGE)

In their grief and confusion, *nothing* initially is transparent to the disciples. They certainly do not recognize God shining through Jesus' hard-to-understand words. But I imagine that weeks later as they process every detail of that last evening together, they remembered their Teacher's powerful words of comfort and hope. Jesus assured them just as he assures us today: You can live where I live—in the heart and home of God.

**PRAYER: Loving God, today may I be fully at home in you. Amen.**

## THURSDAY, APRIL 17 • Read John 14:5-14

During the 1970s I was part of a network of churches that believed they were uniquely called to restore the Christian church to its original mission and vitality. While this movement nurtured a heartfelt commitment to Christ, it also became an exclusive club whose members alone had the inside scoop on God's will and desires. After leaving that group, I realized how very small my understanding of God had become and determined not to tread that pathway again.

Jesus declares, "I am the way, and the truth and the life. No one comes to the Father except by me." Jesus offers a wide-open invitation to know God by getting to know Jesus and his way of living out love. And who is this Jesus?

- He is the one who preached, "Blessed are the poor in spirit, for theirs is the kingdom of heaven.... Blessed are the merciful, for they will be shown mercy" (Matt. 5:3, 7, NIV).
- He is the one who truly engaged with all whom he encountered—tax collectors, foreigners, lepers, Roman soldiers, priests, and prostitutes.
- He is the one who described himself as a Good Shepherd saying, "I have other sheep that are not of this sheep pen. I must bring them also" (John 10:16).

Quaker Hugh Campbell Brown said that we "have glimpsed God through a Christ-shaped window." He says many people "receive the light of God through other-shaped windows, and recognize it as the same light of the same God. But until we are prepared to say that some other window is more illuminating, and that we have to identify ourselves with that path, we cannot afford to disassociate ourselves from Christ in any way."*

**PRAYER: Jesus, help me walk in your way, your truth, and your life. And in doing so, help me catch a glimpse of God. Amen.**

---

*From *Faith and Practice of New England Yearly Meeting of Friends*, 1985 edition, page 92.

Stephen, an efficient administrator of the food-distribution program for the church in Jerusalem, was also a powerful preacher. Like Jesus, his preaching did not sit well with the established religious order. Like Jesus, Stephen was charged with blasphemy and brought before the Sanhedrin.

Stephen's words of defense sound more like a sermon, and they anger the council. He accuses them of being "stiff-necked" and "forever opposing the Holy Spirit." In the words of Frederick Buechner, "The authorities were naturally enraged and illustrated the accuracy of Stephen's analysis by taking him out and stoning him to death."

Stephen's dying prayer closely parallels his Lord's final words from the cross. Stephen releases his spirit to Jesus and prays that those who have harmed him be forgiven. Saul, who later becomes the apostle Paul, hears Stephen's parting words, "Lord do not hold this sin against them," and approves of the killing.

I often wonder how Paul came to terms with being instrumental in Stephen's death. How did he deal with the agony of regret? Scripture does not tell us. But I imagine that Paul prayerfully breathed in both Jesus' and Stephen's final words of grace over and over again until forgiveness seeped into his very bones and healed his heart.

Paul must have experienced the lightness and freedom that comes with forgiveness. For he wrote these powerful words to the Romans: "I am convinced that neither death, nor life, nor angels, nor rulers, nor things present, nor things to come, nor powers, nor height, nor depth, nor anything else in all creation, will be able to separate us from the love of God in Christ Jesus our Lord" (8:38–39).

**PRAYER: God, nothing can separate me from your love—not even my regrets. Help me breathe in your forgiveness and know your healing today. Amen.**

**SATURDAY, APRIL 19 • Read Acts 7:55–60**

As a librarian, my mother often came home with "preview books" for her three daughters to read and review. One day she gave me a young adult book on church history. I couldn't put it down. The stories of those who died because they lived out their Christian beliefs haunted and challenged me.

The stories still challenge me—but in new ways—because of Tom Fox. Tom joined Christian Peacemaker Teams in 2004 and went as a civilian to witness, pray, and work for justice and peace in Iraq. He was abducted in Baghdad in November 2005, with three others. On March 10, 2006, his body was discovered.

Because the Quaker world is very small, many of my friends knew Tom Fox well and loved him deeply. They spoke of his gentle and silly ways, his commitment to community, and his determination to live out Jesus' call to love our enemies. When Tom was abducted, we prayed and cried out for his release. When Tom was killed, we mourned, interceded for his family, and started to grapple with the hard questions his death raised.

We are also seeking to learn about forgiveness. Tom made this public statement in October 2004: "We reject violence to punish anyone who harms us. We ask for equal justice in the arrest and trial of anyone, soldier or civilian, who commits an act of violence, and we ask that there be no retaliation on their relatives or property. We forgive those who consider us their enemies. Therefore, any penalty should be in the spirit of restorative justice, rather than in the form of violent retribution."

Stephen prayed, "Lord, do not hold this sin against them." Tom wrote, "We forgive those who consider us their enemies." I wonder, *How might I more fully give and receive forgiveness?*

**PRAYER: Loving God, forgive us our sins as we forgive those who sin against us. Amen.**

SUNDAY, APRIL 20 • Read 1 Peter 2:2-10

First Peter was originally directed to Jewish and Gentile Christians whose lives had been virtually turned upside down. The Jerusalem Temple had been destroyed in 70 CE; faith communities were scattered, and believers had to evaluate once again what it meant to live out their faith in new and challenging circumstances. To this struggling community the author writes these words: *Be encouraged. You've tasted and known God's goodness in the past. So once again, like a hungry newborn, drink deeply of spiritual milk. Grow into God's wholeness, healing, and love* (AP).

The author is saying: "Drink up and be filled, spiritual babes!" And my initial response is negative. "Hey, who do you think you're calling a newborn? Are you telling me that I need to start over? To begin again?"

After a bit of reflection, I realize the answer is yes. While over the years I have mercifully done some maturing, every morning is still a new beginning. Every day I choose to listen (or not) to the Spirit's guidance. Every day I set aside some time and energy (or not) to breathe in the living Christ. Every day my cup needs filling. I have discovered that while I am able to live on reserves from yesterday, it is not the same as fresh manna for today.

My Alcoholics Anonymous friends teach me so much about the need to begin afresh every morning. Sallie explains that while she annually celebrates her sobriety anniversaries with great joy—it is still very much a day-by-day-by-day journey. And so it is with our spiritual walk. Today let's drink deeply of Christ's spirit.

**PRAYER: New every morning is your love, great God of light, and all day long you are working for good in the world. Stir up in us desire to serve you, to live peacefully with our neighbors and all your creation, and to devote each day to your Son, our Savior Jesus Christ. Amen.**

*Upper Room Worshipbook* (Nashville, Tenn.: Upper Room Books, 2006), 8.

# Divine Dialogue

*April 21–27, 2008 • Robert J. Stamps*[‡]

**MONDAY, APRIL 21 • Read Acts 17:22-31**

Do you agree with Paul's approach to the Athenians, specifically his references to "an unknown god" and the city's pervasive religiosity? What would you do? Karl Barth didn't agree with Paul. He thought the apostle wasted his time trying to "warm up" the fellows of the academy, attempting to find an inroad for the gospel. It is better to get to the good news straightway, Barth advised; let the message build its own bridges. Whatever the approach, the results in Athens that day were scant.

I agree with Paul's method. The onus is always upon the church to find common ground for conversation with its world in every generation and culture. Must the peoples of the world familiarize themselves with our categories, the nuances of our perspectives in order to understand us? I think not.

The work of Bruce Olson, celebrated missionary to Stone Age peoples of the Amazon, is exemplary. Olson states that when he moves in with a tribe, he trusts that God has already prepared its culture for the message of Christ. It is the missionary's responsibility to seek the common ground God has cultivated if the missionary and the people are ever to understand each other. Olson has likewise committed to weave the message of the gospel into the fragile garment of the culture without violating it. His labors among the Motilones consumed his life, yet the culture of this native people remains intact, even enhanced, for its contact with Christianity. It was this kind of dialogue Paul was trying to start on Mars Hill.

**PRAYER: Help me, Lord, to find those bridges you have erected between my world and me. Give me courage then to cross over. Amen.**

---

[‡]Retired clergy, Virginia Conference of The United Methodist Church; living in Richmond, Virginia.

Paul is finally mocked after his rather amiable sermon on Mars Hill because he refers to the resurrection of the dead. The Greeks laughed at the notion of bodies being raised. The body for them was a prison from which the spirit would fly free at death. Most Christians today would identify more with the Greeks than with the apostle. Believers tend to think of the resurrection as the triumph of eternal spirit over transient matter. We clergy can recall discussions along these lines in seminary: "Cadavers can't be resuscitated!" The church typically tames the mockers. When as pastors we bury a young spouse or a child, we will speak of the dead in a more concrete way.

Some people quote Paul: "It is sown a physical body, it is raised a spiritual body" (1 Cor. 15:44). In other words, Paul was really a Greek at heart—right? Then why didn't he explain himself on Mars Hill? For the Jew, a spirit is never the whiff of smoke as it is for the Hellenists. Spirit is a solid thing, more solid than mortal bodies. C. S. Lewis says colorfully that the blades of grass would cut our feet if we should walk on the green in heaven in our present bodies. Spiritual reality is the enduring stuff.

The questions about body and spirit and what we mean when we speak of the resurrection of the body come up time and time again. The conversation engages us very personally, and it connects with our witness to others. As we follow the Christ, Paul's discourse in Athens stands before us as a way to engage those who stand outside the community of faith. We take seriously all questions asked by those who seek spirituality and respond by offering the way of Christ.

**PRAYER: Easter is always our praise, O God, as the risen Christ is the precursor of our victory both today and always. Sustain us that we may engage the larger culture in conversation about Jesus Christ. Amen.**

Having served half a dozen parishes over forty years, I have never stopped longing for one that would afford a "spacious place" for ministry. Each church has offered a place for service, but in every one there were those who sought to pin down or hem in both the ministry and its ministers. Read again verses 10-12a. They remind of those protracted periods of struggle each of us has known, some of which felt like they would never end. But after all, the work of the kingdom did go forward.

Our daughter called today from New York City expressing unhappiness in her work. She has put out her résumé and is ready for a change. As I put down the phone, I asked myself, *Have I ever really been happy in this labor of love?* Well, yes and no. I've loved the people and have been loved by them. I've relished preaching and the ministry of the sacraments. I've rejoiced to see unbelievers come into the church and the children of the church come to fullness of faith. But I have never served a church that did not offer its share of resistance. So much of this calling is accomplished only through dogged hard work.

William Carey, the pioneer missionary to India in the eighteenth century, was queried once as to the secret of his ministry. His simple answer: "I've learned to slog." I'm convinced no good and lasting work for God can be accomplished without it.

What the Christian worker must be willing to accept from God is what Paul found in prison: contentment (Phil. 4:11). Paul had come to believe that despite his discomfort and frustration, God was still working (Phil. 2:13). The place of contentment is finally that "spacious place" we all desire.

**PRAYER: Gracious God, it is never your will that the hearts of those who serve you fail or falter. Kindle anew our hearts to the fires of your love, that we may pursue our work and duties this day with unfeigned joy and willing contentment, through Christ our Lord. Amen.**

Most would define conscience as "a sense of right and wrong innate among human beings." But human ethical systems derive from the mores and scruples of the world's diverse peoples. What one time or culture understands as good or evil, another time or culture may not.

This passage from First Peter tells us that for believers, finding and maintaining a good conscience or a clear conscience originates not in us but in God. We dare not trust any human sense of guilt or lack of it, for as Jeremiah tells us, the "heart is devious [and . . .] perverse" (Jer. 17:9). The writer of First Peter suggests that we appeal to God for a sense of right and wrong that is grounded in Jesus Christ. Any human standard, even one devised by intelligent people, can lead us far afield of what God wants.

Helmut Thielicke, German pastor and theologian during World War II, wrote that the more intelligent the Nazis were, the more cleverly they could reason that their genocide was really best for humanity. The Western church over the last decade has endured the revelation of a host of sexual predators among its clergy. Many of these have been among the church's most educated. Some continue to insist that their behaviors were not only acceptable but beautiful. These examples indicate how morally bankrupt human ideas can be.

I once heard a pastor speak on discerning right from wrong. She held an open Bible and declared, "The word of God must finally be our conscience." What God has said, not just in scattered verses but in the whole of scripture, should be the arbitrator in our moral questions and choices. As the author of First Peter goes on to say, we are to live "no longer by human desires but by the will of God" (4:2), which we come to know by grounding ourselves in scripture and the example of Christ. In Christ, God offers us new life and an enduring standard of right and wrong.

**PRAYER: Help us, Lord, always to do what is right in your eyes. Amen.**

The Bible highlights the virtue of a prominent person taking the side of the underdog, but nothing in the history of God among us illustrates this quite like the story of Jesus Christ. This Righteous One has come over to the side of the unrighteous, not in some tangential way but substantially by virtue of who he was. The Son of God was not just a visitor among us but "flesh of our flesh." Bishop Gerald Kennedy has said that in Christ, God "ploughed [God's] self" into humanity. Neither did Christ live among us as an alien, residing here but really belonging somewhere else. He was altogether at home where we worked, loved, and failed. Not repulsed by sinfulness, he sat down with those dispossessed to advocate for them against their accusers. At the cross where humanity descended (in its rejection of Christ) to its lowest place, he proved to be there with us, holding us to the heart of God, refusing to release us to the end we rendered him. Finally, both Easter and the Ascension confirm that the mind of Christ has not changed: he is still on our side; one day, we will be at his side.

At a Christian college at the height of the drug counterculture, a newcomer named Graham arrived, determined to remain drug free and to follow God. More than once he lapsed, was caught, and disciplined. After several infractions, he was summoned to the dean's office and expelled.

The young fellow broke down sobbing as the university president walked into the office unannounced. Graham turned and fell at the feet of the only person who could save him. Mercy was granted, but the president imposed a hefty monetary fine that the penniless student would find almost impossible to repay. Graham expressed his gratitude and left the office. Then he heard footsteps behind him and felt a hand thrust something into his pocket: a wad of bills for the amount required of him by justice that day. The man who made the rules paid the debt.

**PRAYER: Dear God, grant today that I advocate for one who is undeserving, as Christ has done for us. Amen.**

At my local church during the 1950s, the doctrine of God I learned was apparently based on a subtle, though unexpressed, unitarianism. Even though we sang hymns that praised the Trinity, I cannot remember a sermon on it. Christ was referred to as "divine" but in a lesser, secondary sense. Only God the Father was *really* God.

Our text today is a corrective to that view. Christ's sacrifice for us is sufficient to save us because he *is* God, and we are told to "sanctify Christ as Lord." While Jesus Christ certainly presents God to us, relationship with Christ includes another introduction: Christ presents us to the Father. As Peter says plainly, Christ died for us "in order to bring [us] to God."

A father in New York, a drug addict, left home when his child was a toddler. The son also began using drugs in his early teens and in his twenties was convicted as a felon. After serving several months in prison, the son was free again but miserable. While driving his motorcycle past a church in Los Angeles, he stopped to inquire. Within a few minutes, the pastor arrived on a Harley Davidson. The young inquirer was impressed.

After pouring out his heart and hearing the good news of God's love, the young man received Christ. The two continued to share more details of their lives. The young man told of his father's leaving New York and how he had always wished to know what happened to him. The pastor asked for specifics: where he had lived, his mother's name, when his father had left. Abruptly, the pastor became quiet. Then, trembling, he said, "Son, I am your father."

Years and miles had separated them. Neither had known how to find the other. They had met Christ at different times and places; Christ in turn had given them again to each other. This is what Christ offers each of us: reintroduction to and relationship with our Father.

**PRAYER: Of all your gifts, Lord Jesus Christ, to know your God is best of all. For this gift we thank you. Amen.**

On my bookshelf is a volume of children's Bible stories from my childhood. Under one of its many pictures of Jesus is scribbled, "I love him." I was six when I wrote that, and I could not have appreciated all that love includes.

What does it mean to love God? I am still trying to figure that out, as are many of us. We have described this relationship in many ways. Many Christians persist in thinking of love for God as "a divine romance," but better parallels surely exist to describe the way we love God. We might try to discern what loving God means by looking at what the Bible says about God's love for us:

- God loves us as parents love their children. "My Father will love [you]," Jesus says. So our love for God could be like the love of a child for her mother, as in "honor your father and mother" (Exod. 20:12). If we substitute "honor" for "love" in Jesus' mandate: "[Honor] the Lord with all your heart, soul, and mind" (Matt. 22:37), we may see more clearly what loving God means.

- God loves us as a "friend" (John 15:15). So the love that friends have for each other is what God seeks from us. A friend is one we can trust and respect, from whom we can expect good, upon whom we can depend.

These comparisons may be helpful, but we don't have to struggle like detectives to deduce what it means to love God. Jesus made it plain: "If you love me you will keep my commandments." Our text repeats this standard: "If you love me, you will keep my commandments." And a single commandment includes all the rest: "This is my commandment, that you love one another as I have loved you" (John 15:12). To love God is to love those whom God loves.

PRAYER: **Dear God, help us to show our love for you in the way we love those around us. Amen.**

# Christ Our Companion

*April 28–May 4, 2008  •  Kathleen Coe*[‡]

## MONDAY, APRIL 28  •  Read Psalm 68:1-10, 32-35

Who among us has not bent in sympathy when we hear the old spiritual "Sometimes I Feel Like a Motherless Child"? Who among us has not sensed desolation and loneliness at some time?

Today we live paradoxical lives: Even though we treasure our families and are dedicated to their love and care, our work often takes us away from them. We juggle competing demands, at times leaving our children essentially parentless.

A few years ago when my husband and I visited Tuscany, we noted how many family members of the Italian shopkeepers worked with them in the stores. Whether purveyors of fine leather bags or fresh, ripe fruits and vegetables or the brilliantly colored majolica plates and bowls, shopkeepers were rarely alone. There were grandparents, grandchildren, uncles, aunts, and parents too. Their work merged with their sense of belonging.

The psalmist knows about the crucial bonds of family love. Translations of this psalm vary. Some read that God gives a home to the desolate, the friendless, or the forsaken. Another reads, "God sets the lonely in families" (NIV). God's vision for the created order is that none of us will find ourselves without a home base or a sense of belonging.

The message of God's love is that we need never feel like parentless children. Even though we may be without a human family of our own, we are always part of God's family.

**PRAYER: Parent of all, help me know today that, thanks to your gracious love, I have a home, a family, a place to belong. Amen.**

---

[‡]Grandmother of four, retired pastoral minister of Jamestown Friends Meeting (Quaker) near Greensboro, North Carolina; prior to ministry she was a piano teacher and church musician; a newspaper writer and editor; and a regional director of Self-Help, a community development financial institution.

Here, in his last prayer, Jesus anticipates the disciples' uneasiness about their relationship with him after his crucifixion and resurrection. And so Jesus prays for his disciples; he prays for you and me as well. In his prayer he speaks of those whom God gave to him. We cannot read this without realizing that you and I were chosen by God for relationship with Christ. Jesus not only understood the relationship of God to each of us; he lived it out in all the intimacy of God's love for God's people. This is also the relationship between each of us and Christ—one of intimate companionship and devotion as members of the beloved household.

Jesus conveys this familial intimacy in his touching use of the term *Abba*, or "Daddy," for God. Within this loving relationship, we experience God's protection and realize the depth of our connectedness to God who wills eternal life for us.

Christ is our loving companion; Christ is the one who will always be there when we arise in the morning and when we retire in the evening. Christ is the one who is with us wherever we go.

Christ is truly, steadily, and eternally family. He is ours and we are his by the loving act of God. Christ asks God to protect us and sanctify us—not to pull us out of the world but to guide us through it.

When someone dear prays for us, we are touched beyond measure. That is the effect of the heartfelt prayer that Jesus prays. He prays it for us.

**PRAYER: Christ, my companion, help me to feel the depth of your heartfelt plea for me as one of your beloved family. Amen.**

My sister is one of those thoughtful gift-givers. Whether her gifts are for Christmas, birthdays, or other occasions, they are always perfect. They are not overly expensive or extravagant, and they may be handmade or bought on sale. Yet their perfection as gifts hinges on the fact that the choice is exactly tailored to the recipient, imbued with thoughtful and loving care.

When Jesus speaks of the Holy Spirit, which the Father had promised and which he will send, he offers a personal gift, tailored to our needs. Christ knows us well enough to know what would benefit us the most.

Occasionally the perfect gift is one that the giver has already known and enjoyed and because of familiarity with us the giver believes that we too will treasure the gift. Jesus himself was gifted by the Holy Spirit. The presence of the Holy Spirit signified the beginning of his ministry as well as the beginning of his disciples' ministry. Just as the dove descended after his baptism, and the heavens rang with God's words, "This is my beloved Son," so also did the Holy Spirit's presence at Pentecost herald the beginning of the "beloved community."

Christ, our brother and companion, knows that the presence and guidance of the Holy Spirit will enable our greatest possible fulfillment. The Spirit brings us power far beyond our imaginations—power given not for our own use but for the purposes of God's reign on earth. Our task lies before us; we need not stand and stare into heaven. The fulfillment of mission does not come in that fashion. Perhaps like those early disciples, our own fulfillment comes when we gather in faith and prayer and unwrap the gift together. Only then will we have the power to be Christ's witnesses. The living Christ knows us intimately. The gift of the Holy Spirit will guide, sustain, and fill us for our mission to the ends of the earth.

**PRAYER: Gracious and loving God, you have searched me and known me. Guide and sustain me with your Holy Spirit. Amen.**

## THURSDAY, MAY 1 • Read Acts 1:12–14

One morning several years ago, when I served as a chaplain intern in a large university medical center, I walked into the room of a man who looked as if he wanted to be anywhere but there. An athletic-looking man, trim and muscular, he spoke with the self-assurance of a markedly successful man. He wanted me to know that he would be out of the hospital in no time.

However, the man's medical chart revealed his testing for a serious, life-threatening illness. We talked for a while, but talking about his condition clearly made him feel terribly uneasy. Before I left, I suggested that we close with prayer.

There, in the silence of that room, the presence of God finally confronted him with the fact of his own vulnerability. As we prayed for physical and spiritual healing, tears filled his eyes, and he began to choke with emotion. "I have prayed about this time after time," he said, "but I always asked for the strength to cover it up. This time I can no longer pretend that I am all right."

Daily prayer alone with God has no substitute, but sometimes praying with others takes us to another level. Praying together can help us admit our deep dependence on the strength of God. Our constant devotion to prayer makes it harder to hang on to pretenses and illusions. When we pray together, we may pray for one another and for the common good. Christ is there with us, understanding and comforting us and empowering us to live in the world as his people.

**PRAYER: Loving God, I need you every hour. I depend on your care. Help me to remember my deep need of you. Amen.**

A young friend was telling an adult Sunday school class about his summer camp experience. "It was cool," he said, "because everybody there knew God personally. It was easy to be good. But when we went back to school in the fall, it wasn't so easy. Most of my friends at school think being a Christian is just stupid." At school, in spite of—or because of—his good intentions, my young friend was considered somewhat uncool.

The adults nodded in sympathy. They too live in a world where the Christian life is often met with condescension. In many of their workplaces and social groups they are considered less than fashionable.

Peter, the attributed author of this letter, was no stranger to suffering. He faced personal persecution as part of the fledgling Christian community in Jerusalem. Later he would see that community scattered throughout the known world. And yet in the post-Resurrection church, he remained "the rock," his faith a constant in the midst of strife.

For the Christians in Asia Minor to whom the first letter of Peter was written, suffering came in the form of isolation. Because of their faith, they were estranged from the communities around them. Instead of the peaceful life they might have envisioned as part of the Christian community, they were surprised by mistrust and suspicion.

The wisdom of this epistle tells us how to move forward—even through our pain: we can cast all our anxiety upon God because God cares for us. We are to discipline ourselves and stay alert. Perhaps only than can we recognize the God who lifts us up, bears our burdens, and gives us the strength to go into the unknown. We can acknowledge the transitory nature of our suffering, knowing it is but for a "little while" in God's scheme of things. God is always there to accompany us forward.

**PRAYER: Loving God, help me face the challenges ahead, knowing that you are my constant companion and my strength. Amen.**

The Ascension of Christ was the glorifying moment for all that Christ accomplished through his life, death, and resurrection. In Acts we read that the disciples, perhaps sensing that something miraculous is about to happen, press Christ to reveal whether *he* is about to restore the kingdom to Israel. But his answer shifts the focus to *them*—from his action to theirs. When the Holy Spirit comes upon them, they will be his witnesses to all the earth.

Throughout Jesus' ministry on earth, the disciples had been training to be his witnesses. Now with his impending ascension, he charges them to assume their role to the fullest. If the Ascension is the beginning of Christ's glorification, their witness—and ours—will continue and confirm that glory.

How can our witness today continue Christ's glorification? Webster says that a witness is someone who "is cognizant of something by direct experience, one who beholds or otherwise has personal knowledge of something." To be a witness in truth, then, one must have personal understanding and experience. Our witness to Christ requires direct experience. George Fox, founder of the Religious Society of Friends, often spoke of the power of knowing God through firsthand experience. Only by knowing Christ in this way can we be adequate witnesses.

How does your life bear witness to the power and love of Christ? Is Christ's companionship a daily reality for you? Does Christ's presence powerfully reverberate in your words and actions? In what ways is your life so attuned to Christ's spirit that it magnifies his glory day by day?

**PRAYER: Christ my brother, be my constant companion, that my life might sing of your love and power. Amen.**

Our intellects are exquisite gifts of God that enable us to understand not only God's world but ourselves as well. They allow us to see within ourselves, to analyze and assess, and to imitate the mind of Christ. But our human intellect is limited. While it excels in the dimensions of space, time, and reason, its vision cannot always penetrate the work of the Spirit. That kind of vision is the work of the eyes of the heart. That is why the author of Ephesians prays that the people of Ephesus might have the eyes of their hearts enlightened.

The disciples observe the risen Christ and his ascension with the eyes of the heart. As witnesses to his real and powerful presence, they too gain the possibility of seeing and understanding in a new way, the possibility of effecting change in themselves and those around them.

When the eyes of Saul's heart were opened on the Damascus road, he recognized the love to which he had been blind all his life. His enlightenment took mere days; with many of us it takes years. When our own hearts are enlightened by the presence and leading of Christ, we come to possess unanticipated power, new hope in the future for ourselves and our communities—no matter how great the rifts we face. When our intellects are enlightened by Christ, our understanding traverses new territory; our comprehension expands; barriers fall away, and we look forward with faith and assurance.

**PRAYER: Gracious and loving God, help me to find this new way of seeing. Open the eyes of my heart, so that I can see that which I had not seen before and do that which I could not do before. Amen.**

# Diverse Gifts, One Spirit

*May 5–11, 2008  •  Paul W. Chilcote[‡]*

## MONDAY, MAY 5  •  Read Psalm 104:24-26, 31-34, 35*b*

A wondrous diversity characterizes the world in which we live. Like a magnificent kaleidoscope filled with contrasting colors and shapes, changing constantly with every twist and turn, creation never ceases to dazzle the eye. The psalmist celebrates the manifold works of God. Only a wise God could have created such a marvel. When my family and I lived in Kenya, we prayed a prayer that celebrates the diversity of God's world. We thanked the Creator for Mount Kilimanjaro and Mosi o Tunya Falls, for fat baobabs and tiny mustard seeds, for tsetse flies and majestic giraffe. The Lord, according to the psalmist, rejoices in all these works.

So why is one of God's greatest gifts—variety—also a source of so much discord and strife? We all know too well how diversity can create barriers: different skin color, strange accent, odd ideas, foreign customs, unusual worship. These manifestations of human diversity, instead of promoting thanksgiving and wonder, can easily lead us down the path to conflict and alienation if we lose the perspective of the Creator.

As we approach one of the greatest celebrations of diversity in the life of the church, the Feast of Pentecost, I invite you to visualize our world from the perspective of the psalmist and the Creator. As you survey God's marvelous works in creation, thank God for the infinite opportunities made possible through diversity. Pray that the glory of the Lord may endure forever.

**PRAYER: Loving Creator, you filled our world with an amazing variety of peoples, animals, colors, and works. Grant that we may find joy in difference and reason to celebrate the variety that surrounds us in life. Amen.**

---

[‡]Seminary professor, author, and frequent speaker in applied Wesleyan studies, particularly spirituality, worship, discipleship, mission, and evangelism; living in Durham, North Carolina.

Our first Christmas in Zimbabwe seemed to come so early. We missed the seasonal changes that heralded the great event; but even more, we missed our family back home. It dawned upon us that we were not alone in our yearning for familiar faces and the warmth of renewed relationships. There were at least ten different nations represented at Africa University that year in the student body, and virtually none of the expatriate students could return home for the holiday. But then the Spirit birthed an idea.

We decided to invite all the students who were left behind to come to our home for Christmas Eve. What an amazing celebration we experienced together! If the students were able, we asked them to bring a dish from their native land. What a feast! After dinner we sat in a large circle in our living room and, one by one, each student shared his or her favorite Christmas tradition and taught us, in his or her own language, a song that celebrated Jesus' birth. We sang in many tongues; but truly, we were one in the Spirit.

We celebrated Pentecost at Christmas that year. How similar it must have been for those Jews—gathered together from so many distant nations, crammed into Jerusalem—pilgrims come to raise their voices in praise to Yahweh. Even more astonishing, as the wind of the Spirit whirled around them and filled them with awe and wonder they heard the story of Jesus' birth and life, his crucifixion and resurrection; the Spirit birthed a new community. They discovered a new family—one family in Jesus—and their lives would never be the same.

PRAYER: **Spirit of the living God, fall afresh on me. Teach me the art of speaking with the accent of your love. In every person I encounter this day, may I find my brother, my sister. Amen.**

The circumstances of the Christian community in Corinth certainly called for Paul's gifts of patience and wisdom. Rich Christians there lorded it over the poor. Cliques formed around charismatic leaders who often touted their spiritual superiority. Adherence to customs brought into the practice of their faith from different cultures and religious traditions threatened the unity of that fledgling community we know as *church*. And so the apostle employs one of his favorite word pictures—the "body of Christ"—to help his new brothers and sisters better understand the true nature of God's family.

Unlike the Ephesian letter where the discussion of "one body" takes on an almost comic tone, Paul's words here sober the Corinthian believers despite their intoxication with their own arrogance and pride. "We were all baptized into one body," he pleads. "We were all made to drink of one Spirit." Only the spirit of Christ can overcome the natural inertia that perpetuates divisions between Jews and Greeks, between slaves and free people. You can almost hear Paul teaching his beloved friends the new mantra of reconciliation and peace: "One body, many members. One body, many members."

When we find it so difficult actually to live this out in our lives, God gives us a powerful sign-act to keep the goal ever before us. As we gather around the table to share together in the Supper of the Lord, many as we are, we all share in one loaf. The words and the actions shape us into the people that God would have us be. "For just as the body is one and has many members, and all the members of the body, though many, are one body, so it is with Christ."

**PRAYER: Reconciling God, who calls us to celebrate our unity in diversity: break down the walls we construct through our own ignorance and folly, and shape us into one body in Christ. Amen.**

When the Spirit begins to work, everything gets turned upside down. All our prejudices and stereotypes must be pushed to the side. Radical equality displaces the hierarchies in which we locate ourselves at the top or resign ourselves to our lot far below. Suddenly, everyone becomes important. Every child has a place. Each person's gift finds expression in God's great realm. God affirms each person, each gift, each call upon the name of the Lord. The Bible bears constant witness to this radical message of liberation and the place of every person in the family of God.

Joel's prophecy, realized on the Day of Pentecost, reflects a radical equality with regard to gender and age in the community of faith. It challenges attitudes and actions that restrict women and reorients our thinking about the place of the elderly and the youthful in the family of God. Wherever God rules, both sons *and* daughters boldly proclaim God's word. Dreams and visions displace despondency and hopelessness as the Spirit breathes new life into every creature.

I spent Holy Week 1999 in Lithuania. For half a century, under Soviet occupation, the church there struggled to survive as an underground movement. The bells of the churches and the voices of the people fell silent. But then the Spirit descended with healing in its wings. Resurrection came to the church through the gifts of the elderly and through children who, for the first time in their lives, felt valued and loved by these faithful people. Women figured prominently in this rebirth. I remember one grandmother who would lovingly ask each child, "And what is the gift that you want to share with the people of God? You see, every person here is important."

**PRAYER: Attentive God, help me to know and feel how deeply you love me and to discover the unique gift you have planted in me to share with your world. Amen.**

Our reading today continues to shed light on our theme "Diverse Gifts, One Spirit." Paul provides a list of important gifts that help build up the community of faith. He describes the building blocks of our spiritual home, the church. These building blocks include wisdom, knowledge, faith, healing, miracles, prophecy, discernment, tongues, interpretation. The Spirit distributes and activates these diverse gifts according to the need. Later in the letter, Paul makes abundantly clear that the beginning and end of all God's gifts is love. The proper use of our gifts extends God's loving mission in the world.

In the wake of several hurricanes that devastated much of the southeastern United States, our whole family decided to join the reconstruction effort the following summer. We were somewhat concerned because none of us possessed skills related to the kind of work we anticipated. As the group took shape, we discovered that many of those involved felt exactly the same way. "What can I do?" was a question on the lips of many. But one primary concern united us: our desire to share God's love with people who were hurting. We wanted those who suffered to know that we genuinely cared and that they were not alone.

The Spirit overwhelmed us during those days in mission. One man had the roofing skills needed at a widow's home. The kids painted and played with displaced children who yearned for friendship. An experienced grief counselor offered her listening heart and planted seeds of hope. By working in solidarity with those we sought to serve, we received the abundant gifts they had to share. The Spirit met every need through the gifts of God's people shared with others in love.

**SUGGESTION FOR MEDITATION: Reflect on a time in your life when the Spirit used your gifts to bring healing and joy to a person who needed something only you could give. How can God's love be activated through you?**

By the time we arrived in Zimbabwe, a terrible drought had decimated the entire southern region of Africa. My wife, working with nurses and health-care workers at the hospital nearby, soon identified five hundred critically malnourished children on the large commercial farms that normally produced an abundance of crops for that nation and beyond. Every family we visited in one particular area revealed unbelievable levels of deprivation and despair. The scenario was the same at every turn. "Where is your food?" we would ask. "We have no food," came the response. "Only God can save us now." Hunger gripped the lives of these poor, desperate children of God and threatened to bring them all to ruin.

Those hungry Zimbabweans undoubtedly resonated with the insight of the psalmist when he, in solidarity with the poor, expressed their total dependence upon God: "When you hide your face, they are dismayed; when you take away their breath, they die and return to their dust." We have seen how our faith makes us one, despite the diversity of the human family. But we are also united by our basic needs. If we are honest, we are all equally dependent upon God for everything.

God provided an opportunity for us to serve those hungry brothers and sisters in Africa. Widows and orphans were most at risk. Whenever we delivered basic food items and supplies to those who needed it most, the women would fall to the ground, weeping; then they would spring to their feet, singing the praises of God. They all looked to God who used us as instruments to give them their food in due season. Our common dependence on God made us one and enabled us to celebrate God's amazing grace and provision together.

**PRAYER: Holy Provider, send forth your Spirit and create us anew, for we look only to you to renew the face of the earth. Amen.**

### PENTECOST

The Gospel text for Pentecost talks about rivers of living water. Water features prominently throughout the scriptures. It is a primal symbol; its counterpart in human experience, of course, is thirst. Like hunger, our thirst for water points us to the perennial need for God in our lives. Thirst, the great leveler, brings us all to our most basic level. Not surprisingly, water is a favorite theme of John's Gospel.

For centuries, Christians have connected Pentecost and baptism. It all makes perfect sense. The coming of the Spirit, the birth of the church, the waters of baptism. These images flow together. They remind us of who we are and to whom we belong. Jesus did not simply bring a message or proclaim a new idea and then leave us to our own devices. He formed a group. He gathered a community and then sent his Holy Spirit to be the unifying center for the fellowship of God's people.

Whenever we celebrate baptism, the church says to the welcomed friend: "You are ours, and we are God's. We claim you as our own, and God claims you through us. You are a part of the body of Christ." In those same actions the church says to itself: "We are brothers and sisters. We are a holy nation, God's own people. So our work together is much more important than our petty divisions. We have been remade into the body of Christ."

After a baptism on Pentecost in one of the churches I served, a determined seven-year-old came swaggering up to the front after the service and asked me, "Where is this baby that belongs to me now? If I'm going to be looking after him, I better know exactly what he looks like." The Spirit birthed the church anew that day.

**PRAYER: Come, Holy Spirit, fill our hearts with rivers of living water and bring to completion your great work of love. Amen.**

# God So Ordered

*May 12–18, 2008 • Connie Davis Rouse[‡]*

### MONDAY, MAY 12 • Read Genesis 1:1-5

As the office manager of a newly formed congregation in Myrtle Beach, South Carolina, I dreaded the Monday-morning chaos that usually awaited me at the office. Saturday's mail! Sunday's leftover bulletins! Notes and suggestions from members! Messages on the answering service! Appointments! Letters to be typed! I felt overwhelmed and always struggled to begin to clear up the clutter that naturally encompasses day-to-day church operations. I often found myself pulled among tasks, completing none, and feeling exasperated and stressed.

Yet, when the world was new, God embraced the chaotic nothingness and patiently created order from it, one step at a time. God's Spirit lingered over the watery deep, directing that there be light and darkness, day and night, evening and morning. Then God ordered divisions in the water, upper and lower, to create heaven and earth. As God crafted each new gift to the world, God acknowledged it as good and then moved on to the next task.

Life overwhelms us at times. We find it challenging to maneuver through the chaos the world imposes so that we might see the order God intends for our lives. Yet God's intention leads to wholeness and peace. Peace is not the absence of chaos but the ability to persevere and thrive in the midst of the confusion.

Let us work diligently each day until we find the good. With each new step, may we allow God to create a good work in and through us.

**PRAYER: Lord, calm my soul in all that I do and say this day. Let my life and actions glorify you. Temper me with patience, and let your peace order my steps. Amen.**

---

[‡]Writer/columnist for South Carolina United Methodist *Advocate*; Christian educator, retreat speaker; living in New York, New York.

My younger daughter deeply respects the earth that God has created. She believes that a fitting response to her gratitude is recycling, everything from plastic to glass to cans to all forms of paper. Not only does she recycle, but she kindly demands that her housemate, neighbors, friends, and visiting relatives (mothers included) recycle as well. Complying with her wishes voluntarily on a recent visit, I felt that I was part of something good, almost holy.

I contrast the many ways in which we recycle paper, plastic, glass, and metal with the vision of creation presented in Genesis 1. Many people recycle in the hope that we will heal the earth. In Genesis we see the earth presented as good, as blessed. It comes as a gift. In fact, it seems that everything in the book of Genesis is a gift of grace. We look from this vantage point and weep for a paradise lost, an unspoiled creation.

More than simply weeping for the devastation of the earth, we are invited to serve as stewards of the earth. A number of environmental groups have led the church back to its responsibility to exercise stewardship of the earth. Will we come to a new day when God will again look at the waters and the dry land, the sun and moon and stars, the creatures of sky and sea and earth, and respond as God once did: "And God saw that it was good"?

God so ordered the creation that we care for the earth as a gift in response to God. May we be worthy proprietors of this good and valuable gift we call Earth.

SUGGESTION FOR MEDITATION: **In what ways are you being a good steward of the land?**

PRAYER: **Creator God, you called forth creation and blessed it. In gratitude we pray to live as stewards of creation. Amen.**

My older daughter is a youth pastor, and it is not unusual to find her patrolling the streets late at night, searching to find and feed the homeless. She once picked up a group of inebriated teens who were trapped in the snow and delivered each one safely home. But dogs terrify this brave, young woman who, as a child, was attacked by a large dog.

Many cannot understand her fear because they view dogs as loving pets. Pet lovers often try to use force or ridicule to help her master this fear.

Why do some of us fear God's creatures? Why can we not call all of them good, as God does in the creation story in Genesis? Genesis 3 tells us: One of the consequences of the first humans' disobedience is enmity between humans and animals. We still see many examples of this break.

For example, the owners of two pit bulls who loved their dogs set out to convince their community how harmless and "good" the animals were. They allowed the dogs to roam freely until they attacked the neighbors' three-year-old daughter as she played in her backyard. These animals lost their lives because of their owners' unwise actions.

It is not wrong to love our pets with all the intensity God placed within us. Animals can become special "members" of our families who serve us and others well. Yet we must also always remember that we live in a fallen world. The prophet Isaiah tells us of a time when the peaceable order God created will be restored, when the wolf and lamb will lie together, when no one will hurt or destroy (Isa. 11:6-9). Then my daughter and all of us will be able to live without fear, in peace and safety.

**PRAYER: God, help us to create a safe environment for all of creation, where all can live without fear. Amen.**

As my husband maneuvered the car through the great Smoky Mountains for what would be my first time, I sat in awe. The mountains towered so high that the tips were invisible, secluded in the grandeur of the clouds. The heavens seemed to mysteriously open up and embrace the peaks, caressing them with majesty. For a moment, I was breathlessly frightened as I read the signs that stated, "Falling rocks." We were powerless against those colossal mountains that God had marvelously carved. In my frailty and fear, I recognized that if this landmass chose to rage against us, we would be met with a most formidable and unbeatable foe. I became more afraid.

My husband, who had journeyed around and through these mountains many times before, uttered calming words to me. "Look at what God created for us!" A peace rested upon my soul. I moved from a state of anxiety into one of humility.

God had made it all for me, for us. God created this grandeur for humankind to enjoy and care for. The land would provide for us if we would provide for the land. How marvelous a gift!

Psalm 8 is the first song of praise in the Psalter. It exalts God and affirms our vocation in tandem with God for the care of creation. The psalm is bookended with a phrase that proclaims God's name as majestic; God's character and essence through the "name" is known in all the earth. And there in the middle of Psalm 8 comes the primary question of the psalmist: "What are human beings that you are mindful of them, mortals that you care for them?" We, as creatures of the Creator, find ourselves bounded on all sides by God, framed by God's name and identity. Our dominion comes to fruition only in the realm of God's sovereignty. Only in divine partnership are we a little "lower than God." An amazing relationship; an awesome responsibility!

**PRAYER: God of awesome power, may your name and love bound me in all I do, especially in my care of your creation. Amen.**

Elliot had learned to tie her shoes. "Want me to show you?" she asked one day in liturgical dance class. This five-year-old did not carelessly proceed but declared that there was a method, an order, to the task she was about to embark upon that would most definitely produce the expected outcome. She meticulously outlined the directives her mother had given her.

Hurling her body to the floor with a loud plop, she quickly untied her shoelaces. Elliot, being right-handed, took the left string and pulled it over the right string and locked the two together. Then, bending the right and left strings in half, she looped the left string over the right and pulled it through the hole. Tightening it, she announced with joy, "See! It worked!"

Paul often closes his letters with words that articulate his real concerns about the community and its needs. Here, in the benediction of his second recorded letter to the church at Corinth, he admonishes the Corinthians to "put things in order," "agree with one another," and "live in peace." If they follow the plan, he assures them that it will result in the love and peace of God being actualized through the Holy Spirit and manifested in their lives.

How often we want a simple plan for living, and here Paul offers it. To live together in harmony, we, like the cantankerous Corinthian believers, need to "put things in order." What might our lives look like if we chose to agree with one another and live in peace? In our world of violence and chaos, how would we implement such measures?

Paul goes on to include a visible sign of peace: a holy kiss. And he then reminds us that we are not in this undertaking alone—but with all the other saints! Perhaps together we can truly live as God so ordered.

**Suggestion for meditation: What in your life needs ordering? What would change in your life if you were to "put things in order"?**

## SATURDAY, MAY 17 • Read Matthew 28:16–20

Jesus has been raised. The eleven disciples journey to the mountain in Galilee to which Jesus had directed them. Some worship him, and some doubt. Yet he states that all authority in heaven has been given to him. Then Jesus gives the Great Commission, telling them to go and make disciples. "Going" is part of what Jesus envisions for his followers.

My husband is a third-generation United Methodist pastor, and moving is totally ordinary for him. Not for me. When we moved across the country, it saddened me in ways I could never have imagined. One day, depressed and with no destination in mind, I got into my car and drove. After about an hour I realized that I was lost. I did what any Christian would do—I searched for a church where I could ask for help. Finding no United Methodist church, I went to a Baptist one. The doors were locked. Then I remembered the Jewish synagogue I had passed and rejected as an option. I reluctantly went back. Hesitantly and apprehensive about how I would be received, I walked through the doors and told the receptionist that I was lost and needed directions. Then, surprising myself, I asked, "May I pray?" Not only did she allow me to pray; she prayed with me and went and got the cantor to sing a prayer for me. They weren't Christian, but they respected my speaking of my love for Christ. I thought of the story of the Good Samaritan. Their actions and attitudes in helping me were more like the Samaritan's than mine had been as I bypassed the synagogue. Instead of my reaching out to them, they reached out to me.

Jesus came to reconcile not just a select few but the entire world to God. I had forgotten what Jesus said. I want to be more like those two people who showed me the love of God. Maybe then I will be more effective in doing what Jesus told us.

**PRAYER: Lord, help me go and make disciples. In the name of the Father, Son, and Holy Spirit, I pray. Amen.**

Mrs. Jones doesn't like Mrs. Smith because of something that her sister said to her forty years ago. Sue doesn't want to sit beside Jane in the choir because she is jealous of her great voice. No one likes the pastor because his sermons are far too long. Just a typical Sunday morning all over the country!

What does it mean to keep the sabbath holy? Is it simply going to church? I have discovered that some of the unholiest moments can occur in the church, especially on Sunday mornings. It must be more than that.

It can't be as simple as not working on Sunday, because ministers, choir directors, Christian educators, and youth pastors "work" the hardest on Sundays. It must be more than that.

God created perfection and then stopped to rest in holiness. That divine resting concludes the creation. Sabbath belongs to the created order. Clearly God patterns the need for a rhythm of work and rest. So how can we rest in holiness? How can we rest in the sacred and spiritually pure? Where can we find sabbath moments on Sundays even when it's a workday?

Many companies allow employees to gather on break for prayer. A work break might become a time given to personal meditation or prayer. Reading excerpts from an inspirational book or using your lunch time to volunteer at a soup kitchen can provide sabbath moments.

God rested, and creation's completion resides in our resting. Sabbath, part of God's creating work, becomes the time when we focus not on ourselves but on attending to God and God's ordering of life. A balanced rhythm of life—both work and rest—offers a wholeness that can restore and renew.

Seek the holy. Dwell within it. Rest with God and then arise renewed and invigorated to continue to do God's work.

**PRAYER: Lord, keep me holy. Make me spiritually pure. Help me to be one with you. In Jesus' name, I pray. Amen.**

# A Calm and Quiet Soul

*May 19–25, 2008* • *K. J. Wuest*[‡]

**MONDAY, MAY 19** • **Read Isaiah 49:8-13**

It seems strange to remind people of their responsibilities when they are in exile, having lost their land and heritage. Yet, these words come to Israel—a swift reminder that they are "a light to the nations." As a covenant people they are given to others so that God can act through them to

- restore the land,
- reassign desolate inheritances,
- announce to the prisoners, "Go free,"
- call to those in darkness to "Show yourselves."

It is good to be reminded both of God's intention and God's amazing ability to work through us even when we find ourselves bombarded with myriad difficulties. Our own experience of life's dark moments does not remove us from being of use to others for God's sake.

We may be surprised by the grace afforded us to respond when God calls. A while back I spent many hours waiting in the outer office of a cancer clinic. Many people came and went throughout the day. A few patients came alone for treatment. I had no reason or real intention of making contact with them, but it felt natural to pray for them while they waited their turn for treatment. God comforts us in our suffering through others. How? A smile, a kind word, a willingness to pick up something that is dropped, or help someone undo a stubborn water bottle cap, a small conversation, or just by looking persons in the eye so they know someone noticed they were there that day.

**PRAYER: Compassionate God, whose love knows no bounds, help me to open my heart and life more fully to you and your purposes. Amen.**

---

[‡]Ministry Associate for Visitation and Faith Formation, Kent Lutheran Church, Kent, Washington.

Some people seem to come with a built-in gene for worry. But, in truth, worrying is just a habit; and habits are learned. We learned to lean on worry somewhere along the line; and, if Jesus is talking about it, then clearly it has been a mode of coping with life for quite some time.

Jesus uses ordinary examples of food, drink, birds, lilies, and grass to show that all worry is worthless. Worry has its basis in fear. God knows more clearly than we ourselves do what we need, and God will provide for us. Our fears of not *being* enough and not *having* enough are brought on by trying to serve wealth and knowledge, wisdom, control, and the like. Much and too much are still not enough.

I finally acknowledged that I had learned the habit of worry from my mother—as much as I protested that it was not so. At the time of this discovery, I was leading a small-group study on the subject of stress. One approach we tackled was unlearning patterns by replacing them with something healthy. We would let one bad habit go and fill the void with something worthwhile. I chose to eliminate worry and replace it with prayer. I wrote a few simple and easily memorized breath prayers that I could immediately turn to when my mind shifted into the worry mode. While this venture was not a snap, it was fruitful; and I still practice this approach.

How do you make a habit of trusting God instead of giving worry too much power in your life? Who needs your encouragement to do the same?

**SUGGESTION FOR PRAYER: As you breathe in, breathe in hope; as you breathe out, breathe out fear. (Repeat as necessary.)**

## WEDNESDAY, MAY 21 • Read 1 Corinthians 4:3-5

It takes a tremendous amount of trust not to take judgment into our own hands. From a young age we are taught to exercise good judgment in behavior, making choices, knowing right from wrong, and in choosing friends. In the first three examples we judge ourselves, and in the last we are put directly in the situation of judging someone else. These kinds of judgment seem necessary for our life and our well-being.

Participating in the level of judgment Paul warns about in his letter to the Corinthians has a much more oppressive intent. To be judged the way this world generally judges us—by our religious affiliation (or lack of ), our racial background or class standing (real or imagined) or by the standards of fashion and all things skin deep—is almost immediately painful, destructive, and distracting. But how do we develop the internal strength not to fall into participating in such judgment and reacting when it happens to us?

One healthy practice for building such internal strength involves developing a desire to examine our own purposes of heart. Ignatius of Loyola is credited with a prayer practice called "the examen," which invites us to spend a short time each evening examining our day step-by-step. There are traditional and contemporary formulas for walking through this practice. They lead us to a deeper knowing of our heart's purposes. How we spend our time, with whom, and for what reason, can be eye-opening. Another benefit of such a prayer practice is the opportunity to see God at work in, around, and through us on a daily basis.

**PRAYER: Bless me, O God, with a growing knowledge of my own heart. Give me courage to look within and to pay attention to what I find there. Amen.**

"I have calmed and quieted my soul." Even to say these words moves me in that direction. On those all-too-frequent hectic days when my mind whirls and eventually my heart protests to my schedule's running my day, these calming words make a good walking meditation. They are an even better breath prayer to slow my pace and to bring me back to my true center:

> breathing in: "I have calmed"
> breathing out: "and quieted my soul."

The image of a child at peace in its mother's arms is an inspiring image of a soul quiet in the presence of God. For a child at peace like this is not even holding its own weight. It rests totally against that which it knows to be completely trustworthy.

Several years ago during a time of unexpected crisis I claimed the gift of some similar words, "Quiet my soul in your presence with the stillness of a wise trust." These words and the comforting image they firmly established in my imagination as I repeated them over and over carried me through many rough days. This prayer kept me within myself in a sense. It kept me from jumping to conclusions and encouraged me to rely on God's presence day in and day out.

What word or phrase leads you to a sense of peace in the midst of your life's chaotic moments? Don't have one? Try the one above, or a short phrase from a favorite psalm or scripture. Sometimes a single word like *peace* works well.

**SUGGESTION FOR MEDITATION: Settle yourself in a comfortable chair. Relax all your muscles completely. Close your eyes and picture yourself in God's arms. Breathe slowly and deeply in and out using your breath prayer or word as needed to bring yourself to your calm center. Rest in complete confidence that God holds your every care. God holds your hopes, fears, and dreams. God holds your life.**

I have just come from the funeral of someone dear to me. She was portrayed as a person with a firm certainty. Even though she confronted many difficulties and losses in her long life, she never lost that certainty. Some people are confident to the point of arrogance; the confidence she lived had less to do with her and everything to do with being a child of God. The assurance that carried her through this life stemmed from being claimed and named by God on the day of her baptism, and because of that she faced every today with the confidence of the eternal tomorrow. That assurance allowed her to be generous and kind.

Solomon's wisdom eventually led him to an accumulation of things. Much as we are tempted to use what wisdom we have in the same way, Jesus points out that this is not where our wisdom or effort is best directed. Rather, Jesus encourages us to strive for the kingdom of God. Put our faith into action. Let our lives and our hearts be open to the activity of God in our midst today. Stretch our faith. God knows what is necessary for us in this life. Our challenge is to live, trusting God to provide the necessities, both large and small, as we do our best to serve God faithfully.

Who inspires you to stretch, to serve, to grow, and to give generously? Have you thanked them lately? Who is looking to you to be that inspiration in their life?

**PRAYER: Generous God, help me to be confident of your love, not to the point of arrogance but instead that I may become less fearful and more generous. You know my heart and my needs. Guide me as I discover more and more what it means to be your child and a servant of your kingdom today. Amen.**

"Look! See for yourself—you are like my own fingerprints—that is how close you are to me." That is what the image of being inscribed on the palms of God's hands brings to my mind. God's promise is never to forget, to hold us fast.

These phrases of comfort and consolation to a people in exile can be strong words of hope and encouragement to us as well. Many experiences and situations in this life lead us to feel forsaken, forgotten, and in deep pain. Chronic illness, cancer; loss of a loved one, a career; or the betrayal of a friend are just a few examples of events that can take us into a type of exile these days.

Each brings its own form of mind-numbing grief that can overwhelm even the most well-adjusted individuals. It is too easy to turn to alcohol, drugs, gambling, or other additions to distract us from the pain. But, truthfully, the addiction only adds another layer of pain.

There is One who is always with us. One whose care, concern, and compassion far outweigh anything the world can offer. God can shoulder our pain, fear, anger, tears, and doubts when they threaten to overtake us. As improbable as it is that a mother would forget her nursing child, that is still more possible than God's forgetting us. This is cause for celebration—cause for the mountains, the earth, and even the heavens to break into songs of joy!

**PRAYER: Compassionate God, you promise never to forget me. Empower me to reach out to those whose hearts and lives are broken by the weight of whatever exiles them. Help me to bring your powerful word of promise and joy to those in need. Amen.**

To be called servants of Christ is one thing, but how about bearing the title "stewards of God's mysteries"? What might this involve? A steward is someone who has been entrusted with the management of another's assets. Life is the biggest continual mystery I can think of. But let's think even bigger. Let's consider the mystery of our life in Christ. Seeing ourselves as stewards entrusted with caring for our life in Christ calls for nurturing its growth in ourselves and then also in others—and in that order. We cannot help others grow in their love of God, in their desire to serve, in the growth of and living out of their faith, if we ourselves do not attend to the same concerns in ourselves.

I have one particular soul friend with whom I explore the question: "Is it well with your soul?" When we meet in person after a long absence, this beloved question is the first point of discussion in which we engage after we set aside the hubbub of travel. We each take a turn to listen and to talk.

Sometimes there are tears of laughter or sorrow at life's twists and turns and acknowledgment of God's presence in all. At other times the question fosters a deep need for silence.

What am I reading for nurture; how am I praying; and what am I doing for self-care? Whatever comes in the answering, it is a time of soul discovery and a needed redirection of my attention. Afterward I feel more capable of carrying on as a servant and steward, more open to the mysteries of God.

Is it well with your soul? Who helps you care for the life of Christ within you? Who in your life might need you as a soul friend?

**PRAYER: May your strong word of life, feed and guide all who seek to be stewards of your mysteries, O Lord. Amen.**

# Faith and Trust

*May 26–June 1, 2008 • Daniel H. Mundt[‡]*

### MONDAY, MAY 26 • Read Psalm 46

The psalmist begins with a marvelous affirmation of God as our refuge and strength, but then the psalmist immediately leads us through a litany of natural disaster that sounds as if it came straight from a contemporary news source. Though the earth should change, the mountains shake, earthquakes happen in the midst of the sea, and the waters roar and foam, God remains our refuge and strength.

Whether in life in biblical times or life today, change happens. What do you feel when change seems overwhelming? Sometimes change in our lives, whether positive or negative, causes us to race around frantically. Change upsets our routine, and we no longer take care of ourselves, much less pay attention to God. Natural disasters such as earthquakes and tsunamis cause us to notice grand-scale changes within planet Earth. Like the psalmist, we find it quite probable then to seek refuge in God.

We may find it more difficult to notice the effect of changes in our communities or our personal lives. Sometimes change comes at a pace far more gradual than the calamitous change referred to in Psalm 46. Sometimes we may not recognize change as it happens. As we spend time in daily quiet and meditation, we pray that God will make us aware of and open to change.

How do you seek refuge in times of change? Slow down and listen for God, letting God shelter you in the midst of today's changes. As you face them, stay open to God and trust the refuge that God extends.

**PRAYER: Almighty God, you are our refuge and strength. Though the waters of change may roar and the mountains quake, sustain and guide us this day. Amen.**

---

[‡]Attorney, lay minister, speaker, Bible study leader, former college teacher; member of Glen Avon Presbyterian Church, Duluth, Minnesota.

Noah's faith and trust in God results in actions that witness in word and deed to others. Noah's story shows us one who uses gifts and abilities in God's service.

How do we respond when our task seems impossible or when God's invitation to us seems impossible? What task, because of its enormity, seems to immobilize you? What tasks do you face today or this week or this month that you cannot conceive doing by yourself?

Perhaps we receive a call from God and dismiss it as an unlikely call or a simply impossible challenge. The task may not be to build an ark prior to an impending flood. Maybe your church needs a Sunday school teacher. After prayers of discernment within the community of faith, congregational leaders invite you to consider teaching as an act of service. You have never taught. Teaching scares you. You list many reasons why you cannot do this task; however, as more people hear of the invitation, they say that you are the perfect choice and that they support the invitation. You ask why and the response only mystifies you. You agree to test the work. You pray for guidance before you prepare, and you pray throughout the week for your students. You pray each Sunday, and you pray that the seeds of faith will grow in each student. Soon you recognize that your relationship to God has grown because you teach.

This challenge is not as large as the one faced by Noah, but it puzzles us as something equally improbable. Noah did not know the full scope of God's intent, but Noah surely believed that God would guide and provide a path. We have no certainty other than the ultimate assurance that we receive from God, who is our refuge. Like Noah, we risk ourselves in ventures of faith.

**PRAYER: Nurturing God, gather us in the ark of your love and help us to venture and risk ourselves as we witness to the gift your love. Amen.**

Noah trusted in God and followed God's direction, even into the unknown. God led Noah to dry land. The story of the ark comes to a conclusion when Noah leaves the ark and steps on land with his wife, his sons, their wives, and all the paired animals. How would we feel had we been in Noah's place, going out into the unknown after the flood? Would we have left the ark when we could see only a different, difficult life ahead?

A number of years ago at our cabin property, my wife and I experienced two storms with downburst winds of up to 150 miles per hour. We lost over 5,000 trees between the two storms. The devastation and the mess were overwhelming. We were without water and electricity for over a week. We got a small taste of what people go through with hurricanes, typhoons, earthquakes, tornados, and tsunamis. As many have done in the face of such disasters, we cleaned up for several years and planted 3,500 trees.

The challenge to trust and follow comes when a major problem confronts us. Will we be able to go on? Only with faith and trust in God did my wife and I receive the strength and guidance to continue to seek and follow God's direction.

Noah totally committed his life to God. To him success was following God's lead whatever he was called to do and wherever he was called to go. That understanding of success is consistent with the biblical witness. We see similar understandings of success in the prophets, in Paul, and in Jesus. Commitment to and trust in God allows God's grace to fill our lives; we can then follow, leaving the results to God.

**PRAYER: Lord, when our lives are turned upside down, give us faith and trust in you to lead us through every event in our lives knowing that you provide. Amen.**

## THURSDAY, MAY 29 • Read Romans 1:16–17

Christianity began as a revolutionary concept. Paul and those to whom he wrote believed so strongly in following Christ that nothing, not even death, stopped them from living as they understood they were called by Christ to live. They lived in radical obedience because their lives were made new by God's love. Those who followed Christ in the first centuries of the Christian movement risked government persecution and potential martyrdom. That remains true for many Christians today.

The culture in which I live often brings more confusion than clarity to life. Customs, standards, and values in society contradict how Christ would have us live. Television programs value untalented celebrity and greed. We celebrate political power and military might and fail to see the effects of acts of violence upon the least known in our culture and elsewhere. We wear masks to hide our allegiance to Christ, possibly because we don't want to disclose our faith in a society that doesn't live like Christ or because we feel it necessary to conform to the culture around us.

Paul clearly is not ashamed of identifying with Jesus Christ. He is convinced that the gospel is the power of God to turn upside down the values of the world. That gospel worldview stood in opposition to the perspectives held by emperors and kings, Caesars and Herods who felt threatened by the revolutionary Christian witness.

How do we show others our faith? Do we demonstrate our faith only within the sanctuary, or do we demonstrate our faith throughout the week? Do we let it impact the way we vote or speak or act? Do we show our faith and trust in our deeds?

**PRAYER: God, who shelters us and offers us refuge, encourage us to speak your truth today in the midst of the challenges that come. Help us to tell the story of Jesus Christ. Amen.**

Grace is God's unmerited, free, spontaneous love for humanity. God takes us as we are, warts, wrinkles, and all. We may not want to accept this gift. We may have the misguided notion that God does not love us because of our sin. Or we may believe that we have to achieve on our own, using our own resources. Yet, over and over Paul writes that Jesus Christ makes God's love known to all and that nothing can be done to earn that love. We confuse God's love with the conditional ways in which humans often show love.

God's grace comes through Jesus Christ, which empowers us to accomplish things that we cannot do by ourselves. We can take up our work in God's kingdom because this grace brings with it God's active involvement in our lives. We demonstrate God's grace in our lives through our acts of love and support for others. When Paul discusses true righteousness in Romans 3, we learn of the radical impact of Paul's life-giving encounter with the Christ. Everything in Paul's understanding of God has changed; now God's love and grace empowers his life.

Do we hear God's voice calling us to do acts of *kindness* and *mercy* that tell others we belong to God? Perhaps that action is as simple as sending a card, making a phone call, visiting someone who is homebound. It might be providing food in time of sorrow or reaching out to one who is isolated or neglected. How do we respond in these situations?

We can become involved by *listening*, becoming God's ears to a world of people to whom no one listens. Perhaps we share best the grace of God when we *listen* to others. As my wife has told me many times, "I don't want you to solve my problems or suggest answers. I want you to *listen*." Our world is full of those who want to tell what they think. We are called by grace to show others we care about them by listening to them.

**PRAYER: Lord, may we daily receive your grace and go forth to show your grace in word and deed with others. Amen.**

What is your foundation, the bedrock of your faith? In today's text Jesus clearly contrasts building on sand and building on rock. He refers to a basic awareness about the location of building projects. Building on sand is dangerous. Sand shifts. When we build our lives on Christ's teaching then we have built a life on rock that will not collapse when faced with adversities, problems, and sufferings that will surely come.

Jesus clearly states that if we listen and follow his teachings our strong foundation will enable our house to stand. On the other hand, if we hear but do not listen and follow, then we are like the man who built on the sand. Our lives will collapse when the storms of life assail us. What foundation are we building on?

Many said "Lord, Lord," but did not follow Jesus' way. They fooled themselves but not God. Words, unless they come from the heart and soul and are followed by action, are pretense. Faith without works is dead.

Jesus' words about building on rock and sand conclude the Sermon on the Mount. Scripture says that he astounds his audience because he teaches with authority. Jesus expects each of us to live a life of obedience to his teachings. Our lives will stand or fall based on the foundation upon which we build. Jesus invites the people then and us now to build foundations on the bedrock of trust.

SUGGESTION FOR MEDITATION:
**On Christ the solid rock I stand,**
**all other ground is sinking sand;**
**all other ground is sinking sand.**

(Refrain to "My Hope Is Built," by Edward Mote)

Psalm 46 celebrates God's ultimate victory. The psalmist proclaims the ultimacy of God's truth: though "the nations are in uproar" and "the earth melts," God is our refuge. The psalmist repeats the words, "The God of Jacob is our refuge." We remember that God alone is our peace.

Notice this attribute of God in Psalm 46: "A very present help in trouble." Consider life in the present. Our life with God may not seem easy at times, but it is the authentic life. What does it mean for God to be "a present help"? In what direction does the psalmist point us?

Some regular practices help me each day to stay rooted in God's presence. These practices will not surprise readers of *The Upper Room Disciplines*:

- Read the Bible daily for inspiration and understanding.
- Set aside a regular time for contemplative prayer—to listen for God.
- Seek to know God's love and justice for this day.
- Pray for needs in your community. Pray for the wounds of the world. Pray with the news headlines as your guide.
- Seek ways to worship God in your home.
- Worship with a community of believers.
- Participate in a small group to stay accountable as a Christian disciple. Share meditations and inspirational readings with the group.
- Witness to others and allow them to witness to you.
- Practice gratitude. Count blessings, not troubles.

Today seek God, our refuge and our present help.

**PRAYER: Holy God, you are our refuge and strength, a very present help. Therefore, we will not fear. Let your perfect love drive out the anxiety and fear within us. Amen.**

# The Next Faithful Step

*June 2–8, 2008  •  Harriett Jane Olson*[‡]

**MONDAY, JUNE 2  •  Read Psalm 33:1–5**

Our first reading for this week begins with an outburst of praise. The psalmist addresses the righteous and the upright, calling them to praise the Lord. Is this a case of "like calling to like," with those of us who do not consider ourselves righteous standing apart from this glad reciprocity? This does not sound like the God we know, whose love is poured out on us.

In fact, scholars suggest that this psalm is a continuation or a response to Psalm 32, which concludes with an instruction to the upright and the righteous to be glad in the Lord and rejoice. Psalm 32 begins by recounting the blessing of being forgiven and having no iniquity imputed by God. These blessed ones—the forgiven—are the ones who are then accounted righteous and who "qualify" to respond in joy to God.

The psalmist invites them and us to offer melody and skillfully executed music in praise to God, accompanied by loud shouts—a rather intimidating invitation if it were merely a call for the musically gifted or for excellence. But what if these verses are calling for our best and most exuberant offering of praise?

How blessed we are to be invited into this chorus of rejoicing through the loving-kindness of God! During this week we will see again and again how God extends grace, forgiveness, and healing to those who might have been considered and who might consider themselves to be outsiders.

**SUGGESTION FOR MEDITATION: What makes me feel like an "outsider"—unwelcome or unable to offer suitable praise to God? Can I trust God to see me truly and receive me and my praise? What do I communicate to others that makes them feel similarly unwelcome or unworthy?**

---

[‡]Senior Vice President for Publications, Editor of Church School Publications and Book Editor, The United Methodist Publishing House, Nashville, Tennessee.

The stories of Abram and Sarai are foundational in the biblical narrative. They teach us something about our spiritual DNA. As this couple follows, fails, and fulfills their calling, they alternately provide models and warnings for us. In these verses they hear God's command and promise, a clear word that they understand very concretely in their daily lives.

The narrator gives no detail about how and where Abram hears the Lord. Is it a vision? a dream? a visitor? We don't know. Perhaps that's just as well. Each of us probably hears God in his or her own way. It may be that the call to journey seems natural to Abram since his father Terah had been on a journey from Ur to Canaan when the family settled in Haran. We don't have much detail about how God speaks or how Abram feels.

We do know that God says to go and offers promises (land, nationhood, descendants, reputation) of things that were valued then and things that are valued today. In fact, God promises to bless Abram and Sarai as a part of God's providential care for all people. They will be blessed and will bless others.

Are we called to the same purposes? The visible manifestations of God's blessing (such as nationhood or children) to Abram may not be the same evidence of blessing that God promises us, but we are promised the blessing of a right relationship with God as we respond to God's loving action in our life. We are also called so that others will be blessed as we engage in God's good work in the world.

SUGGESTION FOR MEDITATION: **Not long ago I pondered a decision and a wise woman asked me: How have you reached decisions like this in the past? We might well ask ourselves: How have we heard God's call in the past? Are we following? Might we need to listen again for clarity and a renewed sense of how to take the next faithful step?**

So they go. Abram and Sarai and Lot travel from Haran to Canaan with all their worldly possessions, following God's call. They progress in response to God's call in stages. We don't know how long the journey takes or when it becomes apparent that Canaan is the destination or how long they stay in each place. But we can look back over our lives in faith and see the same sort of progress: in stages. We collect experience; grow in grace; fail; face losses, temptations, and disappointments. All the while, our relationships with God, with the community of faith, and with a needy world are being shaped.

How would your telling the story of your journey change if you viewed it as a demonstration of God's blessing you all along the way, as an expression of providential care for the whole creation?

Did you ever record God's work along the way? Perhaps your baptism certificate or a certificate of ordination hangs on your wall. Maybe you monetarily supported the church or the camp or the organization that nurtured your faith in a special way.

Abram and Sarai express the blessing and sovereignty of God by building altars along the journey. In that way they create memorials to God's action and places of worship for themselves. Their action reminds me of the roadside crosses and grottos that dot the English countryside, which record the lives of the faithful who have gone before us. They affirm the confidence that God has spoken and that we are to respond to God's call in daily and deliberate ways.

SUGGESTION FOR MEDITATION: **What moments of calling or response in your own life would you like to mark in some way? How might those memorials prompt your next step in faith, even as they remind you of the journey past?**

This passage takes us back to imputed righteousness. Abraham's faith is praised here as the vehicle for God's blessing—not his works, not the law but his faithfulness. His faith is the canvas on which God's grace can be displayed.

Much to the consternation of Paul's contemporaries, he points out that Abraham is blessed and called *before* he is circumcised. He is blessed and called *before* he has the framework of the law. He is blessed and called because of God's grace and lovingkindness, which precedes our response (whether that response is one of faith or of doubt). God's action paves the way for us, for each of us.

John Wesley preached about the prevenient grace of God that goes before our response of faith. Today we might talk about our faith as a response to God's loving action. It can be hard to accept that we don't earn God's regard, that we are not the cause of God's blessing. But God's nature calls us into relationship. God's very nature, existing in three persons, models relationship for us.

Of course, Abraham's faith also resulted in action. Sometimes his actions seem to have been faithful (making the journey, believing in the promise of descendants) and sometimes these actions seem to be full of self-importance (passing Sarai off as his sister, lying with Hagar). The epistle reading does not take him to task, however. It records God's work in and through Abraham and states that his faith itself was reckoned to him as righteousness.

Paul makes a direct parallel between Abraham and the believer; we do not achieve righteousness through acts of faithfulness but through the grace of God. Christ's justifying work accounts us as righteous, and we are invited to participate in the great chorus of praise.

**SUGGESTION FOR REFLECTION: In what ways do you see your life as a story of faith that is the gift of God, rather than a story of faithful or faithless action on your part?**

**FRIDAY, JUNE 6 • Read Matthew 9:9–13**

Jesus' encounter with Matthew is a story of a calling that differs from that of Abram. This story focuses not on one person or one family but on a person who interacts with a community. Here Jesus reaches out to an obvious outsider, offers no promises, and partakes of Matthew's hospitality. In so doing, he honors Matthew, causing the local elite to question Jesus' motives.

Jesus' listeners would have no trouble identifying Matthew as one of the sinners that Jesus says he is calling. However, they probably find it very hard to identify the many observant religious leaders in the room with Matthew. In the culture of the day (perhaps a little like ours), a person might give a break to a good or law-abiding person but not to an obvious outlaw.

Think about the *A* student and the *C* student. Both submit late assignments. Who is more likely to receive lenient treatment? What about the person with a clean driving record and the person with a history of infractions—who is more likely to get off with a warning when caught in a traffic violation?

Jesus turns this approach on its head and extends his presence and his honor (grace) to the outcast, the obvious sinner. He signals to the religious elite that this extension of grace (redemption) is intentional on his part. Matthew knows his need for healing, and Jesus responds to his need. He also lectures the Pharisees using a reference to Hosea, which indicates that Jesus' action is in accordance with Jewish tradition.

**SUGGESTION FOR MEDITATION: With whom do you identify in this story: the outsider, receiving grace; the religious leader, offering criticism? In what ways are you acting as part of the body of Christ by comforting the afflicted and afflicting the comfortable? What next steps might you consider in view of Jesus' presence in your own story?**

These intertwined healing stories seem very different at first glance. In the framing story, the synagogue leader is a person of authority who makes a public request for healing for someone else. The woman suffering from hemorrhages is an isolated person who seeks Jesus' healing on her own behalf without his knowledge or the knowledge of his disciples. If you have had an extended illness or recovery from surgery or have grieved the loss of someone close to you, you know something about the isolating impact of illness and grief. While our minds tell us that others have had similar losses, our hearts feel very alone. In some ways, every healing is different.

In other ways, these stories have much in common. In each case the person in need of healing is doubly isolated from her society. The first barrier is that of gender. The woman alone seeking healing "should" have had a spouse or father or brother dealing with the matter. The holiness rules also isolated the woman. Her bleeding has made her impure for twelve years. No wonder she does not seek Jesus openly! Similarly, the daughter is a child—not valuable enough to disturb adults outside the family. While caring parents might grieve her death, it would not be as great a loss as the death of a son.

In both cases, Jesus crosses over. He goes with the leader. He speaks to the woman, recognizing and encouraging her. Both cases employ physical touch, another problem for the observant Jew. The woman touches Jesus, and Jesus takes the girl's hand. In both cases, his touch brings healing.

**SUGGESTION FOR REFLECTION: To whom do you relate in this passage? Are you seeking after Jesus? Calling Jesus to the bedside of a loved one? Waiting for the healing Jesus offers? Jesus has already moved toward you.**

The creative and creating word of God is backdrop for this call for reverence or awe. God's power is made known as the source of the various spheres of existence. The heavens and their hosts, the waters of the sea, and the world and its inhabitants are all spoken into existence by the Lord.

God also speaks the order and relationship of the universe—the seas are contained, and the world is made firm. God has given these things their natures and calls them to act accordingly. Again we see God's good providence at work for the benefit of the whole creation. God also confounds worldly powers of nations and peoples.

So, how might we respond to this reminder of the sovereignty of God (over creation and over the principalities and powers of this world)? The psalm calls us to fear the Lord and to stand in awe. We are to be humble in the face of God's power. We are also called to carry out creative acts and to exercise care for the benefit of the whole creation. But we are not called to act instead of God or to see ourselves as independent of God. Rather, we act to further God's loving-kindness when we let the word of God dwell richly in us and make of us new creations.

The psalm also reminds us that God does the initiating. Happy are . . . the people whom God has chosen as a heritage. Like the creation, we are also the works of God's hands. We give evidence of that nature living in us when we are alert to God's work, when we hear God's call to us individually and as a church, and when we work to return the world to the good order that God called into existence. We are not God (or gods); but we are the heritage of God, showing forth God's power from day to day.

**PRAYER: "Let your steadfast love, O LORD, be upon us, even as we hope in you" (Ps. 33:22). Amen.**

# Nothing Is Impossible

*June 9–15, 2008 • Roy[‡] and John[‡‡] Herron*

**MONDAY, JUNE 9 • Read Genesis 18:1-15; 21:1-7**

Sarah naturally expresses skepticism about the Lord's unnatural promise. Sarah and Abraham are two old folks beyond child-bearing and child-conceiving years. Or so it seems. Sarah's doubting is the only rational response; her laughter also is understandable. Both are healthy ways of coping with what she knew could not be. But then God demands, "Is anything too difficult for the LORD?" Sarah conceives, and Isaac is born.

The doctor told Nancy and Roy that the twins Nancy was carrying would not live. He had seen sixteen such cases; thirty-one of the thirty-two twin babies had died. He recommended abortion. After five visits with three physicians in two hospitals, another specialist suggested the babies might yet live. Immediately prayers went up, spread, and continued—until and even after the birth of one of the writers of this story and his twin brother.

"Is anything too difficult for the LORD?" Many things seem improbable. Many things seem impossible. But God repeatedly and continually answers God's own question in ways that surprise and astound human beings from Sarah in ancient days to those of us living in these modern days.

When God can help Sarah become pregnant with Isaac, when God can get Mary pregnant with Jesus, when God can help Nancy bear John and Rick alive and enable them to survive, the question is answered time and again.

**PRAYER: Lord, help us to realize and remember that you are the Lord, that you can do that which is difficult, that you can even do that which we think impossible. Amen.**

---

[‡]Former United Methodist minister, now an author living in Dresden, Tennessee.

[‡‡]Writer, cross-country runner, and student living in Dresden, Tennessee.

The psalmist begins this psalm by explaining why he loves God.

> I love the LORD, because he has heard my voice
>> and my supplications.
> Because he inclined his ear to me.

And what, then, will the psalmist do? "Therefore I will call on him as long as I live."

No fewer than four times in this psalm does the psalmist call upon the name of the Lord. Why does the psalmist repeat this refrain? For the same reason that he loves the Lord: God hears his voice and his supplications; God "inclined his ear to me."

That is the testimony of scripture. Yet sometimes we pray as though no one is listening. We mumble words in prayers we don't expect to be heard, much less answered. People of faith and not a few others in need call for God's help. They call upon the name of the Lord.

Carole King wrote and James Taylor most famously recorded the song, "You've Got a Friend." The song begins by telling the listeners that when they are down and need help, when nothing seems to be going quite right—then "just call out my name and you know wherever I am, I'll come running to see you again."

Like Psalm 116, four times the song repeats the refrain to "call out my name." What better friend and what better name to call than that of our Lord? What better time to call out than in our times of need?

**PRAYER: Lord, help us to call out your name, knowing that you hear our prayers and intervene in times of danger and distress. Amen.**

Paul's poetic logic goes like this:

Rejoice in suffering,
since suffering produces endurance
which produces character
which produces hope.

We once thought that Paul's poetic words were really more rhetoric than reality. Beautiful, but more lines of poetry than means of production. Then we became distance runners. And in distance running we found that Paul describes a basic dynamic of life, the actual dynamic of human growth. Suffering—putting in the miles—really does produce endurance. And when you have built endurance, it changes your character. And the new and renewed character does produce hope.

Some disciplined and joyful runners who inspired us often ran rejoicing in their sufferings. Paul, Porter, and Terrell would call out, perhaps five or even ten miles into a run, "I feel happy! I feel healthy! I feel terrific!" Their enthusiasm was contagious.

One of the most surprising scenes of hope and joy is an Ironman Triathlon finish line. After 2.4 miles of swimming, 112 miles of biking, and 26.2 miles of running, triathletes finish with huge smiles. The suffering has produced endurance that produces character, which produces hope.

One of us coaches cross country; the other runs cross country. High school students struggle to run at 6:00 AM before school. Some come and stick with it. Others do not. The difference so often between those who keep on running and those who don't is learning to rejoice in the suffering, to rejoice in the effort that eventually leads to hope. And hope does not disappoint us, "because God's love has been poured into our hearts."

**PRAYER: O God who goes the distance, help us embrace the suffering, knowing that you will transform it into endurance into character into hope—and your hope does not disappoint. Amen.**

Few organizations emphasize serving or saving others more than the Boy Scouts. The motto "Be prepared" always seems to be implicitly followed by the unspoken words "to save another's life."

Once, when I was a child, another Scout and I saw a canoe overturn in the middle of a large lake. The two duck hunters spilled into the icy, November waters. Fortunately, we knew how to start a motor and handle a boat. We went out to get the men and arrived just in time. The two men wound up cold but alive.

On other occasions, as a Scout or while lifeguarding at lakes or pools, I have been called on to save a struggling swimmer or an overturned boater—but never with any risk to my own life.

We would like to think that we always would act to save a child. And *almost* always to save an adult. But we may wonder if we would have the courage to sacrifice our own life for a reprobate or rascal. Paul says that "perhaps" we might dare to die for a good person. Perhaps—perhaps for a *really* good person. In this passage, however, Paul uses three different terms for those of us for whom Christ died: *weak, ungodly, sinners.*

One thing is certain about the gospel that Jesus proclaimed and Paul taught: Jesus Christ died for sinners, for scoundrels. Not just for the best of us but for the worst of us. Not just for the innocent children but also for the wretched sinners. And in doing so, God "proves his love for us." How great that love must be.

**PRAYER: Gracious God, whose love is greater than all our sins and greater than all our imaginings, help us to feel just how great your love for us is. Help us also to lay down our lives for your children. Amen.**

The crowds were "harassed and helpless, like sheep without a shepherd." But Jesus does not try to get away from them, nor does he view them as a burden, as we so often see and flee the helpless. Instead he declares that "the harvest is plentiful" and sends forth his disciples. This passage gives Christian disciples the ground rules for life's journey: our calling must bring people to Christ and aid society's pariahs, those who have been exiled to the land of the untouchables.

The hallmark of Christ's ministry is that he goes out of his way to champion the untouchables. Jesus sees the pariahs and outcasts as "harvest," as people of God. Later in Matthew 25, Jesus teaches that those who are needy (hungry, thirsty, strangers, naked, sick, prisoners) *are* the Christ. When we minister to these in need, we minister to our Lord. "Truly I tell you, just as you did it to one of the least of these who are members of my family, you did it to me" (Matt. 25:40).

Granted, often it is not antipathy toward a specific group that keeps us from reaching out but the enormity of the problem. We think, *I'll never be able to make a dent in that problem, so why bother?* Yet groups of committed people, when they band together, can change the entire nature of a society. Three recent examples are the India independence movement, the American civil rights movement, and the ending of apartheid in South Africa.

Who would have thought a religion initiated by a carpenter's son in Galilee would have swelled to the size of Christianity today? Don't worry if the cause you want to take up seems daunting. Take the steps you can, and you may be surprised.

The harvest will always remain plentiful.

**PRAYER: Gracious God, give us the strength and drive to stand up for the untouchables. Amen.**

If a dozen people came to you and said they were followers of Jesus, would you want to know more about them? If they said they were called to "heal the sick," to "heal every disease and sickness," would you think them at best peculiar and probably arrogant? If they said they were called to "drive out evil spirits" and "demons," would you wonder if they themselves were demon-possessed?

If they told you they were to "raise the dead," would you call 911 to have mental health authorities take them away? If they said Jesus told them not to take any money or a change of clothes with them, would you call the police to pick up the beggars before they assaulted someone or stole something?

For many of us, our responses to these dozen people might be less than kind—if not fearful. Then there's our friend Kaki who seemed to take Jesus at his word. She helped found an in-patient treatment center for cocaine-addicted mothers and their children. The center was the last stop for these mothers before losing their children. The residents had no job, no family support, no car, no money. Many descended again into addiction.

Kaki's friends marveled at how she went to work each day without losing hope when facing such great need and so few resources. The tasks of those first disciples could not have seemed more daunting. But Kaki was buoyed by the fact that so many of the women, lifted by the love and care at the center, found jobs, went to work, and cared for their children. And many of them stayed off drugs. Kaki brought the word that "the kingdom of heaven has come near."

Having been blessed, Kaki could give. "How can you see the struggles of these families," Kaki said, "and not be grateful for your own blessings—and the changes in their lives?"

**PRAYER: Lord, help us to welcome your disciples, especially those who have little or nothing of this world, as they spread the word about the nearness of the kingdom. Amen.**

Perhaps religions should be less judgmental toward risk takers. If you think about it, living a Christian life is a giant risk with enormous consequences! A Christian pledges his or her life to an intangible God in hopes of ascertaining peace and a place in Christ's kingdom.

In this passage, Jesus tells the disciples and the early church, "I'm asking you to go for it. To follow me, you will have to risk all hopes of a stable, prosperous life. But in so doing, you will win eternal life."

Many modern-day disciples have taken this enormous leap. Usually, however, someone tries to talk them out of it.

Andrew Young, a minister, civil rights leader, former congressman, and former mayor of Atlanta, once told an assembly of ministers of how his daughter, whom he dubbed "the unpredictable one," came home and informed him that she was going to work for Habitat for Humanity—in Uganda.

"Do you realize Idi Amin wrecked Uganda?" he asked.

"Yes, Daddy."

"Do you understand there is no real government in Uganda?"

"Yes."

"Are you aware that anybody can do anything they want to do to you in Uganda, and there is no recourse?"

"Yes."

"And you still want to go to Uganda?"

"I *am* going to Uganda."

Reverend Young said later, "I wanted her to be a respectable Christian. I never dreamed that she'd become a real one!"

For those who accept Jesus' call to radical discipleship, there is no cause for anxiety. Tribulations will assault them, but Christ will manage the ministry and the logistics. By trading in self-dependence for Christ-dependence, we risk all for the kingdom.

**PRAYER: Lord, help me to emulate the disciples and risk all that I have for your sake. Amen.**

# Open Our Eyes

*June 16–22, 2008* • *L. Joseph Rosas III*

## MONDAY, JUNE 16 • **Read Genesis 21:8–21**

Religious wars are as old as humankind. Many evil things have been done in the name of God. But this is not a problem only for ancient tribes and those bound by superstitions. Indeed, one of the greatest challenges faced by people of faith in the postmodern world is that of living in the tension of competing ideologies and loyalties. On the one hand are exclusivistic claims that are blind to any truth but their own, and on the other a relativistic synchronistic pluralism that sees all faith claims as a private matter for the isolated individual. But all truth is God's truth. Religious people often derive as much meaning from whom they exclude as they do from what they embrace.

Abraham is called the father of the faithful. Through his son Isaac the covenant people of Israel will come. But as the Hebrew prophets frequently remind Israel—they are not chosen as a sign of the exclusion of others; they are intended to be a blessing to all the people of the earth.

We, like they, are slow to learn that lesson. We delight in our parochial and sectarian divisions and so dishonor the name of Christ. At the very beginning of God's active covenant with the people who would be Israel is the strong reminder that God also has concern for Ishmael and offers a promise of blessing for him.

Edwin Markham's poem reminds us of this inclusion:

He drew a circle that shut me out—
Heretic, rebel, a thing to flout.
But love and I had the wit to win:
We drew a circle that took him in.

**PRAYER: O Lord, help us to see the wonder of your love for the entire human family and, indeed, for all of creation. Amen.**

---

‡Pastor, Crievewood Baptist Church, Nashville, Tennessee; adjunct professor, Belmont University.

*Then God opened [Hagar's] eyes and she saw a well of water.*

A cousin and I used to try to outdo one another with our worries about life. We enjoyed our shared fretfulness; misery loves company. One day he said, "I'm worried that I have nothing to worry about, and I am afraid something is about to happen and I will be unprepared." Such anxiety seldom prepares us for anything except more worry.

Worry and fear blind us to the possibilities of life. When all hope is lost and we are ready to succumb to resignation and defeat, we might instead ask God to open our eyes to the possibilities. Even in the darkest circumstance, there may well be an opportunity for faith and hope that we would otherwise not see.

In an earlier escape into the wilderness, Hagar had been promised that God was with her and would make her son the root of a great nation. How quickly we forget God's promises in our lives.

Perhaps Hagar felt justified in her lament in light of what appeared to be a failure of promise. The desert is no place to be cast out with an adolescent Ishmael. Her all-consuming fear blinds her to the possibility of any options. In the midst of this life-threatening challenge, it takes God to open Hagar's eyes to see a well of refreshment and life nearby. This is not water out of a rock or some other miracle. It apparently is a well that was there all along.

Often we feel overwhelmed by loneliness, despair, or grief. When we feel ready to give up, ask God to give us eyes to see and ears to hear where God is at work. Who knows? Deliverance may be nearer than we think. May we not be so blinded by our fears and failures that we miss God's presence and provision in our life.

**PRAYER: O God, open my eyes to the rich and varied ways you move and work in my life. Help me not to give up because of the limitations in my sight. Open my eyes that I might see where you are already at work to meet my needs. Amen.**

*Incline your ear, O Lord, and answer me.*

A commercial for one of the nationwide cellular phone services features a man walking just a few steps at a time and repeating at each stop, "Can you hear me now?" The psalmist seems to ask, "God, can you hear me? Are you listening?"

Over twenty-five years ago my wife and I were expecting our first child. It had been a normal and uneventful pregnancy until we entered the third trimester. One morning before she left for work, my wife was aware of some problems. She called her obstetrician and was told to go to bed for the day.

In rapid succession, the events of the day unfolded. By that afternoon we were at the doctor's office where the obstetrician told us in a matter-of-fact fashion, "There is nothing we can do. You are going to lose the baby."

Devastated, we called family members and were on the way to the hospital when another doctor in the office picked up a faint fetal heartbeat. We quickly headed to a hospital with a neonatal intensive care unit that worked with high-risk pregnancies. Early the next morning we were parents to a very tiny baby girl.

Our emotions had been on a roller coaster. At first we wondered where God was. When the baby was born, our hopes were that against all odds our daughter would survive. But less than thirteen hours after her birth, Sara was gone.

I felt that God had not heard or answered our prayers. Over the years my attitude has changed. In a very real sense God *was* listening and answering—just not in the ways I wanted or anticipated. We experienced the sustaining grace of God through the comfort of friends, family, and church. God's gracious hearing of our pleas for help and strength were answered in the quiet sense of God's presence, hope for the future—and a year later with a healthy baby boy.

**Prayer: Make me aware of your presence, O God, even when the answers to my prayers are not what I want or expect. Amen.**

*Consider yourselves dead to sin and alive to God in Christ Jesus.*

I rebel at wearing name tags. I suppose I resent the notion that people think they know me just because they know my name. In fact, our true identity is hidden much deeper.

How often have you been introduced to someone who asks, "And what do you do?" The question is usually directed at how you spend time making a living or preparing for a vocation. This is a much easier question to answer than, "*Who* are you?"

"Who are you?" can simply be a query about your name. But at a deeper level it asks fundamental questions of life: Why am I here? What does it mean to be "me"? And how should the answers to these questions affect how I live my life day by day and make a difference in the way I do whatever it is that I do?

Socrates observed that the unexamined life is not worth living. That was not a problem for the apostle Paul. He had examined his life and found it wanting. He had the religious pedigree and educational credentials that would define both who he was and what he did in his society. But he had an encounter with the living Christ on the Damascus road, and his life was turned right side up.

Paul came to distinguish between the "old self" that was in bondage to the habits and pattern of sin, the vestigial remains of his attempts at self-righteousness, and the "new self" of all that he was called and created to be in Christ.

C. S. Lewis said that we each become more a creature of God or a hellish creature by the thousands of little decisions we make everyday. Paul encourages us to live in light of the fact that we are indeed dead to sin and alive to God. In other words, live in light of the truth of who you are and whose you are, and the outward pattern of your life will express that reality.

**PRAYER: Dear God, you have called me and are making of me a new creation. May I live according to my identity in Christ and not the passing values of this world. Amen.**

*Have no fear.*

These verses do not paint a picture of "gentle Jesus, meek and mild." Jesus warns his would-be followers that just as he and his message are rejected by many, so those who are his servants should not expect to be above their Master. The kingdom of God may bring painful division. Jesus says in effect, "Cheer up, things will get worse."

But in the face of this blunt assessment, Jesus reassures us that God is aware and providentially involved in the day-to-day affairs of our lives. If God knows when a sparrow falls and has the hairs on our head numbered, surely God can be trusted with the larger issues of life and death and faithfulness in kingdom living.

Several years ago logo wear took on a new meaning when clothing was labeled to communicate what might be a larger message. Take the "No Fear" clothing, for example. Was there more to this than a brand label? Were consumers wearing this clothing as if to proclaim bravery in the face of the challenges and dangers of life in a postmodern world?

We may never know if the advertisers printed a subtle existential message on a t-shirt or if this were just another catchy way to have us spend money we don't have to buy things we don't need to impress people we don't like. But fear is a reality of life. Uncertainties in daily life include concerns for the economy, personal health, or the health and well-being of those near to us and the threats of war, violence, and pestilence around the globe.

Jesus does not glibly say, "Don't worry, be happy." He acknowledges the difficult realities in following the kingdom way. However, he also encourages us to depend upon a God who knows the details of our lives, is involved in our daily existence, and has an eternal purpose for us. "Have no fear."

**SUGGESTION FOR MEDITATION: God is with us is the good news of Incarnation. Reflect upon the ways you sense God is with you in your daily life. How does this presence make you feel about the fears you face?**

*A disciple is not above the teacher.*

Several years ago the acronym WWJD was all the rage. A rabbi friend told me he thought it meant, "What would the Jews do?" Not a bad question. More recently some have suggested, "What would Jesus drive?" But originally the question was: "What would Jesus do?" That may be part of our problem. We want to figure out what Jesus *would* do—as if he is not with us and in us here and now. Perhaps a better question would be "What would Jesus have *me* do?" Or even: "What is Jesus doing here and now, and how may I join him?"

We take our direction from Jesus. Too often we are busy trying to do for him in our own strength and power. Jesus said "Apart from me you can do nothing" (John 15: 5). We can be busy about a lot of things but bear no fruit apart from an ongoing and vital connection with our living Lord.

Jesus is the teacher, we the disciples. He teaches us as much through how he lived as by what he said. Jesus' earthly life was characterized by a radical dependence upon and obedience to God. Jesus spent frequent time in prayer. He showed grace and mercy to the poor, powerless, and "least of these" that he encountered daily. Jesus declared and inaugurated the kingdom of God. By his death, burial, and resurrection he demonstrated the unique love of God for us.

Too often we assume control. We set priorities and make plans in Jesus name. But he is no honorary chairman of the board no longer up to the rigors of the real world. He is Lord of all, and we are to follow his lead. As we continue to listen and learn from him, we will gradually come to realize that Jesus is in fact working in us. We mature in faith as Christ himself is fully formed in us.

**PRAYER: Jesus, help me see you in the "least of these." May my life reflect your radical dependence upon God. Amen.**

*If you test me, you will find no wickedness.*

One of the first books in a long line of self-help psychology that continues to flourish into the twenty-first century was *I'm OK, You're OK*. Its basic thesis was that we should accept ourselves and others as fundamentally good—and seek to live accordingly.

The psalmist certainly approaches life in this manner. He calls his a "just cause" and says his prayer is "free of deceit." In complete confidence he invites a divine examination of his inner being. Meanwhile, he simultaneously asks that God vindicate him from all enemies.

The Psalter is the prayer book of both Israel and the church. Billy Graham reportedly reads five psalms and one chapter of Proverbs everyday—a discipline that would have one reading through these books of poetry and wisdom almost every month.

But how do we pray a psalm like this one? We are never in more danger than when we think we are beyond danger. Certainly David's song can be read as a testimony to his genuine righteousness at this time in his life. At least he is asking for God's vindication rather than trying to impose it self-righteously by his own hand.

Sometimes we are in the right, insofar as we can see. We do not fear sharing with God what we see, feel, and experience in our own life. Better to tell God than others how we know we are right. God has ways of gently confirming what is the good, true, and beautiful in us. And God also has ways of revealing the deepest heart of hearts and all that is within us.

We can certainly pray that our lives be above reproach as characterized by this psalm. But we need to be very cautious in exacting vengeance when we think others are in the wrong. Like the psalmist, we might best leave vindication to God.

**PRAYER: God, may I be open and transparent in my relationship with you and others. When I am wronged, may I trust your faithfulness in my life and the lives of others. Amen.**

# God's Faithfulness

*June 23–29, 2008 • David Moffett-Moore[‡]*

## MONDAY, JUNE 23 • Read Genesis 22:1-7

What must that morning have been like? They rose early, prepared quietly, traveled silently; foreboding knotting up in Abraham's stomach. He is to present his son "on the altar," his only son, the son God had promised him, the son that same God required of him. So Abraham and Isaac set out for a God-chosen altar as an act of faith. No parent wants to see the death of his or her child, especially at his or her own hand. Sometimes we are led where we do not want to go.

In John 21:18-19 Peter declares his love for the risen Christ and hears Christ respond, "'When you were younger, you used to fasten your own belt and to go wherever you wished. But when you grow old, you will stretch out your hands, and someone else will fasten a belt around you and take you where you do not wish to go.' (He said this to indicate the kind of death by which he would glorify God.) After this he said to him, 'Follow me.'"

Dietrich Bonhoeffer, a German pastor during the Nazi regime, wrote, "When Christ calls us, he bids us come and die" (AP). Bonhoeffer lived out the truth of his faith, resisting the Nazis. He left his teaching post in America to return to his homeland, to be a witness for the resistance. In the waning days of World War II, he was marched out of his prison cell early one morning and hanged.

As Christians, we are all called. I believe in free will and think we all have choices; but if we accept the call of Christ on our lives, there is a sense in which we have signed a blank check. "Whatever you ask, Lord, I will do." And so we set out toward a God-chosen altar, knowing that God will provide.

**PRAYER: Lord, I do not know what you will ask of me this day. I only ask that you will give me strength to say yes. Amen.**

---

[‡]Pastor, St. Peter's United Church of Christ, Frankfort, Illinois.

As humans, we are finite. To be mortal does not just mean that we will die. It means some things are beyond us, beyond our ability to comprehend or to accomplish. We are limited creatures who bear the image of the infinite, unlimited, eternal God. As Paul declares, "I am speaking in human terms because of your natural limitations."

We are born with desires, longings for something else, something other. These desires, when played out in our mortal bodies, Paul calls our passions. These desires can become addictions—even good desires. Physical exercise, prayer, attending worship can all become addictions. As humans, we have a natural propensity toward addiction, just as Paul explains that we have a natural propensity to sin.

Naturally we deny our addictive natures or are blind to them. We think that somehow we are immune to their effects. But we are only human! We are born wanting that which is by nature beyond us. Too many of us spend too much of our time accumulating stuff and things that fill our time but do not fulfill our lives; we seek more and more and obtain less and less.

Augustine spent his early years in this maelstrom of materialism, this whirlpool of acquisitiveness, repeatedly discovering that having more did not make him more. He finally confessed, "Our souls are restless, O Lord, until they find their rest in thee."

Paul reminds us that Christ has broken the reign of sin. We as Christians become responsible to make sure sin does not rule our lives. What are we seeking that does not satisfy? For what do we hunger that leaves us empty? With the psalmist we confess, "Who can detect their errors? Clear me from hidden faults" (Ps. 19:12).

**PRAYER: Much will fill my time this day, O Lord. Yet you alone fill my soul. Remind me, O Lord, that only you can make me whole. Amen.**

Jesus tells his disciples, "Whoever receives you, receives me and the one who sent me." He emphasizes the importance of hospitality by continuing, "Whoever receives a prophet, receives a prophet's reward. Whoever receives the righteous, receives the reward of the righteous." Hospitality plays an important role in our witness. Sometimes, we forget.

Often we greet strangers as unknown threats; in church we ask, "Who is that sitting in my pew?" We may be warm and accepting of one another but cold and aloof to visitors. We don't know them, so we don't greet them. We are not sure what to say to them, so we say nothing. We feel uncomfortable toward them, and they sense that tension.

The early church evidenced a sense of warm hospitality by greeting new people and welcoming inquiry, even when it might have been dangerous for them to do so. It was part of how they understood their faith. As Hebrews 13:2 reminds us, some have entertained angels unaware.

In The Upper Room Academy for Spiritual Formation, I learned a Shaker greeting prayer: "The Christ in me greets the Christ in thee and draws us together in love." When we realize that the Christ in us is also in all the people we meet, it affects how we approach the day. In the crowds on the sidewalk, the crunch in the elevator, the gridlock at rush hour, we are surrounded by Christ. Each person we encounter is Christ coming toward us. As we meet, Christ approaches him or her, unbeknownst to the other and usually to us as well. But our awareness of the hidden Christ not only affects our day, it affects the day of all those around us.

Jesus says that even those who give a cup of cold water as an act of discipleship will receive their reward. How would our lives be changed if we greeted everyone as we would greet Christ?

**PRAYER: Lord, in all I see today may I see you; all I do today may I offer to you. Amen.**

At the right time, at the perfect time, when we least expect it, God rescues us. This is repeatedly the message from both Testaments. The testimony of scripture is that God is a God who constantly surprises us, whose abundance overwhelms us, whose grace amazes us, whose love leaves us dumbfounded. "Who would have believed what we have seen?"

Days into the wilderness, traveling to a foreign land and a strange place, Abraham sets about his awful task with a heavy heart. When his son Isaac asks, "Where is the lamb?" Abraham says words he hopes are true: "God will provide." Abraham may not have believed the words on his lips, but God knew them to be true. We know God as the one who provides, who makes good on the promises, who fulfills the word, who steadfastly surprises us. Yet it can be difficult to "let go and let God."

In seminary I took a course on the theology of joy. The intense experience of seminary had seemingly robbed me of joy, and I needed some in my life. I met with the professor to talk about how I my experiences of joy in the past. In retrospect, I noted that joy often came when least expected as a surprise package, an unexpected gift. What we seek to control, we cannot enjoy. Our desire to control can eliminate the possibility of joy.

Abraham responds to God with the words, "Here I am," and sets out. We can imagine the knife blade glinting in the sun as Abraham's hand rises to strike. That blow never falls. His hand is stayed; Isaac is spared. In this God-directed act of faith, Abraham's willingness to "take, . . . go, . . . offer" affords a new vision of God's surprising rescue.

In our lives, where have we given up our desire to control? Where are we open for God to provide us with joy?

**PRAYER: This day, O Lord, may I count the ways you surprise me with rescue and joy. Amen.**

Years ago Bob Dylan experimented with an album of songs inspired by his understanding of the Christian faith. One song was titled "Gotta Serve Somebody." To whom would we present ourselves as "obedient slaves"? If we don't consciously decide, we may end up serving only our sinful selves. This is shortsighted because the quest ends at our grave. Life gains meaning and purpose when we are willing to spend it for something greater. We can serve our community or serve our country; Paul warns of serving our passions. Or we can serve the Lord.

Paul's writing calls to our minds two epic stories: that of Christ and that of the Exodus. As Christians, both stories encompass our lives and make claims upon our daily living as we become obedient from the heart. We have been released from slavery for a greater service. Freed from slavery to sin, we now face Paul's "so now." What is the "so now" that encompasses our lives, that requires redirection and reorientation?

We can give our lives for things that lessen us, or we can give our lives for things that stretch us, that cause us to dream and hope and aspire, that make our lives meaningful.

Only a great hope can make a great human; only a great cause can make a community; only a great promise can make a great people. Christ did not come to make our lives easy but to make our lives great, not to fill us with ease and comfort but with the energy of a great cause. Are we ready to give ourselves, fully and completely, to the cause of Christ? Are we ready to fill our lives with the cause for which Christ emptied his? We've got to serve somebody; shall we not with obedience from the heart find ourselves free from sin and "enslaved to God"?

**PRAYER: I call you Lord and Savior, for that is what you are. As Savior, you rescue me from aimlessness and meaninglessness. As Lord you call for my commitment. May I serve you this day not only with my lips but with my heart, not only with my words but with my life. Amen.**

Water is a necessity of life. Our bodies are 80 percent water. We can survive several days without food but only a precious few days without water. Water is necessary for life on the planet. As we explore the universe, scientists are discovering that water is a rare commodity. Just as our bodies require water, so our souls require the refreshment of God's spirit: "My soul thirsts for you; my flesh faints for you, as in a dry and weary land where there is no water" (Ps. 63:1).

In expressing our welcome and acceptance of others, Jesus reminds us to care for the needs of the least among us. A cup of cold water merits reward. We can often see more plainly the refreshment offered on a physical level than a spiritual one.

Most boys of my generation grew up on stories of cowboys and Indians. I grew up on legends of King Arthur and the Round Table. One of my favorite movies is *Excalibur*, which tells the story of King Arthur and his knights. In one scene the wounded Arthur, weak and lingering, drinks from the Holy Grail, the cup that Christ blessed at the Last Supper. Immediately revived, Arthur says, "I did not know how empty was my soul until I tasted and it was filled." The physical tasting filled his soul.

That's the story for us when we gather around the Lord's table, a physical sharing that fills us spiritually. Our souls thirst and are quenched. It's the story of every missionary who has offered Christ in the form of food or clothing, medicine or teaching. It's the story of congregational outreach in communities by offering the spiritual presence of Christ in and through the physical presence of human comfort and compassion.

Whatever we do, in word or in deed, we do for Christ. Even offering a cup of cold water.

**PRAYER: Lord, remind me this day that whatever I do, I do for you. Amen.**

My prayers usually begin, "We thank you for your steadfast love and your abundant faithfulness." That prayer is based on Psalm 115:1: "Not to us, O LORD, not to us, but to your name give glory, for the sake of your steadfast love and your faithfulness." Contrast the relative peace of those words with the opening of Psalm 13: "How long, O Lord. . . . How long will you hide your face from me?" Four times we read the words, "how long." Four times we come away without answer—only the questions. The psalmist hides nothing. The words strip away any pretense or social veneer from the psalmist. The lament speaks from the depth of the psalmist's soul.

Most of the time we do not live at the psalmist's level of honesty. We keep up appearances. We maintain our facades before one another. Our friends and coworkers often know little about our lives away from work. Those at church may know us because we sit in a certain spot, but know nothing of our inner lives. We struggle to maintain our facades even before God.

We all have done things we're ashamed of; thoughts that would embarrass us if they were made public; feelings that we bury just below the surface, hoping no one knows. But of course, God knows. Our thoughts, our feelings, our secret hiding places are all made plain and revealed before God who sees and knows them all. That thought alone might fill us with fear.

The only One who counts already knows everything. But God is love. Not just "like" love or "sometimes" love or "if we are careful and proper" love. God is love without bounds or limits. God will never forget us or hide from us. However much we may hide from God in our deep, dark, hidden recesses with our secret sins, God will not hide from us. We can trust in God's steadfast love; God has dealt bountifully with us.

**PRAYER: When I think of myself, O God, I think of my broken-ness and shortcomings. When I think of you, I can only rejoice. May I be mindful of you, O Lord, as you are mindful of me, that I may always sing your praises. Amen.**

# Lessons in Love and Power

*June 30–July 6, 2008* • *Barbara Dick*[‡]

## MONDAY, JUNE 30 • Read Genesis 24:34-38

A love story in three parts: A faithful servant speaks the prologue; enter the girl; a marriage made in heaven. In today's passage, Abraham's servant establishes his credentials for Rebekah's family. The wealthy Abraham—whose wife Sarah gave birth to a beloved son in her old age—has sent this servant to find a wife for Isaac. The servant has sworn an oath to seek this wife from among Abraham's own kindred.

We already know all of this from Abraham's own lips (see verses 2-4). Why repeat it? Repetition helps us remember important details. These details are important because this is God's story, revealed through this family. Sarah's old age reminds us that it is God who gives life. The transfer of status from Abraham to Isaac and the emphasis on maintaining purity in the bloodline remind us of God's covenant with Abraham and Sarah. God promises to be with them and their descendants if they will be God's people. Repetition also reinforces the integrity of the servant. He is faithful both to the spirit and to the letter of his mission, unwilling even to eat a meal until he has established his credentials.

Why so much attention on setting the stage for a love story? If we don't trust the servant, the story that follows has less power. And this is an important chapter in God's story, seen through the Genesis family saga. Isaac's wife cannot be just anyone. Therefore, the servant who finds her must embody Abraham's faithfulness. He is the critical link in maintaining the family's reliance on the power of the one true God to lead God's people.

**PRAYER: God of Abraham and Sarah, help us to be faithful in our tasks, to fully embody the One who sends us into the world, and to put aside our own needs in your service. Amen.**

[‡]Editor, Abingdon Press, The United Methodist Publishing House, Nashville, Tennessee.

Psalm 72, like the family story in Genesis, presents a potential ideal of humanity in relationship with a faithful God. The Genesis love story offers an ideal illustration of individuals entering into family relationship. Psalm 72 is a prayer for guidance and support of the king (named as Solomon) in the ideal use of social power.

The prayer paints an extraordinary picture of power: justice in judgment; prosperity for the people; defense of the poor; deliverance of the needy; the oppressors crushed; a long life in peace and prosperity; dominion from sea to sea; tribute, gifts, and service from defeated foes; abundance in grain, fruit, and offspring; all nations blessed in God.

Look at that list! Is this ideal attainable or sustainable any more than the ideal of human relationship glimpsed in the Genesis story? The Genesis family couldn't do it. Solomon (a descendant of that family) couldn't do it. Even with God's gifts of understanding and wisdom, Solomon could not withstand the temptation of wealth and power over the long haul.

What ruling power has ever existed on earth that could hold both extravagant fortune and true justice in balance? Why do power and wealth lead to loss of compassion and injustice for the poor and marginalized? Is it inevitable? What does such repeated failure tell us about ourselves? about God?

Verse 18 provides the key: "Blessed be the LORD, the God of Israel, / who alone does wondrous things." We are not God. We are subject to the limitations of our imperfect being. No amount of money or power, not even God's gift of wisdom, can save us from temptation. God alone does wondrous things. Let us put our trust in God. Only when we let go of our illusion of power do we truly become God's power in and for the world.

**PRAYER: "Blessed be his glorious name forever; / may his glory fill the whole earth. / Amen and Amen."**

In this second installment of our love story, we meet Rebekah. Abraham's servant continues his story: he came to the spring and put all in the Lord's hands, asking that the young woman who responds to his request for water be the appointed wife for Isaac.

The servant says that even before he finished his prayer, Rebekah arrived. Her response reveals significant aspects of her character. The custom of hospitality requires that she give water to any stranger who asks. But Rebekah does more. According to verse 46, "She quickly let down her jar . . . and said, 'Drink, and I will also water your camels.'" Her response is immediate and generous beyond the requirements of custom.

The servant now relates the discovery that Rebekah is not only kin to Abraham but is the granddaughter of his brother and sister-in-law, Nahor and Milcah. We hear again of the servant's prayer of thanks to the Lord and of his gifts to Rebekah. His prologue finished, he asks the all-important question—will you agree to the marriage, or must I continue searching? The answer and the outcome comprise the final chapter in our love story.

If we read only these verses, we might be tempted to think that God's answer to prayer is always immediate and positive or that, if we are nice, people will be extravagant in their gratitude. We know that's not true. God's answer to prayer is often much slower and less clear than we would like. Acts of kindness are sometimes ignored or even resented. But God is steadfast. Prayers offered in trust and thanksgiving, and kindness given without thought of reward all carry their own kind of joy. It's important to recognize and celebrate the small moments of grace in our lives. They are the true embodiment of God's power and plan.

**PRAYER: Lord, help us to trust in you and to give without thought of reward. Amen.**

The love story of Isaac and Rebekah gives us an ideal glimpse of new love. But life is not a fairy tale; human love changes over time. Paul provides the corrective when we come face-to-face with reality: "I do not do the good I want, but the evil I do not want is what I do."

In the call to discipleship—feed the hungry, clothe the naked, free the oppressed, care for the sick, and visit those in prison—I want to respond, but I am overwhelmed. The little I do seems pitifully small in the face of the world's great need. Paul's assertion convicts me on the public stage.

In personal care—diet, exercise, rest, treating my body as a temple—I fail often! Oh, I make my attempts but, again, they feel feeble and inadequate. Paul speaks to me on an individual level.

In relationships—kindness, patience, humility, trust, and integrity—I like to think I do better. Then someone cuts me off in traffic or I'm tired or have a busy day, and my manners take a backseat to my desires. Paul haunts me in interpersonal relations.

Paul's words apply in every arena of life. When we rely on our own judgment and strength of will, we fail every time. Does this mean we are inherently evil? I don't believe that. I believe in the goodness of God's creation. We are not created evil; we are imperfect. We are not God. While our bodies and brains have amazing creative capacity, we are creatures, not creator. We are offspring, not wellspring.

Paul calls us to be "in Christ." When we trust in and rely on God, we are filled with power to act for the good of others and our own well-being. In tiny moments of forgiveness or grand gestures of self-sacrifice, God's grace works through us to bring healing and wholeness to the world.

**SUGGESTION FOR MEDITATION: In Christ we are filled with the power of grace.**

These few verses record the fairy-tale ending of Isaac and Rebekah's story. A marriage made in heaven is so cliché that we gloss over it to the more interesting (read controversial, conflict-ridden) biblical stories. We know that Isaac will try to pass Rebekah off as his sister and that Rebekah will scheme with Jacob for Esau's inheritance. We know that happily-ever-after—isn't. But we also know that without the strength and intensity of first love, many marriages will not survive the inevitable storms of life. Let's not miss this lovely story.

First, Rebekah's family asks if she is willing to go with the man. Custom does not require her agreement to the marriage or the timing of her departure. It's significant that her family consults her. Rebekah's simple, dignified response is, "I will." No flowery phrases or protestations of sacrifice or longing.

Next, enter the hero Isaac. We last saw him bound to an altar with a knife at his throat. Since his mother's death, Isaac has moved out to the Negeb, away from the family compound. In true fairy-tale fashion, he looks up, sees Rebekah, and immediately moves toward her. In the same moment she looks up, sees him, "slip[s] quickly" from her camel, and asks who he is. They move toward each other as the music swells. . . . The rest of the story takes only a few sentences: they meet; they marry; he loves her; she comforts him—The End.

The Genesis family saga illustrates a broad spectrum of human relationships. These verses gave us a tiny glimpse of new love that's simple and true. Abram and Sarai are already married and aging when we meet them. Jacob has to work and scheme for his Rachel. And those are just the parents! That's the key—this is all God's story. People don't need to be perfect; God is perfect. Thank God!

**PRAYER: In our imperfection, Lord, help us to be a perfect vessel for your love. Amen.**

Psalm 72 offers an ideal image of social power and wealth balanced with justice and compassion. In our Gospel passage, Jesus mocks the hypocrisy of those who abuse social position.

John the baptizer fasted, mourned, and dressed in rags. Jesus ate, drank, and partied with sinners and outcasts. The religious authorities condemn both of them. What happened to justice in judgment and defense of the poor, that expressed ideal of Psalm 72? Jesus exposes the reality of social authority that has forgotten that God is the source of all power. Solomon forgot; the Pharisees and Sadducees forgot. Civic and church leaders today have forgotten.

Have you and I forgotten too? This wake-up call is not just for the rich and powerful. It's directed at the crowd (that's us) as well. We see what we want to see. With our eyes, ears, and hearts closed to the truth, we sit in judgment of those around us.

The poor and needy cry out—we do not hear. We don't even see them. The devastation of Hurricane Katrina in 2005 revealed horrific societal inequities. Have we yet heard the cries, or are we still deafened by comfort and privilege?

We encounter people who live different lifestyles from our own. Are we able to see the joy and abundance of God's love in their lives? Or do our rules lead us to blind condemnation of anything different?

Jesus says, "Wisdom is vindicated by her deeds." Look at the faithfulness and power of John's ministry and message; look at the joy and hope Jesus brings to those marginalized by prejudice and custom. What is our legacy of faith? Are we like the crowd that Jesus compares to children sitting in the marketplace and calling to one another?

When will we hear? When will we see? When will we remember that this is God's story and that God's love is the source of all power and justice?

**PRAYER: Lord, help us remember to love. Amen.**

Rest. Sabbath rest. Stop wrestling with power, fear, temptation, and guilt. Take the yoke of love onto your shoulders and into your heart. Let it become your only burden.

I used to struggle with this passage. How can the yoke of Jesus be light? He took on the weight of the entire world's pain and suffered cruel death, abandoned by most of his closest companions. Light? easy? How can that be?

But the yoke of servant love is light. Paul was right. On our own, we cannot escape guilt and sin. But in Christ we are free— free to forgive and be forgiven, free to serve others with joy, free to rest from our labors in the arms of a loving God.

That sounds so wonderful and, when it works, it is. But it's hard to remember, hard to hold on to. The lure of comfort, wealth, and control are so strong. We like to be in charge, to be right, to be comfortable. The only way to sustain the radical freedom of servant love is in the company of others, in loving community.

When we get tired and forget, our brothers and sisters in Christ remind us, help us rest, nurture us until we remember and can begin again. Sometimes that takes just a moment; a hug, a phone call, or a reassuring smile can give us enough space and time to remember who and whose we are. Sometimes it takes much more—more time, more energy, deep prayer, and lots of patience. Always it requires study, worship, and service together, as well as trust in God and in one another.

SUGGESTION FOR PRAYER: **Come to God in Christ, all you who struggle in fear, fatigue, and guilt. Come to God's love in the community of faith and find the joyful burden of accompanying one another in love. Come find rest from your labor, help in your task, and strength for the journey together. Amen.**

# Fishing, Waiting, and Praising

*July 7–13, 2008* • *Mozelle Adams Core*[‡]

## MONDAY, JULY 7 • Read Psalm 119:105–112

"Accept my offerings of praise, O LORD," the psalmist cries. Does God need or desire our praise? Is it anthropomorphic thinking for mortals to assume that divinity requires praise? Perhaps the truth lies more in *our need* to praise.

Praise seemed a natural response for my three-year-old granddaughter as we sat on the lowest of the steps leading to my porch. Above us an ornamental cherry tree abounded in glorious blossoms. A soft breeze caused showers of snowy white petals to fall again and again upon the sidewalk and upon us. With abandon, Elizabeth arose and began to dance and sing a paean of her own making, "Oh, God, you are the special person of love!"

Jesus tells us to become like little children if we would enter the kingdom. Might this mean never outgrowing our childlike appreciation for and enjoyment of God's world and our awareness that we belong to a God who loves us?

Praising God places us in right relationship with God. We think of God as creator of ourselves and all that is. We consider God's goodness and are thankful. We reflect on God's promises and faithfulness and are reassured. How often the psalmist praises God for "steadfast love." Is it God who needs to hear that, or we who need again and again to remind ourselves of it?

As in human relationships, it is natural to praise the one we love and so strengthen the bond between us. Praising God binds us ever closer to our loving Creator and Sustainer. How many times in a day or a week do you lift your thoughts to God in praise?

**PRAYER: Let the people praise you, O God. Let all the people praise you. Amen.**

---

[‡]Educator, active member of Belmont United Methodist Church, Nashville, Tennessee.

TUESDAY, JULY 8 • **Read Genesis 25:19–34**

To several prospective parents scripture tells us God revealed clearly the divine dream for the promised child: Abraham and Sarah; Rebekah; Hannah; Zechariah and Elizabeth; and Mary, mother of Jesus.

I find it interesting to consider the difference in the ways Rebekah and Mary responded over time to the revelation of God's dream for their sons. Both messages must have been puzzling to these mothers-to-be, and, in Mary's case, overwhelming. The roles these two women assume in child rearing, as best we can tell in the little information we receive, seem to be markedly different. Mary seemingly allows God to take the lead ("Let it be as you have said"and "Mary pondered these things in her heart.") Rebekah seems to think that she must take matters into her own hands to bring about the realization of God's dream.

We tend to think of Rebekah as conniving and manipulative, but we could take a more generous attitude and see her as striving to do whatever she could to see that Jacob did, indeed, become the "stronger" of the twins as God had promised. As parents we sometimes try to take the reins into our own hands and control our children's lives rather than humbly allowing God to work through us and through our children to fulfill God's dream for their lives.

I remember sensing my mother's disappointment when, after beginning my career as a teacher in college, I turned at last to directing day care for children of low-income families. This did not follow the dream either she or I had for my career. Only in retrospect have I realized that in following this relatively inauspicious career I might have been following God's dream. I had no clear sense of direction, but God kept opening doors of opportunity that led to preparation for the ultimate task. I kept following God's lead to the dream's fulfillment.

**PRAYER: Divine lover of all children and all parents, help us as parents and grandparents to prepare our children in all the ways we know to hear your voice and follow your dream for their lives. Amen.**

I like to fish. I have taught all my grandchildren to fish and enjoyed it with them. The reason I can keep at fishing all day long, even on a "slow day," is that I fish not only with hope but with expectation that I am going to get a nibble, get a bite, get a fish! I need similar patience and expectation when I ask God for help and guidance.

This psalm is a strong plea for help. The psalmist seems to trust God's faithfulness fully and to expect that God will help him. But even with this seemingly good relationship, he knows there is more. The psalmist wants to know God more fully.

A person good at fishing comes to know the nature and habits of the fish he or she is after, such as what season of the year that fish is running, what the spawning times are, what time of day and in what part of the lake the fish may be feeding. Likewise, the psalmist asks to be taught the ways of the Lord, to know more fully the God in whom he places his hope of salvation. "Teach me your paths. Lead me in your truth." The psalmist already knows and depends upon God's steadfast love and readiness to forgive, but he knows there is more for him to learn. He trusts God to lead him, teach him, and bring him into full friendship.

For this the psalmist waits expectantly all day long. And just as I must keep my eye on the bob as I wait for the fish, the psalmist's "eyes are ever toward the LORD," awaiting the help and the guidance that will surely come.

**PRAYER: O God, we turn our eyes to you, trusting that you will lead us through the day and teach us your paths. May we "fish" with hope and expectation. Amen.**

Paul urges us to live into our true identity as Christians. My grandson recorded a case of identity trauma in his third-grade journal. When roles for the spring play were assigned, John got the role of "bird." "The teacher thought I raised my hand, but I didn't. I didn't want to be the bird," he writes. The situation worsened when John learned the bird had to stand with the flowers. The flowers were all girls! John's parents went to work quickly to make a remarkable bird costume, but nothing helped. At the play's conclusion, all the actors moved upstage, removed their headdresses, and stated their names. John wrote, "I felt like saying I am *not* John Bearden!"

Have you ever felt you did not want to claim the identity others assigned you? I find praise and blame almost equally hard to deal with. When I have received undue praise or undue blame, I have wanted to say, "I am not the person you think I am." At times, however, blame was justified and others have had to confront me as Nathan confronted David saying, "You are the man!" (2 Sam. 12:7).

I recall such a confrontation when I directed a day care center. The staff asked for a Sunday afternoon meeting to help me see the error of a decision I had made and had stubbornly refused to reconsider. I had to claim my negative identity and seek forgiveness from the staff and from God. Fortunately, I did not have to tell God my name. God knows me better than I know myself. The "Spirit of God dwells" within me. That Spirit stands ready to forgive, loving me and longing to shape me into the fullness of my true identity as a beloved child of God.

**PRAYER: God of love, help us each day to claim the identity Paul describes and live joyfully "in the Spirit." Amen.**

When I read this parable, I find elements of myself in each of the kinds of soil Jesus pictures for his hearers. I know that at times I have been the soil of the path, unresponsive and almost unaware that Christ is casting seeds my way, paying little or no attention to what God may be trying to do with my life.

At other times, I have delighted in receiving the seed upon hearing a good sermon; attending a helpful workshop, conference, or small-group experience; or perhaps having an hour or so with a spiritual friend. I have gone home full of excitement and readiness to serve. Then somehow the glow of the experience fades, and my life goes on much as before. The seeds that were planted spring up, but I do not nurture them; and they soon die.

At other times I have been keenly aware that the seeds have been sown in me, and I struggle to tend to them but find myself so buffeted by life circumstances or so caught up in seeking fulfillment of my own desires that the seeds go unattended. I am the soil full of weeds and briars choking out the life of the seed.

But I am thankful that at times I have had the experience of being the good soil. And I have known the joy of bearing fruit in far greater proportion than I thought possible. It is a wonderful gift that God can make useful soil of us when we fully yield ourselves to God's purposes.

**SUGGESTION FOR MEDITATION: Which type of soil have I provided today, this week, for the seed God wants to sow? How have I been resistant to the seed? What has God sown in me that I have allowed to go unattended? Where has my interest in bearing fruit waned?**

**PRAYER: Gracious Sower, may you find in me good soil for the planting, that I may yield an abundant harvest. Amen.**

What does it mean that "there is now no condemnation for those who are in Christ Jesus"? For Paul the condemnation refers to our final judgment before God. And the good news of this passage is that the condemnation has been effected in the cross. In verse 2, Paul moves to the second person singular: you. He addresses every individual who hears or reads his message, including you and me.

This "no condemnation" offers compelling hope to those of us who don't feel good enough or perhaps we feel we don't do enough. Often we feel like failures. Yet I believe that when we bring our failures to God, God is faithful and just to forgive. God's power can redeem our failures.

One day as I entered the lobby of my retirement home, Ellen, a woman whom I knew only in our poetry group, called me to her and said through tears, "I have lost my faith." I fumbled for words and finally replied, "I read this morning that a faith never doubted is not a very strong faith." I said little more and, almost with a sense of escape, took the elevator to my apartment. I felt awful. I had failed both this woman and God. Within three days Ellen became ill with pneumonia, was hospitalized, and died. When I asked her husband if she had regained her faith, he said no.

My failure preyed on my conscience. My pastor heard my guilt and my desire for redemption. Together we recognized the need for more persons to see themselves as ministers to the spiritually hungry, especially to those who are elderly, infirm, or for other reasons cut off from their congregations. My pastor took action, applying for and receiving a training grant. Now fourteen volunteers in our church have taken intensive training that enables them to help people continue to grow toward God and to accompany them through their last years, even through their dying. My painful failure is now redeemed and bearing fruit.

**PRAYER: Merciful God, we thank you for your forgiveness and redemption in Jesus Christ. Amen.**

$P$salm 25 reminds me of my own tendency in prayer. It is a prayer full of praise, requests for forgiveness, expressions of faithfulness in prayer and waiting upon God. Then it becomes strong in personal petition. The closing words "Redeem Israel, O God, out of all its troubles" seem almost an afterthought, a tack-on to the "real" prayer. I consider praying for my country and the world urgent and essential, yet I often make it a tack-on prayer.

I aspire to pray as did Elizabeth, an elderly, blind friend, now deceased. One day after visiting her wonderful flower garden, I asked her to tell me about her prayer life. She replied, "In the morning I pray for my family and those on my prayer list. At noon I pray for my church, my country, and the world. In the evening I pray for myself and my relationship to God." Far different from a tack-on prayer, specific time and thought were given to prayers for church, country, and world.

The morning I heard the Berlin Wall had fallen, I soon began to hear the fall attributed to the power of prayer. Guiltily I thought, *Not my prayer.*

I read that Henri Nouwen found it easier to pray for the world when, through prayer, he had cleansed his heart and made a small space for God. When God occupied the space, God expanded it so that Nouwen could invite in thousands of suffering people. Nouwen's image made me think of the promise that when we do not know how to pray, the Spirit prays within us, interceding on our behalf and that of the world.

**SUGGESTION FOR MEDITATION: When do you make time to pray for the world and its suffering? How does that affect your sensitivity to world situations? How does that prayer empower you to feel that you make a difference?**

**PRAYER: God, who made and loves the world and all that is in it, create in us a love for the world so that we pray for it as devoutly as we pray for ourselves and our families. Amen.**

# Holy Revelations

*July 14–20, 2008 • Cynthia Langston Kirk*[‡]

**MONDAY, JULY 14 • Read Genesis 28:10-15**

People often travel daily via the escape route or move through the geography of life focused on a place named Promise. Jacob's journey from Beer-sheba to Haran is both as he runs from his brother's rightful anger and walks toward the hope of finding a wife. Fatigue and guilt give way to weariness. He chooses a rock pillow for rest, and that's just where God wants him—supine, quiet, with his mind disengaged for God's message to be experienced.

In spite of Jacob's abuse of power, God gives Jacob an in-the-moment, life-changing reiteration of the covenant made with Jacob's grandfather. The most scandalous and reassuring utterance of that nighttime revelation is the reminder of God's identity. God is Faithfulness, the maker and keeper of covenant.

People often think their actions merit divine abandonment or their locales are too ordinary for the Lord of all to appear. In a desire to avoid the current state of affairs, they look back to decisions made, wise or foolish, or forward to the horizon of greener grass or sufficient security.

Now as then, with each and every one of us, God calls us to be still and present. God longs for us to hear and see God's promise: My faithfulness is unwavering.

Are you ever still enough to see the angels descending and ascending? Are you ever quiet enough to hear God whispering that you are in God's keeping wherever you go? Like our ancestor Jacob, you and I do not always act in accordance with God's will, but nothing "will be able to separate us from the love of God in Christ Jesus our Lord" (Rom. 8:39). Nothing.

**PRAYER: God of steadfast love, give us dreams and visions to sustain us. Teach us that rocky spots and quiet places can offer encounters with you. For that, we are grateful. Amen.**

---

[‡]Ordained United Methodist minister serving in the Desert Southwest Annual Conference; poet, writer; living in Tucson, Arizona.

How quick is your pace, how keen your observational skills? Think about this. A hundred or a thousand times a day you pass a place where someone has encountered God. Perhaps he or she did not have the deep regard for stories that connect and form the generations or the wherewithal of Jacob to set up an altar to God. If they had, we would walk past monumental stones stained with oil throughout our days. Our landscape would be dotted with monoliths that would cause us to come face-to-face with each altar of encounter and to remember.

When our speed is too rapid and our focus too narrow, we fail to notice the shades of green in creation or the sound of the bird's song. We fail to see the pain or joy on another person's face or take time to hear their conflicted or celebratory story. Or we are so inundated with demands and despair that we seek to numb our senses or escape in any way we can. We often fail to be aware on our own behalf.

But when we observe, when our pace is unhurried and we permit ourselves dream time, we are more open to experience God. Our souls and pores—every fiber of our being—absorb the reality and wonder of God's presence. That holy moment takes our breath away, and it is not surprising in the least that we deem the spot as God's house and heaven's gate.

Then we may be propelled to lift the rock of our choosing, anoint it with oil, and declare, "God was in this place and I was not even aware of that life-changing truth." When that happens, we might be privileged to see the rocks of other generations glistening with oil.

**PRAYER: O God, slow our pace and allow us to experience your grace. Flood our paths with your mystery so we cannot help but cry, "Holy, holy, holy Lord." Amen.**

## WEDNESDAY, JULY 16 • Read Psalm 139:1-12

Two years ago I participated in an international clergywomen's gathering in Chicago. "Cynthia!" different persons exclaimed as we waited in line, or as I walked out of closing worship. These people know me from two years together in the Academy for Spiritual Formation; serving in ministry in Arizona; being long-time friends; and, for two sisters across the country, from my officiating at a son's wedding or a brother-in-law's memorial service. These people know me by name. They know some gifts and warts. Some know me in a deeper way than others; but in all those circumstances, I was thrilled to be called by name, embraced, and known.

But God knows us in the deepest sense—all our gifts and our shortcomings; all our potential, labors, sluggishness, fears, compassion, courage, monstrous thoughts, words of grace—everything. God knows our best intentions, kindest acts, and the times we sorely miss the mark. God knows.

Is that fact not enough to unnerve you, to make you ponder the words and deeds of your day and feel connected to love eternal by some of them and remorseful of others? Does such knowledge fill you with fear? And does it also elate you that the Creator of the universe knows you, loves you, and will never let you out of caring reach? Doesn't it fill you with peace, gratitude, and boldness?

It is not always easy to be known, but it is a gift. God's knowing allows us to know ourselves more deeply and become the person God knows we can be. God's knowing enables us to be audacious and tenderhearted servants. God's knowing allows us to hear our names called, to feel the embrace, and to beam with joy at the profound recognition.

**PRAYER: Tender God, you know us more intimately than a mother knows a child. We praise you this day that your knowledge of us can breathe new life into our souls. Amen.**

Amy and her scent-discriminating, tracking, trailing dog Kaia comprise a search-and-rescue partnership. Most people never consider what goes into such a team until a crisis crushes upon them, altering days or sometimes lives permanently. This team of woman and canine must be ready at all times. They do not wait until disaster strikes to begin their work. Daily they involve themselves in the discipline of exercise and training. Through mock drills and practice, Amy and Kaia have come to know each other and are rehearsed in how to search and find. Their training often makes it possible to bring someone back to safety.

We act as if the spiritual journey is an enormous trust leap, like falling backward blindfolded into the arms of someone we do not know and who might not be up to the task. When we read the psalmist's plea for the Lord to search and know, we often feel fear in the face of such intimacy that allows God to search even the darkest corners of our hearts.

Three factors make all the difference: (1) God already knows us through and through. (2) God loves us beyond measure. (3) God is rehearsed in bringing people from bondage and through wildernesses to the place of redemption.

The Creator of the universe has already searched our hearts and knows us. When God tests us and finds our ways wicked and our thoughts lacking, it is not to judge us to the point of destruction. God is for us, planning for us, searching for us, cheering for us, bringing us to the "good and broad land" (Exod. 3:8), to the everlasting way. When we allow, God shines a light on our failures and offers us the grace of redemption.

PRAYER: **God of the nooks and crannies, thank you for shining your light into our beings, for illuminating all that we need to see and who we can become because of you. Amen.**

Loves initiates liberation. Certainly, blood, sweat, and toil contribute; but it begins in the womb and heart of love. Love liberates and gives us a new identity.

The universe watches expectantly. Candles in the darkness bear witness to prayers for peace. Water tanks scattered in the Arizona desert stand as reminders that all God's children need and deserve a cup of water, even if it is not cold. Foster parents and adoptive parents offer places of healing for the physical and emotional abuse of thousands of children. Hammer and nails construct homes and hope for those held hostage by poverty.

All of creation cries, "Save us from ourselves and from each other," and love responds. Slowly Christ unbinds us from the sin that holds us captive. We are freed from the shackles of violence and the bondage of narcissism. Gone is the desire to lord money, power, position, and place of privilege over anyone. Gradually, we are filled with a reverence for life. That journey in and toward redemption is our current reality and the future for which creation labors.

The Spirit of God who hovered over the waters at creation's birth bears witness with our spirits testifying before the universe that we are children of God. In Christ, we become brothers and sisters of the Prince of Peace, members of the family of compassion and care.

**PRAYER: God of Love, remove the chains that imprison us. Free us to be your joyful children, your large-hearted heirs of grace. In Christ's name we pray. Amen.**

Hope is the twin of faith, the mother of patience. Sure-footed and never afraid, hope goes before and behind with faith. Hope moves slowly with wisdom and courage, for it is not in a hurry. Hope shines a light—sometimes a penlight—into the darkness.

If you visit a field of white daisies, hope would not be there. Hope is the seed in the dark, fertile soil of winter. Hope lives in hospital rooms; with the young couple who prays to conceive; with the social worker who, year after year, advocates for children.

If God gave us the ability to see the future, to know the outcome of rehab or that, in nine months, a couple would have a baby, there would be no need for hope. If we knew that elections would yield results that would meet all the basic needs of children, we would not need to hope and work. If we could see into the future, patience would not develop and grow. It would be of little use. But God holds the future, short term and for all eternity. *Chronos* patience can be born in that *kairos* reality.

Hope is not dreaming and scheming or romantic, soft-eyed wishful thinking. It is not crossing fingers and toes and waiting. Hope allows us to live with our eyes open even when confronted with the unthinkable or life issues that appear insurmountable. Hope points to the One who is our constant and steadfast companion. Repeatedly, hope motivates and energizes us for the creative life of freedom into which God calls us.

**PRAYER: God of all hopefulness, thank you for living with us in the darkness where hope grows. Thank you for giving us your Spirit who, in the midst of waiting and chaos, offers us peace beyond our comprehension and beyond our ability to manufacture. Amen.**

Sometimes an idea, passion, revolution has been growing for so long that no one can recall when the first seed was planted. What springs forth brings great change and confusion. It may bring intolerance for questions and for that which appears different or threatening. So much so that people begin to strip the sanctuary, select stones for casting, substitute words of faith for secular language and, at times, even throw the proverbial infant out with the bath water.

Growing season in the farmlands offers a similar challenge as weeds and wheat emerge side by side, and temptation woos the farmer to rip the menacing weeds from the soil and rush to the nearest waste receptacle. Yet the farmer waits patiently, discerning and unafraid in the face of life. Fear can cause the grower to move too swiftly and act too harshly.

Jesus instructs us to allow the tares and grain to thrive side by side. Timing and discernment are important. If plucked too soon, the wheat could be immature. Worse yet, if we do the uprooting, we could mistake the grain for weeds.

We might even be tempted to view this parable strictly from an exterior world perspective rather than from an interior spiritual perspective as it relates to our souls and lives. We all have weeds and wheat, shadow and light, wisdom and foolishness. If we do the judging and pulling, we may mistake the weeds for wheat.

Only God and God's angels will determine what chokes out life. They will distinguish what bears life: the light of the righteous. Thanks be to God whose judgment is unsurpassed, whose grace extends to all, and whose mercy is ever-flowing.

**PRAYER: Shine your sun upon us, Merciful One. Take away the lure of judging others. Grow the wheat of our lives into that which serves and pleases you. Amen.**

# The Surprising Grace of God

*July 21–27, 2008 • Paul L. Escamilla[‡]*

## MONDAY, JULY 21 • Read Genesis 29:15-28

The opening sentence of this reading gives us a clue that Laban is an individual for whom self-interest wears the mask of magnanimity. First of all, we have no indication that Jacob had planned to place himself in the service of Laban. He has come to find a wife, not employment. (See Genesis 28:2.) Second, we know from an earlier account that Laban tends to ask leading questions, which open like doors to deals made on his own terms. (See Genesis 24:31.) Jacob names his wages; Laban appears to agree but never gives him his word, only words.

Jacob, schemer, dreamer, and restless soul that he is, is yet strangely bridled by the subtle power of his love for Rachel, his chosen. His seven years of serving seem to him but a few days. Seven more are exacted of him by the machinations of Laban, but neither are they more than scarcely mentioned. Fourteen years pass virtually unnoticed because of one person's sense of devotion to another. Thus, while Rachel and Leah appear to be mere objects in a transaction, they prove here and later to be far more.

Having succeeded in outwitting both his brother and his father, Jacob truly meets his match in Laban. It is all the more remarkable that through this biblical period in which deceit often lies with trickery, the good promise of God will yet find its way.

**SUGGESTION FOR MEDITATION: Meditate on the many ways in which God works through earthen vessels.**

---

[‡]Pastor, Spring Valley United Methodist Church, Dallas, Texas.

## TUESDAY, JULY 22 • Read Psalm 105:1-6

The Psalms are, of course, the songbook of the scriptures. Here are songs of lament and despair, as well as songs of joyful celebration. Before (and after) studying this psalm as a text of scripture, we would do well to enjoy it as song—not Israel's song only but ours as well.

There is the pleasure of praying a prayer-song written ages ago and ample enough to be spoken and sung meaningfully ever since. Beyond this we can derive important lessons about the life of faith from looking closely at the words we are singing. In this case, we see in the first six verses of Psalm 105 a rare and beautiful integration of four faith dimensions: memory, worship, seeking, and proclamation. In other words, the faithful are called in the same breath (1) to remember God's "wonderful works," (2) to praise God for them, (3) to seek God because of them, and (4) to tell others of them.

The expression of these imperatives is so natural here that we are apt not to notice them as distinct features but to see them, as the psalmist does, as one gathered expression of gratitude for God's faithfulness. It is perhaps only more recently that we have compartmentalized Bible study, spirituality, worship, evangelism, and so on, understanding each as a separate pursuit or emphasis. In this delightful song, all of these are strands in a single cloth.

**SUGGESTION FOR PRAYER: Pray or sing (in your own created melody) Psalm 105:1-6 as a prayer.**

**PRAYER: God, may remembering your faithfulness emerge in my life as worship, seeking you and sharing you with others. Amen.**

These five verses begin to do what will occupy the remaining thirty-nine verses of this psalm: recounting certain central episodes in the historical faithfulness of God. The "call to worship" of verses 1-6 in the psalm charges the hearer to "remember the wonderful works God has done." These verses provide all the help we need in order to do so.

The narrative of God's faithful action moves right away from the general to the specific, from the universal to the concrete: God's judgments span the earth; God remembers a covenant that has been made—even to a thousand generations. Specifically, this covenant, our covenant, was made with Abraham and ratified with Isaac and Jacob. The content of that covenant? To give God's homeless chosen people a home in the land of Canaan.

Notice the collective tone of the psalm so far. The plural form of address speaks to all, not just to one; the episodes recited are the community's stories, not those of one individual. The goodness of God can only be fully comprehended by all of the people together. It makes sense to speak of God's goodness to me only in the context of considering God's goodness to us and to all. After all, as someone has said, some things are true even when I am asleep.

**SUGGESTION FOR MEDITATION: Reflect on God's mercies toward you, your faith community, and all creation.**

**PRAYER: God, in singing the songs of your faithfulness, teach me the importance of sharing the singing with others and of finding my place in the songs that others sing. Amen.**

If some things are true even while we sleep, then, according to Paul, it is at least partly due to the Spirit's matrix of care and intercession in our lives. Whereas in the Psalter the gathered community is the sign of memory deeper than my own and faith greater than my own, in Paul's letter to the Christians in Rome, the Spirit becomes such a sign.

My prayers falter; the Spirit completes them. My soul yearns for things too deep to put in words—to have a profound hope realized, to see creation whole, to be with God (vv. 18-25). I cannot even begin to speak these yearnings, "but that very Spirit intercedes for us with sighs too deep for words."

In the charismatic movement of the 1970s, this verse was cited as a warrant for praying in tongues. With all respect to that particular form of prayer, Paul's intent here goes deeper and ranges wider, so as to say that prayer need not be verbal to be expressed or heard. From this understanding we can begin to see the value of many nonverbal prayer forms, such as gesture (movement, dance, exercise, kneeling, lifted palms), silence (meditation, deep contemplation), and vocalization (chants, humming, deep breathing, praying in tongues) as vehicles for prayer.

In this discussion, you and I are considering things we do not claim to understand, things literally "too deep for words." The assurance of Paul is that in the midst of such depths, the Spirit will help us; all we need is given.

**SUGGESTION FOR PRAYER: Introduce into your prayers today a nonverbal prayer form such as one of those mentioned above.**

Coming from just anyone, we would suspect the words that open this passage to be pollyannish and simplistic: "We know that all things work together for good. . . ." But they are spoken not by an ivory-tower academic or an armchair positive thinker but by an apostle who has experienced firsthand the gamut of crises listed in verse 35: hardship, distress, persecution, famine, nakedness, peril, sword.

When one who has emerged from such wreckage speaks about hope and providence, every word is gospel. This closing segment of chapter 8 is a consummate elaboration of the truth pronounced in its opening verse: "There is therefore now no condemnation for those who are in Christ Jesus." In these verses Paul names all the demons, all the threats to our sense of well-being, to our very lives. He lines them up in daunting fashion *twice* (v. 35 and vv. 38-39). Then he says, in effect, "What matters finally is more profound than these or any imaginable circumstance: we are held eternally in God's care, freedom, and love because of God's saving work in Jesus Christ." In one of the most triumphant passages in scripture, we receive the bold assurance that nothing "in all creation will be able to separate us from the love of God in Christ Jesus our Lord."

I have heard that a particular Roman Catholic religious order lists "hilarity" as one of the lifelong virtues. What is meant by this, I think, is a sense of holy perspective on the ultimate outcome of things. By all appearances, things may be desperate or even deadly. In universal scope, however, even death has lost its sting (1 Cor. 15:55), and that particular truth, like Paul's closing verses of chapter 8, is suitable for dancing.

SUGGESTION FOR MEDITATION: **Read thoughtfully and prayerfully Romans 8:37-39. Read these verses again. What special word for you or your congregation do you find in them?**

SATURDAY, JULY 26 • **Read Matthew 13:31-32**

We have in today's parable a nest in the shade during a long, hot season. But to whom is the shade due? Presumably, the mustard seed was planted for the purpose of reaping its harvest later on, mustard being a cash crop with various medicinal and dietary uses. But Jesus' parable does not lead us to that end; the sower is removed from the story early on and never returns.

Instead, we are led to the conclusion that birds of the air become the beneficiaries of the full-grown mustard shrub. Right away we realize that any birds nesting in such a tree are freeloaders, never having lifted a feather to earn their place in its branches. Did they purchase the land? Did they prepare the soil? Did they plant the seed? Did they cultivate the young shrub to full growth? At best, they were a mere irritation of droppings and chatter along the way. But to them belongs the mustard shrub!

Ezekiel 17 offers a beautiful apocalyptic vision of the nation of Israel becoming a towering tree—great, strong, and noble. But in Matthew we get a dowdy, frumpy mustard shrub. And it is given over entirely to birds who are only in it for the shelter and the shade. Unmeriting, undeserving, uncredentialed, the birds are just there to receive. In this parable, the kingdom of heaven is such a reality: a mustard shrub enjoyed by those who can never earn it, never pay for it, never create it themselves—who can only delight in it.

**PRAYER: Loving God, open my heart to receive from you what I cannot earn from you—your gracious rule in my life. And open my heart to accept others I may have thought unworthy, who benefit from that very same grace. Amen.**

This parable of the yeast instantly appears more conventional than the one about the mustard seed. Even as we read we begin to smell the fresh dough, the dust of flour, the warm air from an oven heating up for baking. But within this one verse is hidden what would be for the original hearers—and even for us—a bushelful of disturbing features!

For the original hearers of this parable, "leaven" would have been a code word for evil and its spread. Jesus inverts the image to suggest that it is goodness, not evil, that spreads inexorably and eventually permeates all. Second, a woman raised to the public level (such as being featured in a parable) would have been problematic at the time. And the image of a woman representing God or the kingdom, a bakerwoman God, still challenges stereotypes.

Finally, the Greek word used here for "hid" or "mixed in with" is *krypto*, which normally has negative connotations of secrecy and deceit. Besides, why would anyone knowingly hide the work of the kingdom, keeping it behind the scenes?

In one brief verse of one innocent-looking parable, leavenness, femininity, and secrecy are all inverted to present God's realm in radically new ways. If these features make us nervous, we might consider the whole picture again—a warm, cozy kitchen and the promise of bread enough for many to share. (Three measures of flour, about fifty pounds, enough to make over a hundred loaves of bread!)[*] From the abundance of God's kitchen, we are all fed.

**SUGGESTION FOR MEDITATION: Seek to identify workings of the kingdom of God around you and within you that are "cryptic"; that is, those that normally go unnoticed.**

---

[*] Text note to verse 33, from *The HarperCollins Study Bible*, New Revised Standard Version, copyright © 1993 HarperCollins, Publishers, Inc.

# Finding God in the Meager

*July 28–August 3, 2008* • *Travis Tamerius*[‡]

## MONDAY, JULY 28 • Read Matthew 14:13–21

Throughout our entire lives we come face-to-face with our limitations. No sooner do we arrive on the scene than we are sized up and sorted out. We are weighed and measured, compared and contrasted. Once we begin to notice that we are an object of scrutiny, we may also notice that we are not strong enough, tall enough, slender enough, or smart enough.

The disciples of Jesus find themselves faced with limitations. As they look upon a crowd of hungry people far from home, they anticipate a looming crisis. When Jesus orders them to feed the crowds, they say what seems so sensible to say at the time: "We have only five small loaves of bread and two fish" (CEV).

*Only.* It is a word that puts boundaries on the limitless possibility. It fences in our vision to what is practical and reasonable. It pays attention to the obvious. To the untrained eye, Moses was only a simple man with an unskilled tongue, not a mighty liberator of his people; David was only a shepherd boy, not the future king of Israel; the woman washing Jesus' feet was only a sinner, not a model for how we ought to love and worship. And to the stunted imagination of the disciples, the bread and fish could only go so far.

Where do you find yourself "not enough"? Where do you feel limited? Limited by circumstance, by opportunity, by the hurts and mistakes of the past? Recognize that God is able to feed multitudes with all that seems meager and insufficient in your life.

**PRAYER: God, give me enough faith to trust that you are able to do abundantly more than I can ask or think, according to your power that is at work within me. Amen.**

---

[‡]Pastor, Christ Our King Presbyterian Church, Columbia, Missouri; university chaplain at William Woods University.

The ancient Greeks told the story of Narcissus, a man doomed to the fate of admiring his own reflection in a pool of water. As legend has it, Narcissus was so enamored of his own beauty that he became obsessed with paying attention to his image in the water. He eventually wasted away, lost in self-absorption.

Thousands of years removed from the original telling of that tale, we are still trying to shake free from the clutch of narcissism. If truth be known, we cannot avoid giving ourselves some degree of interest and attention. After all, we live with the self daily, devoting enormous time to making sure the self is well-rested, well-fed, and dressed for success. But to see the self and nothing more is to feed on delusions and lies about who we are and what it means to live this life well.

An alternate approach to the way of Narcissus is the way of the apostle Paul. As our scripture passage indicates, Paul isn't lost in his own reflection. Having located the beautiful in God's gracious work of awakening him to life, he doesn't stop there by simply admiring his own good fortune. Rather, the love of self has given way to the love of God and the love of neighbor. As such, Paul longs for his people to come to the end for which they were created.

Paul is heartbroken to discover that the people of his heritage have come up short. His is the anguish of all who want for their loved ones what those loved ones do not want for themselves. This is the measure of a large heart. It yearns for the light of God's love in Christ Jesus to shine in all creation.

**PRAYER: God, help me love you with all my heart, soul, mind, and strength, and help me love my neighbor as myself. Amen.**

Have you noticed how life unexpectedly changes direction? Things are going along smoothly enough—work is satisfying, relationships enriching, health strong. Then suddenly, as if out of nowhere, we seem to be battling for our life: a friendship sours, an old wound reopens, depression descends, an illness lingers, an insecurity about dearly held values remains.

Psalm 17, a lament, cries out for vindication against false accusers. Imagine the psalmist crying aloud these opening words: "Hear a just cause, O LORD; attend to my cry!" How many times have we wrestled with words and feelings similar to the ones evoked by the writer of this psalm? By day and in the middle of the night, we also cry out: How long, O LORD, must we struggle in this unjust world? How long, O God, must we struggle in a world that celebrates power and might and wealth, a world that abuses and exploits so many of your children and your creation?

At those times we do what the psalmist does—we pray. Our questions and our laments form the substance of our prayers. From our own questions and from the prayer of the psalmist, we learn something profound about what it means to be human and in relationship with God. When we are troubled, we feel as if no one is paying attention. The heavens seem silent. Our friends may have deserted us; they are not enough. We want God to notice us. We want to know that God's love is steadfast. When the struggle overwhelms us, we want a safe place to land. When lost and confused, we want a reminder that God cares for us. The psalm writer expresses our concern in these words: "Wondrously show your steadfast love."

Show your love to us, O God. That desire stays within all our hearts. Be our refuge. Be a place of justice in an unjust world. Deliver us from our enemies and reveal your love in our midst.

**PRAYER: Savior of those who seek refuge, grant assurance that you are with the poor and the oppressed and that you love all creation. Show me your love, hide me from harm, and lead me safely home. Amen.**

Recently a friend and I paid a visit to the Nelson-Atkins Museum of Art in Kansas City. My friend, a gifted artist himself, was quite familiar with the gallery and proved to be an incomparable tour guide. With all the passion of an enthusiast and the trained eye of a practitioner, he showed me more than I had ever seen before or ever would have seen on my own. On my own, I would have seen "a painting" and "yet another painting." But my friend Thom drew my attention to qualities of excellence, the refined techniques for infusing light and casting shadows, the skilled layering of paints on the canvas, "the clever way the artist caught the slight lift in the subject's smile."

Whenever we hang around with someone in the context of that person's deep appreciations—carpentry, music, movies, cooking, birdwatching, dog training—we see through his or her eyes all that is worthy of attention and admiration.

It is no different with Jesus. When we keep company with Jesus in the journey of the Gospels, we pick up on his peculiar way of noticing what we so often overlook. In the midst of a great sea of people, with all the commotion of a crowd, Jesus spots lonely and diminutive Zacchaeus, who climbed up in a tree, hoping to find new life. In all such gatherings of the self-important, Jesus calls attention to the outcasts, the ashamed, and the belittled.

Here in Matthew 14, when Jesus "went ashore, he saw a great crowd; and he had compassion for them and healed their sick." Jesus has the eye of an artist. Be assured that he sees you and that he sees you with the eyes of compassion.

**PRAYER: Jesus, help me to see what you see, having your eyes and your heart for those around me. Amen.**

Are you prepared to accept that a dislocated hip can signal both the presence and the blessing of God? Will you allow, if only for the sake of argument, that the loss of creature comforts might itself be a comfort from the Creator?

More typically, we connect divine blessing with favorable circumstances: financial prosperity, a good report from the doctor, satisfying relationships, and safe neighborhoods. If we are really creative and determined to count all our blessings and name them one by one, we might even reckon that getting a good parking spot at the mall is one more indication that God loves us and has a wonderful plan for our lives.

Jacob discovers divine blessing in an all-night wrestling match with a mysterious stranger. In the darkness of night, with his household at rest, Jacob is left alone to struggle and fight. Like two prizefighters going the distance, Jacob and the man go at it, each determined to come out the victor. How the fight started is anybody's guess. But when it ends at the break of day, Jacob is weary in body and soul. He limps from the place of encounter, realizing that he has seen God's face.

Be prepared to locate God's presence and blessing in those places where you least expect to find them: in a broken body, a heavy heart, a painful loss, a winding road, a sleepless night. Learn to trust that God always loves you, even where you struggle—and especially when you think the night will never end. The saints who have gone before us insist that they have often seen God's face in the darkest of nights and the most unlikely of circumstances.

**PRAYER: God, give me the eyes of faith to recognize how you are with me at all times and in all places. Amen.**

The Center for Survivors of Trauma and War Torture in St. Louis started in the early '90s after therapists began noticing the widespread effects of post-traumatic stress disorder within the immigrant community. Refugees from troubled regions of the world come to the Center in hopes of finding healing for their hurts. These men, women, and children—victims of political oppression and social injustice—tell stories of horrific abuse suffered in their homeland. They describe their inability to eat and sleep, the panic that can arise from the slightest trigger, and the disorientation of their emotions.

The clinic director describes how the Center aims to rebuild lives: "So many [immigrants] come here saying, 'I am destroyed,' and part of the Center's job is to change that sentence, to find a seed, so they'll say, 'I am alive.'"

In Psalm 17, the psalmist is under attack, surrounded by those who wish him harm, those without pity who plot his downfall. Tired of living on the run and hungry for home, the psalmist turns to God. And when he does, he finds a beacon of light in the midst of the fog. After all his anxious complaining, he concludes, "As for me, I shall behold your face in righteousness; when I awake, I shall be satisfied, beholding your likeness."

We utter many statements throughout the course of our days that sound similar to the sufferings of the afflicted: *I'm in trouble. How will I ever get through this? When will it ever stop?*

As we learn to speak the name of God into our life, we change the statement from one of dread to one of hope. We learn to say, *I'm alive. I'm alive by God's grace. I'm living in God's care.*

**PRAYER: Gracious Father, cause your face to shine upon me and grant me your peace in this present moment and forevermore. Amen.**

From time to time we hear stories of people who discover something of great value hidden in their home. A seventy-eight-year-old woman was going through some boxes that had been stored in her basement for two decades. The collection contained memorabilia from her grandfather, James Naismith, who invented the game of basketball in 1891. The boxes held photographs, personal letters, an early rule book, a journal record of the first game ever played, and numerous other keepsakes. All together, the collection has been valued at nearly one million dollars.

The apostle Paul is rummaging through the treasure trove that comprises the history of Israel. Opening box after box of divine blessing, he discovers the great Story that was in danger of being ignored and forgotten. Paul finds there the mementos of God's relentless love for God's people: pledges of covenant loyalty and future provision, ceremonies that adorn Israel as God's beautiful bride, testimonies from patriarchs and prophets describing the extravagant nature of God's gracious care. And then there is the Christ, the one who would deliver his people.

Bringing these up from the cellar, the apostle says to his readers: This is your story, your family. This is who you are and where you come from. These are your gifts. Don't overlook the glory that is boxed up in your basement. Don't be a stranger to your spiritual inheritance.

Similarly, we do well to remember the past, appreciating the legacy that has been passed down to us. We remain in danger of losing our way in this world and forgetting who we are. As we reflect upon God's past kindnesses to us, we find strength for today and hope for tomorrow.

**PRAYER: O God, you have been our help in ages past. Be our help today. Amen.**

# Faith

*August 4–10, 2008 • Fred Oaks[‡]*

## MONDAY, AUGUST 4 • **Read Genesis 37:1-4, 12-28**

"Without faith it is impossible to please God" (Heb. 11:6). Faith affirms the sovereignty of God, and the story of Joseph inspires us with an amazing description of God's work in the world despite human frailty and outright opposition. Joseph's family is rent by conflict, yet God works through it in marvelous ways.

Jacob sets the stage for problems when he singles out Joseph for special treatment, oblivious to the jealousy his favoritism fosters among Joseph's brothers. Young Joseph revels in his father's partiality and becomes, from his brothers' perspective, conceited, self-absorbed, and exasperating. Their resentment eventually boils over, bringing terrible consequences. Yet their treachery ultimately serves God's purpose. Their betrayal of Joseph and subsequent deception of Jacob set in motion events that culminate in the fulfillment of the very dreams that so antagonized them.

Evil people oppose God's purposes. Even well-meaning human beings are often inept. Still God's work goes forward. Sin may hinder God's purposes in the world, but it doesn't finally obstruct them and may even serve them. Our text says that it was Jacob who sent Joseph to check on his brothers. Yet faith affirms that it was God who providentially "sent" Joseph to Egypt, enabling him to preserve a chosen people.

God is the object of our faith. God is forever trustworthy. Even when we're bogged down in troubling and seemingly hopeless situations, we can take comfort in the knowledge that God's purposes will come to pass.

**PRAYER: Loving God, we trust in you. Help us know that despite our faithlessness and apparent calamity, we can believe in the unfolding of your promises to bless all people. Amen.**

---

[‡]Pastoral Ministry Program Director, Kern Family Foundation, Waukesha, Wisconsin; the foundation works with leaders to renew older churches.

We have noted that during his youth, Joseph felt secure in his father's blessing to the point of being smug. But God's work in and through Joseph was just beginning. Over the years Joseph proved to be a model of faith strengthened during times of trial.

In our text, Joseph's idyllic early childhood comes to an abrupt end. The warm glow of parental approval recedes into the chilly night of sibling rivalry as he experiences the first in a devastating series of hardships. Spying "that dreamer" in the distance, Joseph's resentful brothers conspire to do him in. They strip him of his prized robe and cast him down into a hole dug for rainwater. Then they nosh lunch and discuss Joseph's fate while he listens intently from below.

Is God at work in this chilling chain of events? It certainly must not have seemed so to traumatized Joseph. Yet as Christians eventually come to affirm in ways even more profound, God uses the weak to bless the strong. (See 1 Cor. 1:25.)

A winding road takes Joseph far from home to Egypt, to prison, and eventually to Pharaoh's court. At every turn, Joseph proves faithful despite temptations to despair. In the end he passes up a golden opportunity to exact vengeance on his brothers (Gen. 45:1-5). Joseph chooses instead to end the cycle of violence and revenge by offering his brothers a word of grace.

God brought incredible blessings out of Joseph's faithfulness. It can be so in our lives too. Are we struggling under hardships and trials that tempt us to lose hope? Before we succumb to temptation, let us consider how God might use our perseverance to bless others powerfully. Let us seek God's strength to remain faithful: "No testing has overtaken you that is not common to everyone. God is faithful, and he will not let you be tested beyond your strength, but with the testing, he will also provide the way out so that you may be able to endure it" (1 Cor. 10:13).

**PRAYER: God, when hardships threaten to overwhelm us, give us strength to stand, trusting that you will use our faithfulness to bless and encourage others in their faith. Amen.**

Good memories and grateful hearts can bolster faith. This psalm is a unique type of worship song known as a salvation history psalm. The worship leader declares, "Remember the wonders [God] has done" (NIV). Such remembering strengthens faith; one purpose of God's saving acts is to inspire people's obedience.

For a few quiet moments today, pause to consider God's work in the lives of people you know or know about. What stories come to mind? Now think of God's work in your own life. In what moments or seasons of life have you been particularly aware of God's presence and action? Make a list of times when God has come through for you, when you've experienced God's faithfulness. If you like, write a poem structured like Psalm 105 by devoting a line or two to each event on your list. End with "Praise the Lord." You have just created your own personal salvation history psalm!

Foolish, rebellious lives suddenly change when we experience God's loving-kindness. "We ourselves were once foolish, disobedient, led astray, slaves to various passions and pleasures, passing our days in malice and envy, despicable, hating one another. But when the goodness and loving kindness of God our Savior appeared, he saved us, not because of any works of righteousness that we had done, but according to his mercy" (Titus 3:3-5).

Review the events listed in Psalm 105 and your list of God's saving acts until your desire to obey God is strengthened. Offer God the gift of obedience—not out of fear but out of gratitude.

**PRAYER: Thank you, God, for all you have done through the ages. Today we are especially aware of your work in our lives and in the lives of those we know. You have given us so much! Please give us one thing more: grateful hearts that become wellsprings of motivation for faithful living. Amen.**

Prayer feeds faith and focuses action. If the Son of God needs to withdraw regularly for prayer and solitude, how much more do we? We may protest that we are too busy to pray. But in our text Jesus has just presided over the multiplication of loaves and fishes and even taken time to dismiss the crowd. Jesus is more popular than ever before, and the demands on his time are enormous. Even so, he separates himself from everyone else in order to commune with his heavenly Father. Interestingly, this praying comes *after* rather than *before* the time of ministry.

Toward the end of his life, Jesus could say to God, "I glorified you on earth by finishing the work you gave me to do" (John 17:4). What a remarkable affirmation! How could Jesus possibly say such a thing when unmet needs surrounded him on every side? The needy crowds still pressed in on him; the diseased still clamored for healing; and his disciples' grasp of his teaching remained tenuous at best.

Yet Jesus is confident that his work is done. He can know this only because he has faithfully and persistently communed with God in prayer. Through prayer, God refreshes Jesus for service. Through prayer, God directs Jesus in his work. Through prayer, God reveals to Jesus what he is to do and, correspondingly, what he need not do.

If when we relax we feel guilty, if we often feel as if our work is never done, then we must make time to pray. Withdrawing into solitude and simply resting in God's loving presence nurtures a life-giving relationship and prepares us to serve effectively by achieving focus born of clear direction.

**PRAYER: Loving God, when we neglect to pray, our faith, energy, and hope quickly evaporate like sidewalk puddles in the summer sun. When we become overextended and unfocused, call us back to prayer so that we receive the gift of yourself. Amen.**

Faith overcomes fear. The disciples find themselves in a terrifying storm in the middle of the night. The wind and waves furiously buffet their vessel. At first, Jesus' approach frightens them more, but then he speaks. "Take heart," he says. "It is I; do not be afraid." Wind and waves notwithstanding, the disciples recognize that voice. At the heart of this story is Jesus' majestic message to cowering believers. In response, the disciples worship him and make this Gospel's first confession of faith.

Haven't we all played Peter's role in this story? We are at times capable of bold ventures in response to Christ's commands, for those he calls he empowers. Yet, as we gain experience in Christian living, we develop the wisdom to understand that we cannot sustain faith on our own. We know well Peter's awful sinking feeling. We have been in over our heads. The icy fingers of fear have tightened around our hearts, and cries for help have emanated from the depths of our being.

What do we need today? Which is more powerful in our present experience, the world's winds or the Lord's words? In either case he can provide for our need if we but ask. To those who trust him, Jesus gives a share of his power. To those sinking in doubt, he offers prompt assistance.

**PRAYER: Lord, enable us to recognize your voice even when thunder rumbles and winds howl. Empower us to trust you in courageous ventures of faith, and rescue us when we doubt. Amen.**

Faith in Jesus Christ is the means by which we are made right with God. In our text Paul contrasts two ways of righteousness and illustrates them with quotations from the Pentateuch. Moses taught obedience to the law as a means of salvation (Lev. 18:5). Unfortunately, no one has succeeded in the quest to attain righteousness in this way. In fact, for Paul the law functioned only to show us how guilty we are (Gal. 3:19). Thankfully, in God's mercy another way of righteousness has been provided: righteousness through faith in Christ.

Sometimes religious seekers believe that they must accomplish great feats or fulfill demanding quests before they can earn right standing before God. But Paul here states that salvation is "within easy reach" (NLT). "Jesus is Lord" is a simple confession of faith, yet it is still and shall ever be sufficient. Such confessions are empowered by God's Spirit and will one day be on every tongue. What great power resides in this gospel simplicity!

Saving faith is resurrection faith. "If Christ has not been raised, then your faith is useless and you are still under condemnation for your sins" (1 Cor. 15:17). Faith is sorely tested by the reality of death, but Christian hope claims victory over death and assurance of life beyond the grave.

Paul's credentials as a Jew are impressive, but for him salvation is God's free gift to those who place their faith in the crucified and risen Jesus. There are not two ways to righteousness—only one. Paul says that "there is no distinction" between Jew and Gentile in this regard. Earlier in this letter he used this phrase when teaching that all people are lost and unable to win God's acceptance by personal effort (3:9). Now he uses it again to offer all people the wonderful assurance of pardon for sin. Jews and Gentiles alike can be reconciled to God through faith in Christ.

**PRAYER: O God, we confess that apart from your grace we are lost in our sin and without hope. Thank you for providing a way for us to be made right with you through faith in the life, death, and resurrection of your Son Jesus Christ. Amen.**

Faith comes as a gift of God's grace, activated through the hearing of God's word. Paul has established that God "is generous to all who call on him" (v. 12). Now he poses a series of rhetorical questions that lift up the crucial importance of preaching while setting the stage for a deeper exploration of Israel's spiritual condition in the section to follow.

The message of the gospel is designed to produce faith. The words "How beautiful are the feet of those who bring good news!" referred originally to messengers carrying news from Babylon to Jerusalem that the Exile was over at last and Israel's restoration would begin (Isa. 52:7). Paul uses the words here in praise of those who declare the gospel of Jesus Christ. Restoration after the Exile foreshadowed the complete, eternal deliverance wrought for us all by the person and work of Jesus. "Everyone who believes in him receives forgiveness of sins through his name" (Acts 10:43).

The need for inspired preaching is as great today as ever. Yet the task is a daunting one, and no preacher who understands what's at stake dares be cavalier about gospel proclamation. Preachers can take comfort in an observation, attributed to Calvin Coolidge, to the effect that one of the proofs of the divine nature of our gospel is the preaching it has endured. Thank God, when the word goes forth, it never returns empty but rather accomplishes its divine purpose.

Christians called to work other than preaching also play vital roles in proclaiming the good news. Their faithful living and mutual concern authenticate the gospel by demonstrating God's power at work in the believing community. Even those outside the church notice the goodness of Christians and the source of that goodness, which is God.

**PRAYER: Loving God, your good news has changed and continues to change our lives. How grateful we are! Thank you for those who preach the gospel. Bless all those who hear and respond in faith. Amen.**

# Kindred Living

*August 11–17, 2008* • *Leslee Wray*[‡]

**MONDAY, AUGUST 11** • **Read Genesis 45:1-8**

If you go nosing around in a dictionary for a lovely word like *kindred*, you might find the definition "one's blood relations," which can be a bit disappointing. Even the best of "blood relations" can let you down and fall short of anything remotely "kindred." What might inspire mutual respect, loyalty, and trust often ends up dying over the reading of the family will. That just goes to show that being related does not guarantee faithful care of one another.

Maybe that's why we understand Joseph's story. Our attempts at mediation between siblings who protest, "It's not fair!" help us see clearly Joseph's brothers and know why they do what they do. As despicable as their treachery is, we understand it. Our family ties will never be enough to save us from brokenness.

Joseph certainly learned that lesson the hard way; but in the learning, he also found kindred living to be possible with God. Through a miraculous journey of deception, loss, and suffering Joseph found God to be faithfully present. He came to recognize God not as the intentional maker of such travesty but as the Faithful Parent who would care for all of his life and deem it sacred. Like a Master Weaver, God took every piece of Joseph's life—the beautiful and horrid—and wove something redemptive, healing, and good. Such a Weaving Parent lives with us still, embracing every piece in our own lives, weaving together ways and possibilities, bringing new life out of death. Perhaps kindred living becomes possible when we embrace every piece as well.

**PRAYER: Loving God, may we trust your weaving presence to work your saving good. Amen.**

---

[‡]United Methodist clergy, presently serving as the chaplain for Hospice of Stanly County and The Lutheran Home; living with her family on their farm in Mt. Gilead, North Carolina.

Like many of her generation, my grandmother was a saver. Long white gloves and boxes of decorative hats with netting and feathers were stored in my grandmother's attic, waiting, it would seem, to be donned once again when the world came back to its senses. Jar after jar of strawberry jelly lined her pantry because, well, one can never have too much strawberry jelly. And my grandmother had jars of pennies, at least twenty-five of them, dispersed throughout the house—under the bed, behind the couch, buried in a closet corner for any number of saving purposes. My grandmother saw worth in a good many things that the rest of the world had already thrown away.

When I get to this place in Joseph's story, I think of him and my grandmother as kindred spirits. I don't know how he managed his possessions, but he sure considered his brothers worth saving. You remember them. They're the brutes who wanted Joseph dead. And yet, despite everything he endured because of them, he won't throw them away.

With a wave of his hand Joseph can be rid of his brothers, have things settled once and for all. But he won't do it. He's discovered the faithful presence of a loving God. Where once he thought kindred living impossible, now he finds it to be a saving reality. Learning of God's desire to live with him completely, to be with him in a kindred way, Joseph now offers true kindred living to those who once wished him dead.

This part of the story exudes raw emotion. This is no "let's put on a good face" reunion. This is the real thing for Joseph and his brothers. A jar of pennies is one thing; being loved by a kindred God is quite another. It's redemptive.

**PRAYER: Kindred God, redeem us with your saving love. Amen.**

## WEDNESDAY, AUGUST 13 • Read Psalm 133

On those days when it seems as if we humans will never learn to get along, Psalm 133 is a good one to pull out. It's a good choice not because it's the way things are but more as a faithful nudge of what's possible. Believed to be a psalm of "ascent," it was one many worshipers sang on their way to the temple in Jerusalem. It offers a clear picture of how folks might relate and get along, making kindred living look possible. Its vivid wording reads like your dream-house blueprints. You can't walk in the front door yet, but the framing is up. That "outline" compels you to keep building as you see the house for what it will be.

More amazing still, the Southern and Northern Kingdoms have split, drastically changing the covenantal identity of the people of Israel and their spirit of unity. Fierce discord and anything-but-kindred living is in sight.

And yet, this psalm finds its way into the worshiping community of the day. In the midst of dire circumstances and unrest, these folk choose to sing songs and pray prayers of what can be. They look beyond what they see and live into a vision of one day being reunified. They make plans for how their lives will center in Jerusalem once again, praying that a descendant of David will sit on the throne. These dreamers offer worship and praise as if they're already back together, serving God and neighbor. But more than anything, they embrace kindred living where brothers and sisters alike may dwell together in harmony. If only for a brief moment, they live as if it has already come to pass.

That's what singing a psalm like 133 must have done for them. It compelled them to lives of faith. Perhaps it can do the same for us.

**PRAYER: Loving God, may we live as we hope, pray, and believe. Amen.**

In our first year of marriage, my husband and I hit our first "bump." The source of the disagreement is forgotten, but how we cared for each other is not. It came in the middle of the night when one is not always at his or her best to articulate hopes and dreams. First, words were spoken to no reconciling avail. Then the one called "He" relocated upstairs. Finally, "She" left the premises.

At the time, my husband and I lived in a small town with few places to go in the middle of the night. But the twenty-four-hour Food Lion grocery store seemed an obvious choice for a stubborn newlywed who needed to have the last word. After stomping around in the frozen foods for a while, "She" finally settled in at the magazine rack where "She" sadly learned Kathy Lee would be leaving Regis. Nothing like the tabloids to lower your blood pressure and bring you back to your senses.

Finally realizing "She" needed to go home, "She" went out to the parking lot and found a worried-looking "He" coming after her. There's something to be said for living in a small town.

But there's far more to be said about making a covenant with another human being. The day comes brimming over with promise and possibility, with mutual respect and care. You cannot imagine loving any more deeply than you do this day.

Then something happens. You take your covenant out for a spin. It gets muddy; the shine wears off. It no longer looks and feels the same. Is the covenant broken? No. It's deeper, truer, more refined. And you discover a depth of love you're just beginning to know.

It's a grace to share covenant when things are going well. But it's healing to live in unity when you're feeling broken. "For there, the LORD ordained his blessing, life forevermore."

**PRAYER: Healing God, may we remain in covenant relationship, even when we feel broken and wounded. Amen.**

There's something to be said for "necessary disobedience." Sharing lunch with some second-graders has made me a believer. I met them while they were serving a sentence of "silent lunch." For various crimes of disobedience and noncompliance these young hooligans had been exiled to a separate table of no words. One poor fellow, however, didn't get the memo and thought it was lunch as usual. No sooner had he uttered his first word than his teacher whisked him away to a place unknown. I can only imagine he was sent to the jail where he's now doing hard time for talking with his mouth full. This was serious business, and they knew it. Settling in, the group contemplated its lot and the overwhelming intricacies of chicken fajitas.

I know all of this because my own little outlaw sat at the table that day. In fact, she'd been at the table several days. I like to think it was her way of living in solidarity with the oppressed. Her teacher thought differently. So I went to sit with her because we were both short on answers. What I found was a table of revolutionaries.

One by one they glanced at me, smiled, and made silent offerings of their lunch to me. My daughter steadily hugged my arm. I don't think they believed I'd make it on my own. "Silent lunch" was tough, and I was going to need all the help I could get. Though branded with a scarlet *D*, they modeled character development for which any teacher could be proud. I never considered how transforming disobedience can be.

But Paul did. He believed it would be the catalyst that would one day bring the Jews around to Jesus. Sometimes I think we have to say no before we can say yes. Just the other day, I heard some second-graders saying yes.

**PRAYER: Gentle God, transform our disobedience into a necessary grace. Amen.**

About a year ago, I initiated a move from the local church to an extension ministry. My family was in the throes of moving, wrestling with the upheaval that such a decision inspires. Perpetual second-guessing became my M.O. (Method of Operation). Was my decision a sincere response to inward discernment or one of desperation from feeling lost in a vocation I dearly loved? This move would disrupt a lot of lives. Was I being faithful or selfish? Was I directing my heart, or was the One who resided there running the show?

By the time we get to Matthew 15, the Pharisees are ready to rumble with Jesus. Thinking they'll take him to task over his disciples' unprecedented behavior, they pounce, "Tradition!" Only Jesus isn't having it. Like a mad mama bear, Jesus goes after their hypocrisy and manipulating self-interest. Sadly, the Pharisees leave mad and unchanged.

Meanwhile, the disciples worry this run-in will get back to the pastor-parish committee. But Jesus is in no mood to coddle them. So he lays it out plain: Faithfulness doesn't happen by knowing the scriptures cover to cover or having all the right answers. It grows and flourishes as we seek to live out the good desires of God's heart inspired by God's word. It alights when we get out of the way of ourselves and make room for the unprecedented ways of God. The Pharisees missed this. The disciples almost did. The slope of self-preservation is so slippery that we can miss it too. We tell ourselves that our personal heart's desire is what God wants for us as well.

The good news is that we're loved by a kindred God who moves with us in all our second-guessing, hypocrisy, and growth. Openness to such love can make all the difference in what we live out.

**PRAYER: Come, Lord Jesus. Amen.**

Among my children's many lessons to me relates to my apparent inability to listen. Before they complete a question or remark, I chime in with the "untold wisdom" I'm certain is my responsibility to promote as their parent. My atrocious habit has become so familiar that they now say, "Mama, just listen!"

As I contemplate this self-absorbed position of mine, the story of Jesus' encounter with the Canaanite woman offers grace. Some say the story reflects Jesus' hesitancy to respond so the woman will dig all the more for the gift she needs. Others say the Canaanite woman's profession of Jesus as the Messiah is a powerful affirmation of the gospel's being for everyone,

But personally, I think this encounter is Jesus' invitation to look again. Coming on the heels of his conversation with the disciples about the motivations of the heart, Jesus offers himself as an example of what faithful living looks like. Yes, he hesitates with the woman—but even there he reveals the power and grace of faithful discernment. Had he not taken the time to reflect and look again, he might have led with his first impression: the woman was an outsider, a pup wanting prime rib in place of the designated canned food. Instead of leaving it at that, Jesus looks again and discovers a great woman of faith. His honest struggle is both gift and generous example that has not been lost on me.

If I too will look and listen as a mother, I realize I don't have all the goods. I learn that my children have some "untold wisdom" of their own; and if my children, then maybe a multitude of others. Sometimes we miss the boat on faithful living because we haven't found a way to look and listen. Looking and listening makes kindred living possible.

**PRAYER: God, help us look and listen. Amen.**

# Making Tough Decisions

*August 18–24, 2008* • *Wallace H. Kirby*[‡]

## MONDAY, AUGUST 18 • Read Exodus 1:8-22

"Then a new king, who did not know about Joseph, came to power in Egypt" (NIV). In one chilling sentence the fate of a people is sealed. The king, troubled by the increasing number of Israelites and the fear of their joining forces with Egyptian enemies, gives an order to two Hebrew midwives: "When you help the Hebrew women in childbirth, . . . if it is a boy, kill him" (NIV).

Those two midwives are Shiphrah and Puah. Did they work separately in their birthing tasks? Were they sisters? Did they decide together the reason they would give the king for not killing the babies? We do not know the personal history of each one, but we do know that they were courageous women who feared God more than any earthly king. Their allegiance to God gave them the courage to make a tough decision.

These two women play a decisive role in the biblical story. Their brave action sets the stage for a series of events that lead to the Exodus. Two ordinary midwives, despite possible punishment for defying the king's edict, make a momentous decision.

Whatever role we play in life, we have to make decisions. Even when they seem trivial, they still carry shoots of everlastingness in our lives and those of others. God, through prayer, gives us wisdom and determination to make some tough decisions.

**PRAYER: God of grace and love, you have graced us with the gift of life. You challenge us to live with a faith that gives us courage and guidance as we make tough decisions. Grant us the wisdom to make the right decisions. Amen.**

---

[‡]Retired United Methodist pastor, living in Asheville, North Carolina.

"A man from the house of Levi went and married a Levite woman. The woman conceived and bore a son." This story involves three women: the baby's mother, the baby's sister, and the king's daughter. Yesterday we read the harsh decree of the new Egyptian king that all male Hebrew babies were to be drowned in the Nile River. When the Hebrew mother can no longer hide her boy baby, she makes a tough decision. She prepares a waterproof basket, places the baby in it, and floats it in the Nile, trusting that some Egyptian woman will find the basket and take the baby as her own. The baby's sister watches to see if the baby is rescued. The king's daughter comes to the river, finds the basket, and decides to keep and care for the baby. Each of these women made a tough decision.

Many women today live in relationships and situations that require them to make tough decisions. Some choose to stay; some choose to leave.

Alienation had been building in one couple's marriage for years. All the factors that destroy or enhance a marriage came into play: money, relationship, family, religion, sex. She resented his salary when compared to her earnings. They socialized little together. He found strength through prayer, the church, and weekly worship. She ended her relationship with the church. She became pregnant but had a miscarriage. At his insistence they went to a counselor and after almost two years were told that they had to make a decision about their marriage. This was a tough decision for them both; they chose divorce. God is with us in all life's tough decisions, ready to bring new life to us and to others as we go forward.

SUGGESTION FOR MEDITATION: Take an inventory of people whom you know have made or are making tough decisions and offer supportive prayers.

How does a believer offer proof of God's existence? Theologians have proclaimed it. Philosophers have written theories that offer proof of God's being. Faithful believers declare that life experiences confirm God's presence.

Psalm 124 raises the probing question, "What if the LORD had not been on our side?" As the people of Israel recited this psalm in their worship, they would remember the story of Moses, which began with Shiphrah and Puah, his mother and sister and his rescue, the escape from the harsh times under Egyptian captivity. Their answer would sound forth, "Our help is in the name of the LORD."

I often wonder what my life would have been like had God not been guiding and directing me. What way would I have taken? What enemy would have destroyed me? What flood waters would have drowned me?

Had the Lord not been on my side, I could never have left the security of a place in business and society to enter the ministry; I could never have stood in a pulpit and preached for forty years; I could not have endured seeing indifference and apathy in the parish; I could not have faced rejection by my peers; I could not have refrained from revenge when I felt unjust anger and criticism directed at me; I could not have endured the flood of grief when my wife died after a four-year battle with cancer or when my son was killed in an automobile accident. I could not have escaped suicide when overwhelmed with depression. The Lord "lifted me out of the ditch, pulled me from deep mud" (Ps. 40:2, THE MESSAGE).

My friend tells me that life is what happens while you're making other plans. Only with the Lord on my side did I avoid being overwhelmed by the events of life; "the snare is broken, and [I] have escaped."

**SUGGESTION FOR PRAYER: Give thanks for the ways in which God has guided you in the past and continues that guidance, helping you escape life's snares.**

We can be shaped, like a cookie cutter shapes dough, to fit the world's expectations. Or we can be shaped like a seed shapes a flower. Paul appeals to us, "Do not be conformed to this world, but be transformed by the renewing of your minds, so that you may discern what is the will of God." That appeal gives us the courage to make some tough decisions.

When a sudden storm arose at camp, sixteen-year-old Stephanie raced for shelter. Lightning struck a pine tree, and the bolt ran through her body. She lay in the intensive care unit of the hospital for a week, kept alive by a machine that breathed for her. The medical team knew her brain was dead. When Stephanie got her driver's license, she had decided to become an organ donor. In light of their daughter's decision, her parents consented to cutting the breathing machine off and allowing her organs to be harvested.

Bob's drinking had caused the loss of community respect, the loss of his grocery business, and almost the loss of his family. He found it hard to admit that he was the cause of these losses. He did seek help, however, through Alcoholics Anonymous. Six years after that decision, he had regained his self-respect, the respect of the community, a new business venture, and a stable family life. Stephanie, her parents, and Bob made decisions not to be "conformed" but to choose a more godly way.

A student was admonished by the college president because he had broken a campus rule. His defense: "Sir, I'd wager that there are not ten men on the whole campus who wouldn't have done exactly what I did under the circumstances."

The president replied, "Young man, has it occurred to you that you might have been one of those ten?"

**PRAYER: God of grace, renew our minds so that we may discern your will when we have to make tough decisions. Amen.**

We look at the world and the people around us and see incredible diversity. Paul lets us know that God has a design for each of us and that God provides guidance and help in meeting our particular design. Each of us has a place in this diversity, just as the many parts of our human body have different functions.

Twenty-six of us registered for a pilgrimage to the Holy Land. Some folks I knew before the journey because we had spent time together learning the history and geography of Israel. The additional persons in the group were only names on a paper sent by the agency.

As I began to associate with these people I did not yet know, I noted that Karen was a loner. She was always at the front of the line as we walked from site to site. She also often sat alone at mealtime. One evening I sat at the end of a table for six, directly across from Karen. Since the others were conversing, I engaged Karen in dialogue. I asked questions about her hometown, her family, her work.

I learned that she had been divorced for nineteen years, had reared her daughter with no help from her former husband, and was now financing the girl's college education. Karen, a nurse who works in a retirement home, ministers to the elderly residents. A devout church member, she anticipated this trip as the fulfillment of a longtime dream. My impression of this "loner" changed after that dinner conversation. I saw her as a vital part of our pilgrimage.

Paul reminds me of how some of my prejudgments are unfair, and how difficult it can be to approach a person I have categorized.

**SUGGESTION FOR MEDITATION: Think of a person you have categorized or prejudged in some way. Decide to engage that person in dialogue.**

The disciples respond when Jesus asks what people say about his identity. Rumors are swirling; the disciples can easily answer this request. I have tried to imagine which disciple spoke up. Perhaps Philip said, "John the Baptist" because he, himself, was an evangelist like John. Matthew, so steeped in the Old Testament, might have conjectured, "Elijah," for the Jews expected the return of Elijah before the coming of the Messiah. Simon the Zealot might have said, "Jeremiah," for he expected that prophet to be his country's help in time of trouble.

But then the situation gets a bit sticky. Jesus turns to question them specifically about their own thoughts of who he is. Peter, the outspoken one, readily speaks up—and amazingly enough, Peter gets it right! Peter might not have been able to give a theological account and a philosophical expression of what he meant when he said that Jesus was the "Son of the living God." Peter knew that no mere human description adequately described Jesus Christ.

"You—what do you think of me?" That is a question we all must answer. Our knowledge of Jesus can never be secondhand. I might be able to summarize his teachings or memorize the Sermon on the Mount. I can offer my views on Christology. I may know a lot about Jesus, but I must know Jesus myself, for he demands a personal verdict.

The Gospel of John helps me put words to my personal experiences of Jesus: the light of my life (8:12), bread for my journey (6:35), my shepherd (10:11), my Lord (13:14).

**PRAYER: Jesus, bid me come to know you in such a way that I, like Peter, may claim you as Messiah. Amen.**

Ted, one of my friends, made a decision one night in the coal mine where he worked. He was in his thirties, with a wife and two children, and had only a high school education. He decided to leave his job to attend college and then seminary. His life changed that night. Ted's decision was one answer to the question that Jesus posed to the disciples: "Who do people say that the Son of Man is?" Some of the disciples report news and opinion, but then Jesus asks, "Who do you say that I am?" Throughout the centuries, the church proudly echoes the words of Peter: "You are the Messiah, the Son of the living God."

The incident at Caesarea Philippi is a pivotal one for the group that followed Jesus and for all disciples since then. This moment remains the crucial one for the disciples. Our response to Jesus' question sustains and strengthens all the choices that we will make in our daily Christian discipleship.

Two brothers James and John ran a successful fishing business with their father. One day Jesus walked by and called them to follow him. They accepted his call without delay. (See Mark 1:19-20.)

"Who do you say that I am?" Each day we hear Jesus' question as if for the first time. We choose to respond, like Peter, as if this were the first time we responded. Our choice is critical. Being a follower of Jesus calls us to serve God in this day, this moment. We proclaim the good news of the gospel with words and with actions because we are answering Jesus' question. We move forward as disciples or we regress.

Take time to notice how you answer Jesus' question *today*; notice how your response establishes today's priorities.

**PRAYER: Great God, your love is new every day. Each day you invite us to choose whom we will serve. Sustain us by your love that we may choose rightly, through Jesus Christ we pray. Amen.**

# Planted on a Firm Foundation

*August 25–31, 2008 • M. Garlinda Burton[‡]*

**MONDAY, AUGUST 25 • Read Exodus 3:1-12**

By early adulthood, Moses has led a tumultuous life. As an infant, he was marked for death, then rescued and adopted by the daughter of the ruling Egyptian pharaoh. Although he lived his early years in relative comfort, he was doubtless confused, sharing the heritage of enslaved people and the privilege of their oppressors. By Exodus 3, Moses has fled to Midian to avoid a murder conviction, reduced to tending sheep for his father-in-law. He is man with a confused past and no clear direction for his future.

However, God has a plan for Moses and reveals it in a blaze of glory. Moses leaves the sacred mountain of Horeb a changed person. From a man underemployed and of confused loyalties, Moses is transformed into a person sure of his place as an instrument of God's power and justice. He goes from languishing on sinking sand in a strange land to standing firmly on the Rock of salvation.

The chorus of one of my favorite pop songs reminds me that when I stand on the Rock, nothing can defeat me. I sing it as a prayer whenever my confidence flags. The words tell me that each of us has a vital role in the work and will of the God who created us, who saved us, and who loves us fiercely. Yes, challenges confront us; pain assails us; and even death threatens us. But nothing can defeat us if we, like Moses, plant our feet and hearts firmly in God through Christ, the solid Rock.

**PRAYER: As you spoke to a confused and downcast Moses, O God, and showed him his place in your divine plan for the world, so may I too hear your call upon my life. Dear One, use me this day to do your will. Amen.**

---

[‡]Member of Hobson United Methodist Church, Nashville, Tennessee, where she mentors teens and directs the women's choir; General Secretary of the General Commission on the Status and Role of Women of The United Methodist Church.

## TUESDAY, AUGUST 26 • Read Exodus 3:13–15

During Sunday morning worship it is not unusual for people in my congregation to respond aloud to a poignant line read in the morning scripture or a well-turned phrase in the pastor's sermon or even a flawless high note sung by a soloist. Worship at my church is a like a rhythmic dance with swaying and clapping punctuating each fervent phrase.

One woman in the congregation is usually quiet for most of the service. However, if the pastor or liturgist concludes any prayer or reading with, "In Jesus' name," her clear, reverent voice is sure to be heard repeating with emphasis, "Yes, in Jesus' name." With just those three words, this woman can sing psalm-worthy praise or invoke God's help in the most troubled times.

When God commands Moses to go to Pharaoh and demand release of the captives, Moses asks, "Who am I that I should go to Pharaoh?" And he further asks, "Who are you to send me?" God declares, "I AM WHO I AM." In other words, God says, "I am the firm foundation of all that is, the Creator of all people. The Rock of Ages. Whatever you call me, I named you before you were born, and I will be with you a thousand years hence."

I find especially moving those songs, prayers, and poems that use the image of a solid rock to describe the triune God. In that image, I can understand the eternal loving presence, the absolute steadfastness, and the unshakable attendance of God's love. When I sing, "On Christ the solid rock I stand/All other ground is sinking sand," I see the face of my church sister and hear her declare simply, "In Jesus' name"; and I know for sure that in Jesus' name I live, move, and have my being. In Jesus' name, hatred is undone; slaves are freed; swords are beaten into plowshares; and grace is greater than any other force on earth.

What will you do differently today because you stand on the Rock of salvation? because you order your steps in Jesus' name?

**PRAYER: Loving God, amid the confusion and challenges of this day, remind me that I am called to seek justice, love kindness, and move boldly as you call me in Jesus' name. Amen.**

Psalm 105 is a musical recounting of God's great deeds, specifically the release of the ancient Hebrews from slavery in the days of Moses. The first few verses of introduction remind those ancestors of freed slaves that their very being is inextricably linked to that ancient covenant between their forebears and the eternal and almighty God. As heirs of that covenant, they are called to offer regular praise to the One who continues to deliver them from all adversity, and they are to let the world know that God is the Rock of their salvation.

That covenant continues today for us. All of us are invited to share in that sanctified heritage, to build a personal relationship with the God who loves us, and to remember the many stories of God's mighty deeds on behalf of those who have ever been oppressed, enslaved, weary, bowed down, hopeless, or troubled. We are called to celebrate God's presence in our lives, to worship God with gladness and thanksgiving, and to tell our own stories of how God moves and works in our lives.

Retired United Methodist bishop Leontyne T. C. Kelly can preach the roof off the sanctuary merely by reciting with passion the words of the old hymn "How Firm a Foundation." I've heard her preach that hymn many times, and her absolute assurance that she—indeed, all of us—are connected to one another by eons of creation, sacrifices, burning-bush inspiration, salvation, struggle, prayer, and praise always electrifies me. The bishop declares that the words of the hymn, like the words of the biblical psalm, remind us that the same God who created the world and sent Moses and raised Jesus, is the same God who walks with us at this very moment in all our circumstances. The story of the rescued Hebrews is also our story. The psalm of remembrance and celebration is our song. Praise the God of the ages, who has laid for all people a solid foundation of changeless love.

**PRAYER: O God, regardless of my struggles, yours is a love that will never let me go. May I live in such a way that everyone I meet will see the light of your salvation in me. Amen.**

"God is faithful," my best friend, Toni, often says. She should know; Toni embodies God's faithfulness. At this writing, she is caring for her elderly mother who has cancer. Toni lives three hours away from her mom but drives up every other weekend for doctors' appointments and to confer with paid caregivers, pay bills, cook her mother's favorite foods, and style her mother's hair.

Toni usually drives home early Monday morning, straight to her office. She barely has time to do her own laundry, care for her own household concerns, or even take a day's respite before she is back in Kentucky again.

Whenever I wonder aloud about the toll this is taking on her, Toni admits that she is tired. However, she loves her mom, the woman who has been there for her during the best and worst times of her life. Toni feels she is merely returning a little of the love and care she has received. For her, it is that simple.

For twenty-five years I've watched the interplay between this mother and daughter. Before her mother's illness, she and Toni's late father celebrated Toni's quarterly weekend visits home like most people would mark New Year's Eve. Her mom cooked her favorite foods, fixed up her room, and reordered her schedule around Toni's visit. Her mother always reminded Toni that she was a special and irreplaceable gift from God and could always come home.

In Psalm 105, the celebrant recounts the specific events of God's "everlasting covenant" with the descendants of Abraham. It is a reminder that God is faithful, even in times of confusion, fear, danger, and loss. We have only to remember that God loves us as a watchful mother or an attendant daughter loves. How do we express our gratitude? With whom do we share that love?

**SUGGESTION FOR REFLECTION: Someone needs your faithful, steadfast prayers and presence this day. Is it an elderly relative? a hurting child? a prison inmate? a grieving neighbor? an ill coworker? a politician struggling to make the right decision? How will you respond?**

"Present your bodies as a living sacrifice, holy and acceptable to God," says Paul. For many of us, this is much easier said than done. With bodies (and souls) fed by junk food and reality TV, compressed schedules, lack of exercise, family/household responsibilities, and apathy about our spiritual lives, it is sometimes embarrassing to think about what kind of physical offering we are to God.

Last year, I was diagnosed with diabetes. I wasn't surprised. My husband had died of lung cancer two years earlier; when he was diagnosed, I went into an emotional and physical tailspin. I stopped sleeping, hoping, and exercising. I subsisted on junk food. I shut myself off from everyone—including God (whom I blamed for letting my husband die). By the first anniversary of my husband's death, I had gained fifty pounds, my blood pressure had soared—and now diabetes.

When I returned from the doctor's office, however, I picked up my Bible. Inside, I found a bookmark with the poem "Footprints in the Sand," which reminded me that God had not deserted me. In fact, God had carried me through the most difficult passage of all. Even when I turned my back and began to self-destruct, God was there to guide me back to life.

Since my diagnosis, I have been able to control my diabetes with weight loss, diet, and exercise. My spiritual discipline and physical self-care have enhanced my relationships, my work, and my play. I have deepened my dependence on and trust in Christ.

All of us are called to discern and use our unique, God-given gifts. Finding our gift may entail confronting competing concerns that interfere with our embracing the gift. The good news is that God is not keeping score, comparing us by weight, class, hairstyle, income, or status. All of us comprise the body of Christ, and God has given all of us the tools we need to achieve "living sacrifice" status.

**PRAYER: O God, you are my strength and the center of my joy. Help me discern what is good and acceptable to you. Amen.**

As Paul is writing the letter to the Romans, he is in the midst of a great evangelistic endeavor, preaching redemption in Christ, with the goal of engaging Jewish traditionalists and Gentile outsiders. It is no easy task. After all, Paul was once Saul, a harsh Gentile persecutor of those who followed Jesus. The fact that he has made a dramatic about-face and is becoming the best-known apostle no doubt raises suspicion and resentment among the old faithful and the new seekers alike. Some believed that old Saul was up to some trick; others feared new Paul would make the new faith about himself alone.

Most of us have faced this dilemma. When we undertake a needed change in our lives—from extending the olive branch to a former enemy to losing weight or kicking the cigarette habit—some friends are cheering us on. But there are also those who mistrust our motives or claim to have liked us better fat or who accuse us of having a self-righteous sense of superiority.

Instead of fighting against this sentiment with harsh words and denouncements, Paul offers a message of humility, patience, and love. Paul reminds his hearers—and himself—to stay focused on the right things: "Live in harmony with one another; . . . Do not repay anyone evil for evil; . . . If your enemies are hungry, feed them."

I have discovered that my faith-walk is easier when I focus more on doing God's will and less on worrying about what others think they know about me as a Christian. Our task is to live as faithfully as we can, and, to paraphrase Paul, that includes resisting the temptation to repay nay-saying with nay-saying.

**PRAYER: God of forgiveness, someone is trying a new thing, attempting to serve you better in a new way; and it isn't easy. Let your word be a lamp unto his or her path today. Amen.**

## SUNDAY, AUGUST 31 • Read Matthew 16:21-28

In spring 2006, I visited a small church in Bulgaria. An eighty-eight-year-old woman, a church member all her life, recalled that she had lived in the town as a Christian during the most hostile occupation by Communist rulers. Worship in those days was monitored for subversive teachings; people of faith were bullied and pressured on the job; and soldiers would accost her on the street as she walked to Bible class on weeknights. Her faith never wavered, even when threatened with harm by anti-Christian police officers.

As I listened to her story, I thought about the current popularity (at least in the United States) of Christians who espouse "prosperity theology." The idea is that if you're "right with God," you'll get a good job, live in a nice house, and provide for your family. The flip side implies that people who are poor and hungry, who suffer, who are pushed to the economic and social margins just aren't faithful enough. Greed, warring, avarice, and consumerism gone rampant aren't to blame—it is those who suffer who don't have sufficient spiritual fortitude.

When Jesus predicts that his own earthly ministry will end in suffering and death, Peter argues against it. Jesus then denounces Peter as a "stumbling block." Faithful living is not all glory, ease, and flowery epitaphs. Faithful living is a ministry of servanthood that requires humility and sacrifice—sometimes even death.

Does that mean that we shouldn't count our blessings or celebrate our achievements? Of course not. But in a world still bound by trouble on every side, God has called us to trumpet the notion that Christian jubilee is intended for all people. We are to do justice and walk humbly with God, whether the road is easy or rough. Prosperity is not to be found in things and power but rather in a closer walk with the Rock of Ages.

SUGGESTION FOR MEDITATION: **When have I chosen to forfeit my life for the things of the world?**

PRAYER: **Dear God, remind me today that being a follower of Christ has its own demands. Amen.**

# Living in God's Community

*September 1–7, 2008 • Mary O. Benedict[‡]*

## MONDAY, SEPTEMBER 1 • Read Psalm 148

How will we live together? That is a question we face at all levels of experience. The theme of living in God's community emerges in this week's scriptures: the push of Old Testament laws and wisdom and the pull of salvation's coming day in Romans 13, the about-to-be liberated community where no one is left behind in Exodus 12, how we handle grievances within our church assemblies in Matthew 18, and the imperative in Psalm 148 for all animate and inanimate things in the universe to live as community in the praise of their Maker.

The enactment of mutual honor and deference within the divine community (the Holy Trinity) is ever extending the invitation to all creatures living in community. The triune God seeks to gather us into God's own self, where we are one with another in the triune God, living, loving, and praising. As we experience this community we welcome a foretaste of that glory yet to come, when we will no longer see through a glass darkly but will see God face-to-face.

We begin and end this week with attention to Psalm 148 because praise is the portal that honors the Creator of all things. So whether you are star or storm, king or princess, man or woman, old or young, let us praise God together in relationship with all of God's creation. Surely this God is worthy of our worship and adoration. With one voice we bless our Creator.

SUGGESTION FOR MEDITATION: **Try your hand at writing a psalm of praise. Do not ask God for anything. Simply write about the wonder of who God is and how God's wonder affects you.**

---

[‡]Retired manager of The Upper Room Living Prayer Center; living a contemplative life with her husband in Waialua, Hawaii.

She was so open and vulnerable; in that moment of time she became transparent. Her husband had recently returned from the war in Iraq, and the adjustments were major. The emotions of the strain and stress of months of separation on their relationship and the family, now that he was safely home, were free to surface with a vengeance.

Every woman (mostly military wives) around that table could identify with her pain. The Bible study group members moved from the safety of their seats and gathered around her to pray. They reached out with the laying on of hands to minister to her. This way of praying was new to them; the presence of the Holy Spirit was palpable. In this chapel in Okinawa we were all aware that we were standing on holy ground. The law of love had been fulfilled in our midst that very day.

Fulfilling the law of love—putting "on the Lord Jesus Christ" (v. 14) involves action. In the musical *My Fair Lady*, Eliza Doolittle sings, "Don't talk of love. . . . Show me!" As in this reading, love is less about feelings and more about action. Love in action determines the fulfillment of the law of love. We need not keep a handy list of dos and don'ts that we monitor and consider—we need only to love neighbor as we love ourselves.

The sense of urgency in this passage compels us to express love by reaching out to one another to bring what is hidden in the dark out into the light. The imperative to live a life of love is not merely living honorably or respectably; our vocation is to put on the armor of light and to clothe ourselves with the heart, mind, and work of Jesus Christ. The need of the hurting world is the context of living out this vocation, whether in Rome in the first century or our village, town, or city in 2008.

PRAYER: **God of light and truth, give us discernment and wisdom to know how our actions reveal your love in our immediate surroundings. May our intentional loving be salve for the hurting world so that your light and truth prevail. Amen.**

Paul says that love trumps all. His ultimate interest is not legal requirements, social conventions, or political expediencies. Paul focuses on the final result—the reconciliation of all things in the divine embrace. Paul, aware of the demand and obligations of the social and political order, urges his readers to "pay to all what is due them." Yet, when everything is said and done, it is love that fulfills God's law.

The laws listed in verses 9-10 address the behaviors that take place in the "night" of Roman culture. The people Paul addresses would know well the dark side of pagan Rome; they may even be seduced by it. To them Paul says, "Don't live that way. Rather, put on the Lord Jesus Christ and so fulfill the law of love." The commandments cited in verse 9 correspond roughly to the practices of darkness.

However, this passage focuses on more than just meeting moral demands. While observing the law may accomplish a certain end, love not only accomplishes that end but goes beyond it, anticipating the coming "day" of God in living out of relationships with brothers and sisters in the church. Here Paul specifically speaks of loving one another in relationship in the small house churches of Rome as concrete expressions of the salvation that is coming. However, in reading the text for our time, the conviction that love trumps all includes both relationships within our congregation and our relationships in the wider world.

**PRAYER: Gracious God, help us faithfully walk in the light of your love. Reveal to us those times we choose to live according to the rules rather than love. In the name of the one whose love took the form of a cross. Amen.**

The Passover is not an ordinary day. It is singular; God's action sets it apart from all others. It will be remembered and rehearsed every year to come. This meal may have been the first fast food, but it is not just any fast food! This is fuel for deliverance!

This day of deliverance isn't just for one or a few—but for *all* in the community. God calls for corporate participation. God's detailed instruction leaves nothing to chance. Israel's job is to follow through. All in the community will see the hand of God, though they do not yet fully grasp what God is doing. They are to obey, individually and collectively. In so doing, no one will be left behind or left out; no household will be too small. All receive provision.

In Jewish reckoning of time, the new day begins with sunset. In this new day, God extends an invitation to relationship. This collaboration features God's initiating action and Israel's responsive participation. Saint Augustine summed up this relationship, "Without us God will not, and without God we cannot." This is where our faith community's journey began. This is how we* came into being. Each year we tell the story and remember who we are. A delivered people! Ritual is patterned action and a form of enacted story. Each time we celebrate the liturgy of the Eucharist, we rehearse the narrative work of God in Israel and in Jesus Christ, and we find ourselves there in the story! We eat and are delivered. We remember and set out together on the journey. This is our story. This is who we are!

**PRAYER: Delivering God, who are we that you should call us into relationship, that you should love us so much? Cause us to live as delivered people. Empower us to collaborate with you, drawing into your love all those within our reach. In the name of the One who stretched out his arms for all. Amen.**

---

*While this is Israel's story, we Christians also claim the Paschal story, rejoicing in God's mighty action that formed and sustained a covenant community.

Matthew's Gospel was written long enough after Christ's resurrection for internal divisions and wounds to surface within the church. When disagreement turns to dispute and dispute turns to division, Jesus lays out simple (not easy), practical guidelines for recovering the integrity and wholeness of the body of Christ. However, some may remain unrepentant and choose to reside outside the community.

Yet there is a possibility and responsibility that takes the community to a level beyond settling disputes and dealing with sin, whether or not the offending member chooses repentance. "Truly I tell you, whatever you bind on earth will be bound in heaven and whatever you loose on earth will be loosed in heaven." John's Gospel offers a parallel text: "If you forgive the sins of any, they are forgiven them; if you retain the sins of any, they are retained" (20:23). Both statements reflect an ambiguity about what church members are to do with this loosing and binding, forgiving and retaining. What part do we play in extending or constricting God's grace?

As a child, I was molested by a family member. This event haunted me for years; I struggled in my relationship with that person. I admitted to my daughter that I wanted my "day in court." I wanted to be heard; I wanted the silence broken and responsibility acknowledged. When the person who had abused me died, memories of the molestation overwhelmed me, and I cried out to God, "Will these be the only memories I have of him?" When I shared this thought with my daughter, her response stunned me: "Mom, can't you see? Today you had your day in court. He is accountable to God for what he did to you, but, because you have forgiven him, he will not stand under judgment!" Trusting this gospel word, I could now thank God; what I had loosed on earth was truly loosed in heaven!

**SUGGESTION FOR MEDITATION: What situation in your life or in your church binds you and needs to be loosed? What will you choose to do about that?**

## SATURDAY, SEPTEMBER 6 • Read Matthew 18:15–20

This passage offers another dimension of the power of living in community. "Where two or three are gathered in my name, I am there among them." When the community of Christ prays together, God shows up with power to restore, to make whole, and to mend broken relationships.

Those who exercise with a partner are more likely to continue the discipline than those who exercise alone. In Covenant Discipleship groups, the "buddy system" sustains us in mutual accountability. Even in nature we see the power of two. Zebras often stand in pairs, head to tail, tail to head, using their tails to swat flies off the other and act as eyes in the back. Enemies coming from either direction are quickly seen. We commonly say and believe that "there's safety in numbers."

But this text involves more than merely human support and communal power. The community is the context of the continuing realization of the risen Christ. (See Matthew 1:23; 18:20; 28:19-20.) Matthew's Gospel holds a clear vision of Christ with us and among us to the end of the age.

Each of our passages this week explores and affirms that we are communal beings, from the microchurches in ancient Rome to our growing awareness of ecological relationship with all things. As Christians we do not live as lone rangers. Baptized into the Christian community, we acknowledge that solitary piety contradicts biblical understandings of Christian living. Our vocation is to work out our salvation, inward and personal and outward and social, as members (in the organic sense more than organizational) of the body of Christ. In every context, grace draws us up into the love and life of the Trinity. We are invited again and again to know God through the power of community.

SUGGESTION FOR MEDITATION: **When have you experienced God's presence through the power of community? What were the short-term and long-term effects of life in community? How will you strengthen the sense and experience of community for yourself and others?**

The psalmist invokes praise, moving from heaven to the earth to the nations to Israel's covenant community. Our ecologically threatened habitat cries out for religious communities to embrace the planet in the praise of God's name. The psalm is an extended imperative addressed to all of creation to praise its Maker. From time to time, we experience unique opportunities to share in the wonder of creation and the sense that we commune with other creatures in the praise of God. Here is one such moment in my life.

The beach was completely deserted but for the two of us. The monk seal had come onto the beach to rest. Her gaze made me feel she was as struck by me as I was by her. I sat down barely a yard from her. She had beautiful, large brown eyes and did not appear the slightest bit intimidated by me. We simply sat and studied each other. I had never been this close to a wild animal of this size out in nature before. I spoke softly to her. She never broke eye contact. With quiet dignity, we sat like that for almost an hour.

It was a mystical experience for me. I felt uniquely at one with creation. I told her what a wonder she was; and knowing her species is fighting extinction, I prayed for her. I knew her right to this space was as great as mine; for this moment in time, we shared it. I was cognizant that both of us as part of God's creation reflected God's glory. Her very being seemed to praise God. Reluctantly I withdrew and continued my walk on this solitary beach. When I returned, she'd gone back out to sea. Her presence and the moments we shared have stayed with me. I could not help wondering if at times *my* presence is cause for others to praise God.

**PRAYER: Creator God, how fearfully and wonderfully made is your creation. Let all that is crafted by your hand praise you. Cause us to be more aware of your world, so that we live as good stewards. In the name of the One who was with the Father and the Spirit at creation. Amen.**

# The Big Picture

*September 8–14, 2008 • Pat Luna[‡]*

## MONDAY, SEPTEMBER 8 • Read Exodus 14:19-31

If you had asked the Egyptians to describe the heavenly pillar, they would have described it as utter darkness. The Israelites, on the other hand, would have described the same pillar as a great light. Both would have been correct. The same heavenly pillar is both cloud and beacon, depending on where the observer happens to be standing. It is a matter of perspective.

In life, our perspective can often distort the big picture. We think our point of view is the "correct" one because it is the only one familiar to us. We may see disagreements as win/lose events. Blinded by our own perspective, we may fail to give serious consideration to the views of others, especially others who are very different from us. We may even become insulting or intolerant in our zeal to defend the "right" view. And in doing so, we may discard the paradoxical truth. After all, sometimes in God's creation a pillar is both fire and cloud.

As earthly creatures, we all see through a glass, darkly. We are creatures of limited perspective and limited vision. When we rely upon our own sight, we stumble.

Thankfully, however, God provides a way out of darkness. The Almighty God, the God of unlimited perspective, waits to guide us.

**PRAYER: Eternal God, giver of light and life, you see all that lies before us. Grant us strength and courage to be open to other views as we seek to walk in the light of your love. Amen.**

---

[‡]Retreat leader, The Upper Room Academy for Spiritual Formation; President, capital campaign consulting firm; Chair, Board of Discipleship, Alabama-West Florida Conference of The United Methodist Church; member, Whitfield Memorial United Methodist Church, Montgomery, Alabama.

We often see life from the wrong side—like a tapestry that we view from the "back." We see only a tangle of threads with no discernible pattern. We do not see the purpose of the threads that weave our lives together. We lose sight of the vision, of the big picture.

The victory songs here in Exodus remind us of the value of looking at life with a perspective of faith. God's people have come through a difficult time, and they have seen God's power. Moses and Miriam lead them in celebrating what God has done. One of the purposes of sabbath time is to move back from our own limited perspective and to seek God's vision of the world. Detaching ourselves from our own narrow thoughts, cares, and concerns, we seek the things of God. We find a quiet place where we can see God's face and hear God's voice. We sing a new song, God's song.

Occasionally, we catch a glimpse of life from God's perspective. Whether through prayer or meditation or the sound of a child's laugh or the unexpected kindness of a stranger, we are blessed with a gift of a new heavenly vision. In those moments, we rejoice in God's big picture!

The majesty and power of God's loving purposes overwhelm us, and we marvel at the wonder of God's beautiful creation. At those times, we glimpse the tapestry from the front side and see its glorious, harmonious, intricate, and marvelous design. Then our heart joins with the saints to proclaim, "Who is like you, O LORD, among the gods? Who is like you, majestic in holiness, awesome in splendor, doing wonders?"

**PRAYER: Heavenly Creator, thank you for sustaining us with glimpses of heaven on earth. Open our eyes today to see sparks of the eternal in our ordinary world. Amen.**

We are historical beings, limited by our own experience. This scripture reminds us, however, that God is without limits of time or space. God's perspective is infinite, God's power unbounded. We struggle, but God triumphs.

We may see our daily struggles as an evil to be avoided and long to escape the conflicts and tensions of our lives. But in God's eyes, some conflicts may be good and necessary, even holy. After all, tension is a natural part of the creative process.

Consider the ordinary task of knitting a sweater. Each hand works against the other, often pulling the yarn in opposite directions. When seen from the limited point of view of either hand, the process is much like a tug-of-war. In reality, however, a delicate balance must be reached to produce a usable sweater. The tension between the hands must be harmonious: too little tension, and the weave will be too loose; too much tension, and the weave will be too tight. In either case, the sweater will be unsightly and useless unless each hand respects the other and seeks to work together.

Our daily conflicts and struggles can be a holy process. We need not feel compelled to give in or pull too hard to get our way. Instead, we can seek a loving balance and trust that there is value in the struggle.

**PRAYER: Almighty God, help me to see my daily struggles as part of your holy and creative process. Amen.**

## Thursday, September 11 • Read Romans 14:1-6

God alone sees the big picture, and so God alone is qualified to judge us and to direct our efforts, individually and corporately. All that is expected of each of us is to be fully persuaded in our own minds, to respond faithfully to God's call. What wonderful news, especially in times of conflict and change!

Despite this good news, like modern-day scribes and Pharisees we often obsess with proving right and wrong, wanting so much to be right that we are reluctant to trust the Spirit of God that dwells within our neighbor. Our compulsion to resolve conflict compels us to settle for simple answers to complex questions. From there, it is a short step to judgment and from judgment to divisiveness.

If there were no diversity within the church, our constant comparisons might have some merit. If we were all the same, shared the same gifts, and performed the same functions, our comparison would be apples to apples. But as Paul has already reminded us in Romans 12, the body of Christ is composed of many members with a diversity of talents and different roles to play. Diversity exists within the church for a reason. A body full of eyes would not be a body at all, and a hand with only fingers and no thumb to oppose them, is capable of much less than a whole hand.

Thanks be to God, we are not responsible for persuading anyone else that we are right! We are, rather, commanded to refrain from judging. We trust God to direct the hearts and minds of others, just as God has directed our own.

PRAYER: **Almighty God, our Judge and our Redeemer, direct our hearts, judge mercifully our efforts, and redeem our shortcomings. Help us to comfort and heal the body of Christ and restore it to wholeness. Amen.**

At times, our society demands that we judge others and submit to judgment by others. As students, we learn at an early age that we are rated according to our behavior and our intelligence. As supervisors at work, we are called upon to evaluate others and rate their job performance. Retail merchants offer rewards if we will fill out a survey and judge their product or services. Our society rests upon laws of conduct, and we are expected to sit in judgment of others as part of our civic duty. It is no wonder that we have a natural inclination to judge others. It is programmed into us from an early age.

Discerning and careful judgment is often good and necessary. Imagine how unsafe products would be without quality control. Would you want to drive across a bridge designed by engineering students who were never graded on their knowledge of scientific principles?

And yet, Paul's admonition to the Romans is unmistakable, and it is consistent with Jesus' unambiguous commandment: "Do not judge, so that you may not be judged" (Matt. 7:1). How, then, do we perform our civic duty and our work responsibilities without judging others unjustly?

One way to begin is by judging ourselves first. We take an honest look at our own limitations. After all, our ability to assess anyone else is limited by our own narrow perspective. We must seek as best we can to detach ourselves from our own biases, feelings of favoritism, pride, and selfish ambition. To the extent we cannot, we should openly acknowledge our limitations. We must earnestly seek to love the ones we must judge as God loves them. By our love, everyone will know we are Christ's disciples, even when compelled by circumstances to judge others.

**PRAYER: Merciful God, help us to regard others with mercy and compassion, just as you regard us, that your glory might be revealed in and through us today. Amen.**

Whenever I am tempted to withhold forgiveness, I remember seeing this parable reenacted at a state detention facility, and the occasion was an Epiphany weekend. The audience, a group of incarcerated youth, had elected to attend the religious weekend perhaps to escape their normal routine. Many had heard the good news of God's grace for the first time that weekend, and some had already accepted God with grateful hearts. But the leadership team knew that many had also sworn an oath of vengeance. Before that weekend, their life's only firm purpose had been to avenge the senseless slaying of a best friend or the rape of a dear sister. Would they understand and heed the Gospel commandment to forgive others, even as we have been forgiven?

The leaders' reenactment of the parable was silly, the costumes ridiculous. A representative of the institution played the role of the king, and the boys delighted to see him dressed in a cape, wielding a scepter of aluminum foil. What possible difference could this simple story make to them?

After the skit and a homily on forgiveness, the youth were asked to make a list of people whom they needed to forgive. One young man sat upright and tense, staring at his blank sheet of paper. The weight of the world seemed to rest on him. Placing my hands on his shoulders, I pressed down gently and whispered, "Don't you realize that the person your unforgiveness hurts most of all is you?" His tears began to flow, and his hand began to write. He filled up the front of the page and turned it over. By then he was smiling.

**PRAYER: Good and merciful God, you carried the weight of all sin to the cross so that we would never have to bear its full weight. Help us to surrender our pain, with thanksgiving, to you. Amen.**

By staring at an object, such as a bright light, we can cause it to become imbedded in our optical memory, so that when we close our eyes, the image remains. Our spiritual sight works much like our physical eyesight. When we spend substantial time reflecting on an event, we find our thoughts returning there on their own. Paul knew this secret and admonished the Philippians, "Whatever is true, whatever is honorable, whatever is just, whatever is pure, whatever is pleasing, whatever is commendable, if there is any excellence and if there is anything worthy of praise, think about these things" (4:8).

In this parable, the king exhibits extraordinary generosity. The servant asks only for additional time, and the king eliminates the debt altogether. This act of forgiveness is complete, and the servant owes nothing from that moment forward. The servant must have been ecstatic! And yet, by the time he encounters his friend, the servant has lost sight of the king's generosity.

Often we, like the servant, focus on the wrong thing. We concentrate on the details of the unpaid debts of our lives—a hurtful remark, a thoughtless gesture, a lack of respect, a wrongful accusation. Or we allow an injustice to consume us and think about nothing else.

Thanks be to God, we can choose to change our focus. When we meditate on God's generosity and the enormity of the debt that has been paid for us, the wrongs done to us grow dim. When we focus on the big picture of God's love for us, our cares melt away, and God's peace returns to us.

**PRAYER: Generous God, you have secured our salvation through the sacrifice of your only Son. Help us focus on you, so that we will eagerly extend to others the forgiveness you offer us. Amen.**

# Astounding Grace

*September 15–21, 2008* • *Brian K. Wilcox*[‡]

**MONDAY, SEPTEMBER 15** • **Read Matthew 20:1-16**

My neighbor found the parable of the laborers in the vineyard confusing because it pictured God as unfair, and that cannot be true. I reminded her that the story is a parable and ought not be read literally. Now I would reply differently to her. The parable does not depict the landowner, who represents God, acting unfairly. Jesus uses the landowner's unconventional fairness as an irony to teach how God treats us. Grace is ironic, for it does not fit usual ideas of justice.

God's divine economy surprises and challenges us in its unconventionality. Our society seeks to thrive economically through competition and merit. Generally, we assume a person should receive only what she earns, and we speak of fair wages. In our economy grace appears impractical, maybe somewhat odd. Yet the parable teaches that grace arises from God's being, not our merit. God chooses to give us more than we deserve, for that is God's nature.

Today's parable challenges us as much as it did those who first heard Jesus speak it. We are challenged to appreciate the unconditional nature of God's kindness to everyone. Thereby, the parable urges us to cooperate together with God in the divine economy by approaching our relationships with that same grace given through Christ. We, the body of Christ, have been entrusted to share God's overflowing generosity, lavishing kindness on everyone.

**SUGGESTION FOR PRAYER: Pray for help to be gracious to a person you struggle to be gracious toward.**

---

[‡]United Methodist clergy in the Florida Conference, author, and writer for the Web ministry OneLife Ministries; living in Pinetto, Florida.

*God Keeping Covenant*

A Welshman preparing to be a doctor, William Williams (1717–91), committed to Christ on hearing Howell Harris, an itinerant evangelist, preach. Williams too became a traveling evangelist, preaching and singing all over Wales. He penned a song that appeared in a hymnal in England in 1745. The hymn was "Strength to Pass through the Wilderness." Later, the song received the title by which we know it today, "Guide Me, O Thou Great Jehovah." Williams used the wilderness wanderings of the Hebrews to typify the Christian life. The Christian is a "pilgrim through this barren land," but while "I am weak, . . . thou art mighty." Williams prays "hold me with thy powerful hand" and "lead me all my journey through." He rests assured that God will lead him into Canaan and declares, "Songs of praises,/songs of praises,/I will ever give to thee;/I will ever give to thee."

Psalm 105, likewise, stresses God's providence. God is faithful to the promise of land in covenant with Abraham. Lack of reference to Israel's response accents focus on God's gracious loyalty. Psalm 106, which forms a couplet with Psalm 105, sets forth the people's disloyalty, but God's faithfulness is the concern of Psalm 105.

We, like the Hebrew tribes, are a people living under God's promise. The Holy Spirit encourages us on our pilgrimage with Jesus' promise, "I will not leave you orphaned; I am coming to you" (John 14:18). We live in the promise from Matthew 28:20, "And remember, I am with you always, to the end of the age."

The triune God goes with us and in us by the Holy Spirit. We may feel lonely, but we are never alone. God's keeping covenant with us is the ground for joining our ancestors in the psalm's conclusion: "Praise the Lord!"

**Suggestion for meditation: Reflect on ways the Holy Spirit guides you in your Christian walk.**

*Patience and kindness amid complaints*

God raining food in response to the Hebrews murmuring against Moses and Aaron occurs shortly after leaving Egypt. Events in Exodus 15 highlight the discontent, though the chapter includes celebration of deliverance at the Red Sea, the changing of bitter to sweet water at Marah, and the tribes camping at Elim beside water, where there are twelve springs of water and seventy palm trees. Despite all the gifts received by the Hebrew people in the liberation from slavery and the exodus from Egypt, their complaints in the wilderness demonstrate a short-term memory. They seem to prefer slavery to freedom.

Moses and Aaron find themselves in a situation common to leaders. They are caught between the complaints of those they lead and the leadership task that they have received from God. The two men actually receive an example of gracious leadership in God's response to the complaints: God will provide food in the wilderness. The people will receive bread in the morning and meat at night. With their physical needs met, the people may no longer complain.

We know that the story of complaints does not end with the provision of food in the wilderness. We also complain, sometimes bitterly, that our needs are not being met or that our lives were better in another time—perhaps a time during our own bondage to sin. We look toward the future and see a dimly lit horizon that seems to hold only the very worst predictions made by social scientists. Yet from the wilderness comes the basic lesson to take one day at a time, to let the day's troubles be enough, to carry no longer the past into the future. From the wilderness comes the lesson to allow God's grace to be sufficient.

**PRAYER: Gracious God, in the wilderness you provided for all the people. Open my spirit to an awareness of your provision in the wilderness I face today. Amen.**

*Emulating Christ's gracious self-giving*

Paul and the Philippian Christians were especially close. He reminds the Philippians that they participate in God's grace with him. He affirms, "For God is my witness, how I long for all of you with the compassion of Christ Jesus" (v. 8). Paul says he desires the Philippians with the "bowels of Christ Jesus," for the Jews considered the bowels to be the seat of tender affections.

Paul, being in prison, is torn between martyrdom and living. For Paul to live means serving the Philippian Christians. He affirms remaining in the body as more necessary for them and avows, "Since I am convinced of this, I know that I will remain and continue with all of you for your progress and joy in the faith." Paul forgoes self-interest for the church. His intent is its "progress and joy." Paul emulates Christ's gracious self-giving to serve us.

Serving in Christ's name entails not letting self-interest impede our God-assigned role. In Christian service we can wrongfully use those we serve to meet our needs for affection. Paul can express love for the Philippians, but he is clear about his role as spiritual mentor. While we receive love from those whom we serve, their "progress and joy" must take priority over our needs for affection, with the consequence that we, as their servants, can say, "that I may share abundantly in your boasting in Christ Jesus." This sharing gives deep satisfaction to the Christian servant. We can keep this focus of gracious self-giving when we can say, "For to me, living is Christ."

**PRAYER: Beloved, fill me so with joy through daily living in you that I can serve others unselfishly for their joy and growth in the Holy Spirit. Amen.**

*The grace of suffering*

When I was a child, some friends came to my home to celebrate my birthday. We gathered around the kitchen table, and I began opening gifts, finding something new in each package. I came to a small box and thought it might be expensive, for I associated such with small packages. The gift was not expensive and clearly not new. My friend had given me a used toy car.

I thanked him, but I was upset. I wondered why he did not invest effort to get me something new. Years later in adulthood, I came to realize he possibly gave me the best gift of all that day, something so special to him that he wanted me to have it. My response mirrors how selective we can be in estimating what is a worthy or unworthy gift.

When we think of God's grace, we likely think of blessings. By blessings we mean gifts that make us feel good. We esteem highly such gifts. Paul reminds the Philippians, however, that God gives us the gift of suffering for Christ.

We are "to live as citizens of heaven" (v. 27, NLT), rather than be enamored with temporal things. When we allow suffering to be for Christ, the Holy Spirit uses it to transform pride into humbleness and doubt into faith. Suffering leads to a deeper communion with Christians who, likewise, offer their sufferings for Christ. Through suffering we become more receptive to grace, for it transforms inordinate affections, enabling us to act "in a manner worthy of the Good News about Christ" (NLT).

**PRAYER: Holy Spirit, I commit whatever suffering I undergo to Christ's honor and purpose. Use suffering to lessen my pride and increase my love, to diminish my fascination with temporal things and expand my joy in things eternal. Amen.**

*Cooperating with God*

I had not danced with anyone for over twenty years. Standing beside the dance floor, my friend asked if I would dance with her. I declined the offer. While feeling shy about dancing, I actually longed to step out and join in rather than watch. I summoned courage, approached my friend, and accepted her offer. I let myself enjoy the experience. I had such a good time that I danced by myself in the living room when I returned home. It seemed my body had been cleansed of resistance that kept me from dancing with other persons.

Grace implies response. The church has called this response cooperating grace. The Holy Spirit works in us, enabling acceptance of salvation. The early church used a Greek word rendered "synergism" (working together, sharing energy) for this cooperation. Synergism continues in sanctifying grace, whereby the Holy Spirit keeps forming us in Christ's image. Grace enables us to release inhibitions to sharing in the Trinity's life and work.

Israel is to respond to God's loyalty by obeying the law. We as Christians are bound to principles of Old Testament law reaffirmed in the New Testament and church tradition. Jesus spoke, "Do not think that I have come to abolish the law or the prophets; I have come not to abolish but to fulfill" (Matt. 5:17).

This partnership with God comes from the heart, not as a perfunctory duty. Paul affirms, "Thanks be to God that you, having once been slaves of sin, have become obedient from the heart to the form of teaching to which you were entrusted" (Rom. 6:17). By the Spirit's transformation of our wills, dancing with the Spirit becomes a delight.

SUGGESTION FOR MEDITATION: **What opportunities do you have to cooperate with grace daily?**

*The Christian life, a natural life*

For years my Christian walk seemed unnatural. I tried to live in two separate worlds: the world of the Christian life, which many considered unnatural; the other world of the natural life, which many considered sinful. I finally learned the Christian life means living in a natural world naturally.

This natural life, often spoken of as life before the Fall, comes through living the kingdom of heaven. Jesus used monarchical imagery for hearers who were of a long history of monarchy, both theirs and empires that subjected them. But what does the kingdom of heaven mean to us long-separated from imperialism? Jesus' use of *kingdom* shows it is neither a place nor bound by time. The kingdom of heaven appears more as a synonym for God. John Wesley wrote in his sermon "On the Omnipresence of God" that the teaching of God dwelling in heaven is condescension to "weak understanding." God is "the universal God … in universal space." Everywhere is God's dominion. The Eastern Church has taught that we experience God through the glory of God, like experiencing the sun through sunbeams shining on all things and everywhere. God is the pervasive, gracious influence flowing through the Word. It touches all, for God is everywhere and in every time through Christ.

Thankfully, Jesus does not call us to be unnatural. Jesus teaches us to live this life naturally. We do not have to be torn between two worlds as I was for many years. Jesus says, "Look at this kingdom. Look at God! I will show you how to live the way the Creating One intends, and that way is reasonable, natural, and loving." The Holy Spirit matures us in this true life by applying grace for ongoing conversion of heart and mind, and we progressively learn to live graciously in respect for all creatures.

Suggestion for meditation: **How do you see yourself growing in experience of the kingdom of heaven?**

# Danger or Opportunity?

*September 22–28, 2008 • Jerry L. Moore[‡]*

## MONDAY, SEPTEMBER 22 • Read Matthew 21:23-27

Kevin had grown up on these streets until his gang activity put him in danger without opportunity for escape. His aunt moved him from this danger within a few years. After graduating high school and college, he returned to the streets of his early childhood to lead others beyond their limited options. We talked.

"Tell me what led you to join a gang at the age of eight." Kevin stood up and walked me to the window facing a street in the Cabrini-Green neighborhood of Chicago. Thoughtfully, as if seeing all the people of his past gather on that street, he said, "Let me ask you a question, Jerry. You are walking down the center of the street toward school. The street is a battle line for three gangs. Small, alone, and in the middle without support, you know they can make you disappear now or later. Security comes with choosing to join one of these gangs. Which gang would you choose?"

Kevin's question changed all the questions. He knew that wars are fought over authority and turf. Gangs are authorities unto themselves. The privileged among us debate issues from windows. The oppressed among us live or die by questions asked on the street.

Jesus knows the elders are not seeking to debate the law. No answer he gives will keep him from the threat of death. His selfless life disturbs all self-centered people. The transcendent mind of Christ knows all gangs will converge to kill the Truth that threatens their constructs of life. Jesus will soon become dead to all groups of people seeking to protect their own turf—their own way, their own truth, and their own life.

**SUGGESTION FOR MEDITATION: Where do you debate issues and face questions—from the window or on the street?**

---

[‡]Spiritual director, founder and director of Formative Studies of Epiphany Home; pastor, Central United Methodist Church, Dalhart, Texas.

Go, work in the vineyard. One son openly professes he will faithfully follow his father's will; his brother confesses his unwillingness to cooperate. The professing son does not cooperate, but the brother who confesses his unwillingness does follow through with his father's will. Faith is revealed not with words or tone but with responsive steps that lead away from or toward the vineyard.

Jesus uses this story to reveal the difference between faith pretension and faith expression. Jesus turns the tables on those who follow the separation laws. The chief priests declare who is clean and unclean and therefore who can sit at table with the community. Those who are unclean have no provision within the gates of Israel. Therefore, the unclean can survive only by selling their services or their bodies (possibly their only commodity). This creates a vicious cycle. The unclean circle in the wilderness of self-provision, which keeps them from association with those tending God's table.

The economy of the father's table brings with it the opportunity to receive what people cannot provide for themselves. Even the dogs are allowed to eat the crumbs that fall from the master's table. This masterful economy depends upon the father's faithfulness to provide for all who respond to his invitation.

The promise of food and shelter is assured as one takes his or her place in the family. Grace is not about labor exchange that promotes competition among workers but about competent participation as authorized by the father. The master provides both the place at the table and the unique call to participate in the ongoing work of his domain. Anyone who has ever been unemployed and unable to find work can appreciate the gracious compassion of a place at the table.

SUGGESTION FOR MEDITATION: **Consider your work in the vineyard and your place at the table.**

Be careful not to judge our ancient friends as they enter a new wilderness. They have been slaves for generations, taught to busy themselves in mindless tasks, equipped to be tired and content in hopeless busyness. A new mind has been cultivated within God's congregation. The Hebrews know that their pottage will be provided and their water will be waiting—as long as they do not disrupt the fear-driven system designed to keep them enslaved. Some life seminars for enslaved minds might be titled

1. Job Security—How to make bricks that crumble along with your identity in Yahweh
2. Murmuring—How to express your ideas to those like yourself without risk of personal change
3. Blaming and Shaming—How to participate in self-enslavement in a contemporary culture

Here are some leadership seminars for contemporary taskmasters:

1. Conflict Management—How to nurture the enslaved mind among the afflicted
2. Time Management—How to raise up the next generation of mindless, busy slaves
3. Effective Busyness Model—Training slaves to make bricks that will crumble tomorrow

SUGGESTION FOR MEDITATION: **Attend to the enslaved mind, whether it's your own or another's, by**

- **listening for fear-driven reactions (within or without) created by performance-based taskmasters,**
- **considering the source of murmuring demands,**
- **seeking God's face, listening to God's directives,**
- **walking from self-centered wants toward the Source of all.**

**How might your life or that of another change by following through on some of the suggestions above?**

Years of oppression and fearful living have trained God's people to distrust those in authority. The Israelites' fear-driven appetites quickly motivate them to move beyond a demand for water to assuming Moses has a personal agenda to cause them harm. The spokesperson actually accuses Moses of leading them to this place to take their lives, the lives of their children, and their assets (such as livestock).

Moses' question reveals that he seems to know that he has a bigger problem than finding water for demanding people. He has taken formerly enslaved people to a place where they have never been—free from provision of lesser gods. Suffering is familiar. Giving them water on demand will not change the disposition of this abused and angry flock of God.

Shepherding for his father-in-law's flock might have helped Moses discern the difference between the bleating of a thirsty sheep and the bleating of one who is lost and fearful. Though threatened by this new human congregation, he knows the issue is not about water, and he comes to learn that their murmuring is not at all about him.

Therefore, Moses does not ask God for water. He asks what he is to do with this people. God instructs Moses to make this a public meeting with the elders of the congregation. God directs him to use the tools of God's provision and to lead the people toward the God of their beginning.

Privileged cultures are tempted to give people what they want when they become demanding. History proves that any privileged culture can console people by giving them what they want. For the Israelites the issue is not provision; God is reintroducing God's self to a generation of people who have come to entrust themselves to lesser gods and lesser gratifications.

**SUGGESTION FOR MEDITATION: When have you enabled enslaved minds or shepherded demanding people toward new life in Christ Jesus?**

In Philippi men of commerce publicly attack Paul and Silas. The message of these itinerant preachers does not bother these businessmen until one conversion cuts into their bottom line. Paul's ministry changes one woman's life to the point that she can no longer perform her job. (Read Acts 16:16-24.)

This female employee's spirit of divination worked well for this economic group. They used her spiritual insight for profit. Paul frees her from spiritual possession and the economically driven purposes of these men. Participation in this liberating exorcism disturbs more than the spirit within.

These business-minded men are intuitive enough to understand that this apostolic ministry could ruin an entire industry they have developed for their own blessed assurance. To insure cash flow they must keep a target population in constant need of their services. If pastoral direction starts leading people out of spiritual usury, enslaved minds will disappear. Their markets will dry up.

Paul follows in the selfless way of Christ who sought nothing for himself. This obedient outpouring of self for the sake of others can ruin a consumer-driven market that perpetuates the vital desires of people. This makes Paul a natural enemy of self-interest groups geared to nurture narcissistic tendencies within contemporary culture.

Whether you lead enslaved minds from a modern-day Pharaoh or set people free from misuse of spiritual gifts, some people do not want the church to be in full accord and of one mind. The self-promoting world will ignore this ministry until it disturbs the bottom line. Pastors and teachers who lead people out of financial, emotional, mental, and spiritual poverty toward God's compassionate unity in one accord will become a threat to those in the business of enslaving minds for their own purposes.

SUGGESTION FOR MEDITATION: **Whose name is advanced by your prayers, presence, giving, and service?**

Students of Paul know he preaches that we are saved by grace and not by works. He encourages us to understand we are the ongoing work to be transformed by truth and grace. So what would keep us from becoming this graced work of God living in one accord and in one mind? What formative events would facilitate a tremor of fear through the saints and pastoral leaders?

This week Moses has been pursued by the most powerful person in the nation as he attempts to lead God's people away from Pharaoh's table. Paul's simple act of pastoral direction brings the economic and political forces of his day against himself and his friends.

Consider what would have happened if Moses had facilitated the happiness of the enslaved people of Egypt with motivational and hopeful messages of the Promised Land but never led them beyond the reality of Egypt's oppressive order. What if he unwittingly became the motivational voice of Pharaoh's house of provision rather than the pastoral leader of God's people toward true freedom?

What if Paul had ignored the woman with the spirit of divination? She might have been fed and sheltered and been able to maintain some integrity among other working women. She provided a marketable service that did not break the law.

Paul reveals to the saints and pastoral stewards of Philippi that all salvation is by grace. But Paul distinguishes the lesser sources of grace. Some benevolent providers will gladly gratify your faithful efforts if you cooperate with their vital and socially driven purposes.

To whom do you bow your knee for a place at the table?

**SUGGESTION FOR MEDITATION: Can you sit at two tables of provision and be faithful to both?**

Sitting in a cold stone sanctuary in New Mexico, my body resonates as the Benedictines pray the psalm in consonance one with another. My heart and mind begin to run clean like the walls of the canyon being washed by the gently blowing rain. The consonant truth begins to dissolve false perceptions in my mind. Pictures of hungry, impoverished, war-torn families disturb this present moment. The vile pictures and harmonious voices seem to shake me to my knees.

As the monks rise from their seats to leave, tears stream from my chin to the stones of the floor. The gentleness of God's mercy and the harshness of human suffering cannot be retained in one body. The veil has been torn, and the light shatters the darkness of my sleeping mind. My heart longs for the lives outside of this valley to harmonize like the monastic lives of these men coming from many nations and traditions.

During this sabbath, dare to listen and eat at God's table. Discern with compassion the impulsive choices of those who have gone before you. Weep with them as they disappoint the God of our beginning and end. Say no to the lesser gods who seek to seduce you with the immediate gratification served at their tables. Say yes to the God who continues to set the table for those who follow through the wilderness.

In remembrance, become awe-inspired with the Holy One who sends messenger after messenger. Live in awe-filled appreciation of the God who calls, heals, and forgives. As you go, guide others with the gifts and graces given you. Be faithful in one accord and one mind.

SUGGESTION FOR MEDITATION: **Consider God's ongoing formative presence in you.**

# The Greatest Gift of All

*September 29–October 5, 2008 • Mary Lou Redding*[‡]

## MONDAY, SEPTEMBER 29 • Read Psalm 19:7-11

What wonderful power God's law has! If we live by its guidance, it can revive us, make us wise, give us joy, enlighten us. Who wouldn't want these benefits? Who wouldn't hold this law and its Giver in loving reverence?

This psalm in its praise for God's law reminds me of Tevye, the poor but deeply devout farmer in the musical *Fiddler on the Roof*. Tevye talks to God throughout every day as he would to a close friend, rehearsing his concerns and joys and complaining to God when things go wrong. In the song "If I Were a Rich Man," Tevye sings to God about what he could do and have if he were rich. After mentioning the gifts he'd give his wife and daughters and how he would impress the town, Tevye switches tone and sings longingly of one more thing he could do if he were rich: he could sit with the rabbis all day long and discuss the Torah. In the movie version, his face shows joy and wonder and yearning and love. He can imagine no higher privilege than being able to explore the law.

As we treasure the gift of God's message to us in scripture and dig more deeply into it, God's power will transform us. Like Tevye, we come to the conversation just as we are, with all our completely human dreams and concerns. As we do, God meets us, opens to us great treasures, and leads us to fullness of life.

**PRAYER: O God, we hunger to know you and to be filled with your wisdom. Prepare our minds and hearts to hear you speak to us as we open your gift of scripture. Amen.**

---

[‡]Editorial Director of *The Upper Room* magazine, author of books including *The Power of a Focused Heart*; living with her two spoiled dogs, Abby and Annie, in Brentwood, Tennessee, near her almost perfect granddaughter, Rosalie.

Surveys about people's spiritual concerns always isolate some form of this question: How can I know God's will? And it's not just Christians who struggle with this query. Nancy Reeves wrote a book titled *I'd Say Yes, God, If I Knew What You Wanted.* The book's content draws from in-depth interviews with people from many different faith traditions—Christian, Hindu, Islam, Native peoples—about how they seek and receive guidance for their lives. (The interviews reveal amazingly similar processes across faith traditions.)

Continually asking about God's will for our daily choices seems unnecessary if we take to heart the intent of today's scripture reading. If we follow the guidance for living contained in these verses, many apparent dilemmas would melt away. Should I take time to run by Mom's and help her clean out the attic? "Honor your father and mother." Should I agree with my coworker's account of how we got into this difficulty? "Do not bear false witness." Should I use my credit card to buy this outfit that I don't really need? "Do not covet . . . anything that is your neighbor's." Do I really need to give my time and money to church? "Have no allegiance to any gods but me."

Ten items may be more than most of us can manage to remember. That's okay. Jesus summed them up in two clear guidelines: "Love the Lord your God with all your heart and mind and soul and strength," and "Love your neighbor as yourself." (See Matthew 22:37.) We don't have to guess what our priorities are supposed to be or how God wants us to live. That is a great gift.

**SUGGESTION FOR MEDITATION: Look back over your actions in the last twenty-four hours. How would living by the Ten Commandments have made your choices clearer or different?**

**PRAYER: Holy and loving God, make us like you. Help us to honor your name by showing love in all that we do. Amen.**

Many Christians speak of a sharp contrast between "the God of the Old Testament" and "the God of the New Testament," between law and grace, as if the two are opposites. It's almost as if they see two gods.

According to a 2006 Baylor University survey, however, two isn't enough. This survey reported *four* American views of God: an authoritarian God angry at us for our sins, a benevolent God who primarily forgives, a critical God who views us disapprovingly but nevertheless does not intervene, and a distant God who "launched the world" but is "detached from and uninvolved in daily events." Our view of God determines our politics and our daily behavior.

But God doesn't have multiple personalities; God didn't undergo a personality change in the four hundred years between Malachi and Matthew. The God who is as attentive to us as a nursing mother to her child (Isa. 49:15; 66:13), the tender father who loves us in our weakness (Ps. 103:13), the One whose mercies are new every morning (Lam. 3:22), whose "steadfast love endures forever" (Ps. 136)—this is the "Old Testament" God whom Jesus loved and revealed.

God loves us more than we know and from the beginning of time has been trying to get through to us. The rule of life that God gave us in the law calls us to the way of life that Jesus embodied. It is not a new way; it is still God's way. There is no separation; that wall of misunderstanding is our doing, not God's. Paul's lineage and summary of it remind us that God in Christ calls us not to a new way but to an ancient one—the way that leads to life.

**PRAYER: God of Abraham and Sarah, Rahab and Obed, Mary and Jesus, thank you for the gift of your unfailing love that never gives up on us, no matter what walls we build or what sins we commit. Amen.**

Living by the guidance of the fourth commandment outwardly evidences our commitment to the first three. Modern culture offers many idolatries, and keeping sabbath helps us confront them—and our entanglements with them. Doing so is difficult; there is virtually no support for keeping this outward sign of our inner commitment. People eventually complain if we kill others or commit adultery or steal or tell lies and so on, but no one complains because we're busily working hard, especially if we're working for God.

Taking time regularly to rest and focus on God sets us free from the lie that we are in charge, that whether the kingdom comes depends on how hard we work. Keeping sabbath reminds us that God is God—and we are not. This is news to some of us (commandment #1 notwithstanding).

We are all too busy. We have our day planners and our personal digital assistants and the cell phones that have become part of our anatomy and wireless laptops so we can stay plugged in to the action no matter where we are. The result of all this diligence is a world where we never relax and allow God to re-create us. Commanding the sabbath is one way God says, "Stop it. Put down all that stuff. Let me hold you and heal you."

Of course we are meant to do good works; but the spiritual life is about relationship with God, not about performance. When we step back from performing and take time simply to be, to sit in God's presence, we model the truth that God is the center of life and creation. All that we do for God is our gift to God. But God's gift to us is the reminder in sabbath that we are not capable of or responsible for doing all that needs to be done. God was at work in this world before we came along, and God will still be faithfully working when we are dead and gone. So we are called to lay our heavy burden down. For one day each week, we can let God manage the world. Sabbath is a gracious gift.

**PRAYER: O God, help us surrender to you for twenty-four hours the mantle of our busyness. Amen.**

I really wish I liked the apostle Paul more. Maybe then it would be easier to get to the heart of this passage's message for my life. Here he seems to brag about how wonderful he is: "If anyone has reason to be proud based on being a blueblood," Paul seemingly says, "that would be me. If anyone could brag about doing a good job of keeping the law, well, that would be me too. If you're looking for the purest guy around—again, *c'est moi.*" I don't think I'd enjoy chatting with this guy at a party. The first several verses of today's reading make me think of an ad for a church in my town that promises to help people connect with God without becoming an "arrogant, self-righteous know-it-all." Paul might need to visit that church.

But Paul doesn't stop with rehashing his vita. After laying out his credentials, Paul says that they matter not at all; they are "rubbish" (the Greek word is actually cruder than that). Then why bother to mention them? Perhaps because he is addressing "good people" like us—insiders, those who are trying hard to be what God asks, to do what is right. Paul has to command their respect in order to get beyond their image of themselves as God's best advertisements for holiness. Paul talks about himself only to gain an entry to talk about what Christ offers. (Not a bad standard.)

Seeing our flawed efforts at goodness for what they are and ourselves for the eternally flawed creatures we are makes God's grace all the more dazzling. Our hard work is not enough and never will be. God has known that all along. In spite of our wiggling to get away and our arguing about standards, God holds us close. God in Christ tells us that no matter how long we keep trying to earn salvation and no matter how badly we mess things up, we are accepted anyway.

**Prayer: O God, thank you for what you have done for us in Christ. Thank you for saving us. Amen.**

This is quite a strange story, on the face of it. It's one of several Jesus tells in a series of parables about the nature of the kingdom of God, so we should probably read it alongside the others. Who do these tenants think they are, and how is this scenario going to play out? If we were to extend the story, we'd probably say the tenants will seize the land and declare it theirs. Allowing them to do so would overthrow the basic law of private ownership of property. Since those with the gold (the property) make the rules, it seems unlikely this would be permitted. Sooner or later, the tenants will be called to answer for what they have done. Their behavior cannot remain secret, after all.

One of the things I love most about Jesus is that he never lets theory simply remain theory when responding to questioners. With this story, Jesus pushes us to examine whether we really agree with the premise that all of the earth, all of life, all that we have belongs ultimately to God. We say that God is God of our lives, but do we live as if that is so? That's just *one* question this story raises.

This vineyard owner has set the tenants up with all they need to make a good life for themselves and to honor their agreement with him—a vineyard, a winepress, a fence, a watchtower. But in return, they use what has been entrusted to them as if they are in charge and have ultimate say about the ordering of the world. This sounds remarkably like us!

The grace in this story comes in the truth that God is more gracious than humans are. Jesus' hearers assume that the tenants will be killed, but Jesus is proof that God has not given up on humanity, self-centered and cruel as we can be. Beyond our illusions of self-sufficiency and power, God waits—still God, still loving us.

**PRAYER: O God, forgive us for living as if we are in charge. Show us how to honor you with our substance in what we do every day. Amen.**

My friend and her husband lived far from family. He was her rock, her most enthusiastic cheerleader, the love of her life. And he was desperately ill, lying in the hospital with an illness the doctors could not diagnose. His organs were shutting down; the situation was grim. She went home from the hospital late one night with a heavy heart. Fearful and feeling completely alone, she took the dog out into their backyard. It was a clear night, and she looked up at the heavens to see the Hale–Bopp Comet shining brightly in the sky. Somehow she suddenly knew that she was not alone. Now, years later, she remembers that moment as a turning point in her understanding of God's reality. Eventually her husband recovered, but she carried away from that ordeal a deep, personal assurance that God cared and was close.

This psalm reminds us that God speaks to us and reaches out to us in many ways, through the words of the law but without words as well, as to my friend. God is the great opportunist. Wherever we allow the tiniest opening, God takes advantage of it to come to us. As deep and as universal as the human yearning to know God is, God's yearning to know us is eternally deeper. By God's initiative we were given the law; by God's initiative Jesus came; by God's initiative the heavens and the earth declare to us that we are not alone.

Francis Thompson's familiar and sentimental poem "The Hound of Heaven" describes God as one who pursues us "down our nights and down our days." This relentless God will never give up on us, never turn away from us. That assurance is the greatest gift of all.

**PRAYER: O God, thank you for reaching out to us continually, until we realize that you are there and turn to you. Thank you for responding to our hunger to know you. Amen.**

# Lost in Wonder, Love, and Praise

*October 6–12, 2008  •  Robbins Sims*‡

## MONDAY, OCTOBER 6 • Read Exodus 32:1-14

While Moses lingers with the Lord, the Israelites at the base of the mountain are ravaged with anxiety. Desperate for relief, they demand that Aaron produce a god for them. Lacking fortitude for leadership, Aaron loses his nerve and complies. Israel's self-sabotage takes the form of a golden calf, an ominous sign of infidelity that will sully their offspring for generations. The Lord offers them a pristine gift, and they settle for a fake—a terrible loss!

Israel's story is also ours. Faith requires steadiness, but we writhe with worry when the Lord doesn't deliver as quickly or convincingly as we expect. If the God of mystery doesn't address our needs as we perceive them, we clamor for a more familiar, user-friendly substitute. We make our own scaled-down deities and attribute to them God's name and saving power.

The good news is that the Lord's revelation doesn't end with the Israelites' failure or ours! Moses intercedes for the people by imploring God to remain true to God's self. In Jesus, the eternal selfhood of God confronts us with uncompromising grace: "the same today, yesterday, and forever." His enigmatic cross embodies God's irrevocable decision to give us the best, despite our unworthiness or unreadiness to receive it. Easter finalizes God's decision to believe in us. The Holy Spirit works to fulfill God's confidence in us. In the endless end, we are awakened finally to the wonder, beauty, and strength of God's gift. Having spurned so many opportunities, we are all the more grateful that the Lord doesn't give up on us.

**PRAYER: Lord, in the aftermath of my panicked fears, your love remains steadfast. In times when I give up on you, I am grateful that you do not give up on me. Amen.**

---

‡Pastor, Whitfield Memorial United Methodist Church, Montgomery, Alabama.

Some errors are more than embarrassing. They are shameful. Of such, our Communion ritual used to say, "The remembrance of them is grievous unto us." Bearing the grief of these memories is necessary, however, if we are to expose ourselves fully to God's transforming grace. Therefore, the psalmist acknowledges that "both we and our ancestors have sinned." Such confession breaks the spiritual circuits that transmit transgressions from one generation to another.

For me, the struggle with white racism is a poignant example of this principle. I was born in Montgomery, Alabama, in the year of Rosa Parks' momentous defiance of the city's bigoted bus policy. I have spent most of my life in proximity to this epicenter of the civil rights movement. In such a place, it is hard to ignore the truth about my complicity in the scandalous evil of racism. I cringe now to think of my city's racist legacy and how its residue might taint my attitudes and actions. Yet, only in facing my loss of innocence do I receive the grace to truly and earnestly repent of my sin.

This is the goal of sanctifying grace: not that we be condemned but that we be transformed. And so the psalmist prays,

Remember me, O LORD, when you show favor to your people;
help me when you deliver them;
that I may see the prosperity of your chosen ones,
that I may rejoice in the gladness of your nation,
that I may glory in your heritage.

Confident of the goodness of God's future, the psalmist prays to be part of it. In the same manner, we yearn to be saved to the uttermost. We bare the depths of our depravity, not to be defeated or even excused but so that every aspect of our lives might be prepared for the glory of God's kingdom.

**PRAYER: Gracious God, give me grace to confess my sins without fear of condemnation and with a desire to be transformed through Jesus Christ my Lord. Amen.**

Jesus taught us to pray, "Your kingdom come. Your will be done on earth as it is in heaven" (Matt. 6:10). How do we begin to receive the answer to that prayer?

According to this week's Gospel lesson, "The kingdom of heaven may be compared to a king who gave a wedding banquet for his son." The story is laced with messianic metaphors, but its central point is straightforward—the invitation to God's kingdom is the highest of all possible privileges. Being the personal guest of a queen, president, or prime minister could not exceed it. If this is true, then the kingdom comes only as we, the invited guests, appreciate the awesomeness of that to which we are invited. The kingdom tarries whenever we see it as an obligation, a distraction, or an inconvenience. The kingdom cannot come so long as we oppose it or act as if we have better things to do.

Let us examine more closely the exquisite privilege of that to which the Lord calls us. The bestowal of a privilege affirms those on whom it is bestowed. We struggle with our belief in God's kingdom, but that may be the wrong issue. The kingdom's coming depends more upon God's belief in us than upon our belief in God. The kingdom breaks into being when, with breathless humility, we accept God's acceptance of us and of one another. As the kingdom dawns upon us, we begin to see ourselves and one another in a totally new light. Our awareness of privilege expands exponentially. In the fullness of the kingdom we are "lost in wonder, love, and praise"* for the Lord who makes and claims us all.

**PRAYER: Loving God, amid all the opportunities and obligations of my life, enable me to see clearly that nothing matters more than your gracious acceptance of me and of every other person in this world. Amen.**

---

*From "Love Divine, All Loves Excelling," in *The United Methodist Hymnal* (Nashville, TN: The United Methodist Publishing House, 1989 ), no. 384.

If God's kingdom exists in God's acceptance of us and others through Jesus Christ, then our rejection of Christ produces the very opposite. In the parable of the wedding banquet, excuse-making and mockery turn finally into brutality. The vengeance that follows is swift, certain, and ruinous.

At first glance, this part of the parable seems rather punitive. Nevertheless, it is consistent with other texts in which Jesus warns about the fate of the unrepentant. Jesus points to a putrid dump (Gehenna) and a terrifying "outer darkness" to depict the destruction of those who base their lives on anything other than God's universal love.

We cannot dismiss these troubling images of God's judgment, but we need not attribute them to some dark, retributive aspect of God's nature. When we persist in graceless ways of life, the immutability of God's love condemns us. God's uncompromising compassion is the wrath against which we flail ourselves in any and every attempt to go it alone. We are dissipated not by God's desire to make us pay for our sins but by our proud and futile attempts to live apart from the One whose love is life. God's restorative judgment forces us to face the damage we inflict upon ourselves and others when we vaunt ourselves against God's will. It serves as an expression of God's prevenient grace (God's working for good before we are aware of it).

From God's side, the reality is always grace. From our side, the only solution is surrender. The surrender that saves us is not weary capitulation but the cessation of self-justification and self-condemnation. Such surrender doesn't diminish us but binds us to the enduring foundation of God's word.

**PRAYER: Thank you, God, for the ways you bring me to yourself—even for judgment that prompts me to turn from sin and depend upon you. Amen.**

A friend related an experience that reminded him of this part of the parable. He was a new faculty member at a small private school where the art of social refinement was still considered a necessary part of a proper education. Having been reared in another country, he was unfamiliar with the finer points of high-brow etiquette. Consequently, he didn't think twice about wearing clean khakis, starched shirt, corduroy blazer, and his best cowboy boots to the college president's fall reception. He realized his predicament, however, the moment a uniformed servant opened the door to the president's "mansion." Standing before him in formal attire was the educator-in-chief and a room full of similarly clad colleagues, senior students, and influential townspeople. He recalled how the befuddled crowd had turned to stare at him in his innocent but unmistakable state of buffoonery. Still smarting from the embarrassment of it all, he said, "Believe me, I know what it's like to feel out of place!"

God's kingdom is a new creation in which "righteousness is at home" (2 Pet. 3:13). It is the realm of God's rule in which Christ forms us. Spiritual formation is finally a transparent process. There is nowhere to hide, least of all in religion. However polished our pretense, false piety is no more acceptable than plain wickedness.

We take our place in God's kingdom as we "put on the Lord Jesus Christ" (Rom. 13:14). Doing so, we are clothed with a righteousness that is not our own but is nonetheless real and personal. The Holy Spirit teaches us to recognize the subtlest differences between good and evil. God enables us "both to will and to work for [God's] good pleasure" (Phil. 2:13). The more we experience divine grace, the more absolutely out of place sin feels for us.

PRAYER: **Almighty God, by the patient working of your grace, enable me to become a person who truly belongs in your kingdom. Amen.**

Belonging in God's kingdom requires that we get along with others who belong there as well. Paul urges Euodia and Syntyche to "be of the same mind in the Lord." Paul doesn't disclose the nature of their dispute but encourages them to seek sacred mutuality in their common relationship with Christ.

It is difficult to work through differences over things that matter deeply to us. Disagreements over values hinge upon matters we believe to be true, right, and important. Disparities in taste involve our sense of individuality. Diversities of experience affect us at the points where life is most familiar. Divisions born of injury are hard to heal because they create imbalances of power and feelings of victimization. We resist compromise on such differences because we fear the loss of our essential selves.

Christ calls us to self-denial, however. Does this mean we must renounce all that is distinctive about us? I think not. Among other things, self-denial means identifying ourselves with Christ rather than with the lesser attributes by which we are otherwise known. The Lord allows us to claim our differences so long as we don't allow our differences to claim us.

Being of the same mind in the Lord means having the mind of Christ "who, though he was in the form of God, did not regard equality with God as something to be exploited, but emptied himself, taking the form of a slave" (Phil. 2:6-7). Being God didn't prevent Christ from taking the form of a slave. In fact, Christ's self-sacrifice was fundamental to his divine nature. By a radical act of submission, Christ became one with us and reconciled us to God. From the fullness of his grace, we receive our true identity and the power to submit ourselves to one another in love.

**PRAYER: O Christ, beyond all else that defines me, I belong to you. May I be so at peace with you that I can be at peace with others. Amen.**

For now, life in God's kingdom is a way of being in the world. Paul prescribes it as a life of continual rejoicing, gentleness born of God's nearness, and calm, thankful, all-inclusive prayer. Paul promises that for those who live such a life, "the peace of God, which surpasses all understanding, will guard your hearts and your minds in Christ Jesus."

Paul's promise of peace comes with an admonition to search everywhere for evidence of God's grace. Paul is no advocate of isolated Christian community. The world in its present form may be passing away, but it isn't devoid of goodness. God loves this world. It is the arena in which God works. So, Paul says, "Whatever is true, whatever is honorable, whatever is just, whatever is pure, whatever is pleasing, whatever is commendable, if there is any excellence and if there is anything worthy of praise, think about these things."

My wife and I recently stood in a busy airport with a throng of strangers, all of whom were waiting for friends and family members. As people spotted their loved ones, their faces lit up with smiles, laughter, and joyous tears. Happy reunions were punctuated with buoyant greetings and warm embraces. I doubt that all were Christians, but that did not diminish the beauty of what was happening there.

We do well to accept goodness wherever we encounter it. Whether it occurs in or out of the Christian community, all goodness is of God. If we trace any good act back to its true origin, we find God. Every discovery of goodness gives us a reason to rejoice. God is near to us in any and every good deed. The more we recognize goodness in the world, the more able we are to rest in the assurance of God's peace.

**PRAYER: God of all goodness, enable me to rejoice in your goodness wherever it occurs. Amen.**

# A People Set Apart

*October 13–19, 2008 • Lib Campbell[‡]*

## MONDAY, OCTOBER 13 • Read Exodus 33:12-17

Moses has stayed too long on the mountain, long enough for Aaron and the people at the base camp to sin a great sin in the casting of a golden calf. Moses' anger results in the breaking of the tablets upon which God has written the law. Moses begins a conversation with God about whether God will favor Moses and lead the people to the place promised. Moses, the reluctant, slow-of-speech leader, finds the voice of a skilled negotiator interceding for God's presence and favor that the Israelites may be reaffirmed as elect and strengthened for the rest of the journey.

But God's simple assurances are not enough for Moses who asks at least enough favor that others will see how distinctive a people the Israelites are. Moses persuades God to say yes. Despite the people's anger and disobedience, God favors this motley crew of folks, knows them by name, and seeks relationship with them through a covenant of knowing and being known for a purpose. God seeks to be known and worshiped above all gods by an obedient and faithful people.

Faithfulness and obedience to God's word distinguish the people set apart for a purpose even today. How do we look to the rest of the world in our set-apartness? Can the world around us see that we are God's? Moses intercedes on behalf of a sinful people. Jesus mediates that reconciliation on our behalf. Are we living God's purposes for our own lives, or are we waiting for someone else to act yet again on our behalf? These are hard questions for those who still work to cast a golden calf!

**PRAYER: Thank you, God, for knowing my name and for giving purpose to my life. Thank you for the prayers of all those who have made intercession on my behalf. Amen.**

---

[‡]Wife, mother, grandmother; ordained elder, North Carolina Conference of The United Methodist Church; living in Raleigh, North Carolina.

*Known in part*

Drug companies that manufacture antacids know that human beings often do not know when enough is enough. Moses surely doesn't in his requests of God. Moses asks to see the glory of God as proof of divine presence with him.

Asking to see the face of God is asking too much. While God wants to be known by us, God knows that full revelation will be more than Moses, or we, can handle. So the Holy One offers a compromise, allowing Moses a glimpse of God's back, while protecting Moses in the cleft of a rock until the divine glory passes by.

Since the garden of Eden, human beings have wanted to know the fullness of God, to have all mystery revealed, and to see God face-to-face. The closest we come to this seeing is revealed in Jesus the Christ. Why do we always seek more? Would full knowledge increase our faith? Or would full revelation flatten our faith out of existence?

The God who is known in part is with us, as God was with Moses in the cleft of a rock. Paul is right: now we see dimly, then face-to-face. How patient are we in the waiting to see God? How obedient are we in our waiting? Is the back side of God enough to keep a people faithful?

The extent of God's glory overpowers the ability of mere mortals to comprehend. That is why God is God, and Moses and we are not. True faith involves acceptance and love of the partial, knowing that in the fullness of time God's glory will be known to us—not in part but in whole.

**PRAYER: God, protect me from myself when I ask too much of you. Satisfy my soul in your gracious presence. Amen.**

*Known in holiness*

We Christians have a great familiarity with the Jesus who walks with us and talks with us in gardens and along seashores. We tend to view the God of the Old Testament in a different light. The call to know the Lord God in a trembling holiness establishes God's transcendence and other-worldliness that we are too often unaccustomed to praising.

Psalm 99 tells of the enthronement of God in high holy places. And the people pray from places of lowliness and inter-cessory hope. Ascription of praise to the One who reigns exalted above heaven and earth reminds us of the person and place of the God of creation, the God of power and might who hears our cries of despair and from on high directs our protection. How good of God to plan our care in such ways. How can we keep from praising with all the voices of the ages who have shouted, "Holy, holy, holy!"

Kneeling and bowing before kings is foreign to many of us. Yet realization of God's holiness as the one who reigns supreme over all life calls forth such reverence. The psalmist's words become our own when we see ourselves in the posture and alignment of praise and thanksgiving.

Once again we see that God wants to be known to us in God's holiness on high and our increasing holiness as travelers in a process of sanctification. God hears and answers the cry of the people who call upon God's name. May we exalt with praise the One who made us, the One who keeps us, the One in whose presence we are forgiven and made whole.

**PRAYER: Holy are you, Almighty God. From places of lowli-ness, your people praise you and your holy name. Thank you for hearing our cries and forgiving our sins. Amen.**

*Known by our steadfastness*

Paul offers words of greeting and thanksgiving to these of the early church in Thessalonica. Their faith and witness are winning converts to the new church in such measure that Paul offers thanksgiving for their witness, as well as much-needed encouragement. The new converts are known by their faith and distinguished by their witness to Jesus Christ as Lord of their lives, even amidst persecution and trial, and are shored up in Paul's thanksgiving.

*Steadfastness*, the word Paul uses to describe the faith and hope of the people, is an old-fashioned word that is somewhat out of vogue in today's world of planned obsolescence and disposable everything. People are cast aside like a used-up commodity. Marriages are lived until the going gets too tough. People in public service are regularly targeted for criticism. The church too often leaves discussions of justice and poverty off the table. Where is a steadfastness that evidences hope, faith, and love? Haven't there been times when even the most faithful of us have felt like giving up or giving in?

Words of thanksgiving and encouragement keep a people keeping on at the task of discipleship and faithful obedience in the fledgling church. How many times have words of encouragement shored us up through tough times and kept us going? Perhaps steadfastness is the result of embodying thanksgiving and encouragement in ways that keep us at the task of faithful living.

It is possible that our churches, our families, our marriages, our interpersonal relationships, and even our country would be blessed into greater steadfastness and strength with a little more thanksgiving and encouragement on our part. Who needs our encouragement today?

**PRAYER: God, make me an encourager this day. May my life be one of building your people up. May I be steadfast as you are steadfast. Amen.**

*Known in two worlds*

Jesus reminds the Pharisees and us that we live in two worlds and have responsibilities in each. We live in the kingdom of the world with authorities of state. And we live in the kingdom of God under the lordship of Christ. What would the world look like if we lived our Sunday school lessons instead of just teaching them? Imagine this correspondence with Jesus:

> Dear Jesus, your words about rendering unto God the things that are God's and unto Caesar the things that are Caesar's confuse me. I have been in the church since I was a little child. I have professed faith and been baptized. I've worked in missions and Sunday school and taught Vacation Bible School. I have led worship and tithe my resources. Isn't that enough? I do church a lot.
> Sincerely yours, A Confused Christian

> Dear Confused, thank you for your work and faith. I want you to remember that you live in two worlds—the kingdom of God and the kingdom of earth. Ask yourself what the world would look like if you lived God's kingdom ways in the world in real and measurable ways. I'm not talking about kingdom rhetoric; I'm not even talking about the work you do in the church. Remember, *doing* church is not *being* church—my body for the world. I'm talking about justice, mercy, humility, compassion, and love lived out in generous and unselfish ways in the places of your everyday life and work. Sure, give Caesar his due. But remember, you are mine; and I am counting on you to be part of my redemption plan. I love you. Have a nice day.
> Jesus.

**Suggestion for meditation: Make a plan for today to live your Christian witness in your deeds and not just your words. Meditate on how your life bears witness to the world that everything is the Lord's.**

*Known in wisdom and amazement*

Jesus is hardly operating beneath the radar of the religious authorities any more. In Matthew 21:45-46, the chief priests and Pharisees have had about enough of Jesus' teaching and are plotting to have him arrested. Exposing Jesus as an insurrectionist could accomplish just that. They ask that he tell them if it is lawful to pay taxes to the emperor or not

But Jesus, aware of their malice, asks them, "Why are you putting me to the test, you hypocrites?" Jesus does not fall for their plot; his entrapment does not occur at this juncture. Jesus' wisdom buys time. The prophetic voice is not silenced. And the authority of Jesus' wisdom amazes the status quo. Bravo, Jesus! Bravo, righteousness!

The prophet will always challenge the status quo. Knowing who we are and whose we are always challenges authority tainted by self-aggrandizement and self-serving. Those who follow Jesus and seek to live in the same way as he did face the same tests and entrapments. All over the world, those who follow Jesus are plotted against.

In places where freedom rings, how can we sit by and not be prophetic and visionary regarding the church of Jesus Christ? Our Jesus wisdom will confront authority and stand firm against unrighteousness. Thank you, Jesus, for the lesson learned!

**PRAYER: O God, help me not be afraid to speak truth in the face of injustice. Help me stand in small ways and large to promote peace and righteousness at every turn. Though I live contained in time and space, help me be of your kingdom. Amen.**

*Known by our witness*

Paul gives credit where credit is due. The message of the good news of Jesus Christ has not merely been orally transmitted, it has been enlivened and empowered by the Holy Spirit in gracious and authentic ways. The church in Thessalonica is inspired, and the word is going out in powerful and convicting ways. People are being drawn to Christ and into a life that imitates Christ and serves a living and true God.

As a young woman, I attended a luncheon where one of the hosts asked another woman other than me to say the blessing for the meal. The host said, "I asked her to say the blessing because she's the only Christian in the group." Those words from nearly forty years ago still evoke confession in my life.

The day of that luncheon I vowed to God that no one anywhere as long as I live will *not* know I am a Christian. In ways of hospitality, love, generosity, and grace, I continue to work to live Christ for the world every day. Paul's words admonish me even today, "Become imitators of us and of the Lord, . . . so that you become an example to all the believers."

That luncheon long ago became a turning point in my journey of faith. Forty years later, *I* am often the one asked to say the blessing for meals. I give thanks to God always, who through the power of the Holy Spirit emboldens the witness of the faithful in every age and in every place.

**PRAYER: Dear God, may our witness be joy, our lives thanksgiving, our hands praise, our hearts love, our strength peace, and our daily walk hope. May you be known because of the way we live our lives. Amen.**

# God's Tender Care

*October 20–26, 2008 • Anne Pharr[‡]*

## MONDAY, OCTOBER 20 • Read Psalm 90:1-6, 13-17

Just prior to my thirty-fifth birthday, I began experiencing what some might call a midlife crisis. Gone was the sense that a vast future sprawled endlessly before me. Instead, I felt newly aware that—despite what I had believed during my twenties—my life wouldn't last forever after all.

At one point, such a realization might have been cause for fear. Instead, I felt renewed. I began waking each morning with a quiet but urgent desire to choose my activities a bit more carefully. After reassessing what I believed to be my God-given talents and responsibilities, I was compelled to focus more time on what seemed central to my true identity, rather than frittering away my time on things that seemed less vital. I was acting on the truth that life is precious—and that it doesn't last forever.

I wonder whether that might be the psalmist's intention in Psalm 90 when he reminds the Israelites that our human perception of time differs from God's. To some, a lifetime may feel a thousand years long (especially on difficult days!), but from the divine perspective, our life cycle resembles the grass that springs up in the morning but is dry and withered by the evening.

It can be sobering to recall the fleeting nature of a human life, but such knowledge can also lead us to ask God, as does the psalmist, to "count our days" and to "prosper for us the works of our hands." The Holy One will surely respond to such a prayer. And in God's answer comes the freedom to devote our days to what is truly important—the work for which we were created.

**PRAYER: Lord, allow me to be mindful today of life's brevity and of your willingness to establish the work of my hands for your kingdom. Amen.**

---

[‡]Wife, mother of two children; part-time English instructor, Knoxville, Tennessee.

TUESDAY, OCTOBER 21 • **Read Matthew 22:34-40**

It's near the end of an exhausting week, and my husband is work-ing late. My preschoolers, gleefully "sock skating" through the kitchen, unintentionally block my attempts to load the dish-washer. My patience is depleted. It seems all I've done the last few hours is bark instructions over my shoulder while doing house-work. Right before banishing them to their rooms, I realize they need undivided attention rather than more snappish instructions. Reluctantly leaving my tasks, I head to the living room.

I improvise a brightly lettered poster listing "Habits for a Happy Home" and invite my children to snuggle up on the couch. Their little voices enthusiastically join mine as we say the rules together. "We keep our hands and feet to ourselves." "We are kind with our words and our actions." As I imitate someone breaking every rule on the list, they burst into giggles. My irri-tation melts into affection, and they head to bed.

When life's demands overwhelm me, I begin to resemble the Pharisees: I assign myself an impossibly long "must-do" list, then feverishly work to prove my competence by completing each task. Such an approach seemed effective during my days as a pro-fessional; however, it has not served me well as a parent. In my determination to complete every item on the list, I grow oblivi-ous to the needs of those persons God has entrusted to my care.

In retrospect, I realize God prompted me that evening to shift my focus from what seemed important (completing house-work) to what was truly vital: loving God by guiding and enjoy-ing my children.

Regardless of where I spend my day, I often sense God en-couraging me to put aside my own agenda. The invitation not only alleviates the anxiety of needing to prove my competence. It frees me to live out the two simple principles designated as the "greatest" commandments—loving God fully and loving others unselfishly.

**SUGGESTION FOR PRAYER: Ask God to reveal God's desires for you to carry out this day.**

Each time I sing "Jesus Loves Me, This I Know," I take comfort in the reminder that "little ones to him belong. / They are weak but he is strong." Though I consider myself a competent adult, my shortcomings confirm that I am still a "little one" in need of Jesus' strength, guidance, and forgiveness.

The Pharisees admit no such need in their conversation with Jesus. Unable to accept this man as God's son, they want to "test" him—to prove his incompetence and, in turn, reinforce their own superiority.

Jesus follows their test with questions of his own: "What do you think of the Messiah? Whose son is he?"

We can imagine the Pharisees' response, "That's easy. Everyone knows that the Messiah is the son of David." Then Jesus quotes the opening verse of Psalm 110, a royal psalm, and asks a question that silences the hair-splitting logic of the Pharisees: "How can David refer to his son as Lord?"

Jesus overturns the Pharisees' academically accurate answer—and their mistaken sense of superiority. When David, the Pharisees' forefather, calls the Messiah "Lord," he sets an example for them to follow. This, however, would require admitting to something less than self-sufficiency . . . something that might resemble weakness.

The Gospel concludes this passage with the sentence that begins, "No one was able to give him an answer." Though the Pharisees fall silent when confronted with the truth, we can take deep comfort in relinquishing our need to be strong, acknowledging instead our weaknesses and need for God's strength.

SUGGESTION FOR REFLECTION: **Consider the questions that block you from participating fully in God's love. Try to release those questions that bolster your false sense of security and strength.**

How often do I encounter someone who could benefit from a kind gesture: a pot of soup for a sick neighbor, a cool drink for the traffic policewoman, a lunch invitation to the new coworker. As I consider doing a "random act of kindness," doubts arise. My neighbor may prefer privacy. The policewoman might not appreciate the interruption. My coworker might not enjoy my company. What if I'm more a bother than a blessing?

Paul has no such doubts in his ministry. He and his colaborers loved wholeheartedly, despite insults and "great opposition." Scripture suggests that they annoyed a few people along the way, but they didn't agonize about being a bother. Rather, they cared for the Thessalonians like "a nurse tenderly caring for her children," sharing "not only the gospel of God but also our own selves, because you have become very dear to us."

What motivates Paul and his coworkers to love with such abandon? Not the admiration of others, for Paul writes that they were not attempting to "please mortals." But Paul does care about pleasing God. In verse 5, he writes of his unwavering, singular desire to please only God. When we remind ourselves that this too is our focus, other questions quickly fade away.

**PRAYER: Lord, when I next encounter someone who might be blessed by a simple kindness, I pray that my reservations about what the recipient (or anyone else) might think of me won't stop me. Rather, remind me of this simple question: how might I please you by doing something kind for my neighbor today? Amen.**

If I'm honest, I must admit to times of neediness when I could not locate God's provision, times of sorrow when I felt none of God's comfort, times of confusion when I could not discern God's guidance. In those excruciating moments, the compassionate Father described in scripture seems at least distant if not entirely absent from my life.

During such seasons, my prayers go something like this: "God, your word says you are a caring Father, but I feel as if you have disappeared from my life. I'm so afraid. Am I being punished? When will you relent, Lord? Where are you?"

I find comfort in discovering that even the psalmist voices similar feelings in Psalm 90, asking God to "turn," to "have compassion," and to "make us glad as many days as you have afflicted us." The psalmist's words imply that his experience feels like God is purposely distressing the people. Indeed, verses 13 and 15 suggest that God has been unrelentingly stern, not compassionate.

If the psalmist and God's chosen but rebellious people face such challenges in their relationship with God, then my own occasional sense of God's absence isn't as portending. And, though we all prefer those experiences where we can easily perceive God acting as loving Parent, we can feel less anxious when we can't seem to "locate" God. We take hope that other children have walked through seasons without God's discernible presence. We, like they, can continue to pray that God will "satisfy" us with "unfailing love" and "make us glad."

**SUGGESTION FOR PRAYER: Ask God for the ability to recognize the divine presence, even during life's challenging experiences.**

I still remember my Sunday school teacher telling the story of Moses. How Pharaoh's daughter finds him floating in a basket on the river. How he grows up in the palace, kills an Egyptian, and flees. How he encounters God in a burning bush and obeys the command to lead the Israelites to the Promised Land. And how, in the end, God does not allow Moses to enter the Promised Land himself. While many other Bible stories emphasize God's kindness, that well-intentioned Sunday school lesson planted a seed of fear that continued to grow through the years.

How refreshing it was to revisit Moses' story as an adult and to discover a God who is tender, even while delivering painful consequences. God does prohibit Moses from going into Canaan, but God graciously allows him to view it with his own eyes. In doing so, God gives Moses the opportunity to see fulfilled the dream he and the Israelites have clung to during decades of hardship.

Though Moses still has the strength to climb Mount Nebo and the vision to see Canaan, scripture tells us that he soon dies "according to the word of the LORD" (v. 5, KJV). Might God have been sparing him not only the hardships of aging but also the heartbreak of living out his years excluded from this Promised Land? Jewish tradition interprets the phrase "according to the word of the LORD" as meaning that Moses receives an actual kiss from God at his death. Then God buries Moses in a location known only to God.

This passage reveals a God who cares tenderly for Moses. It reminds us, as well, that though we may fear the consequences of our failures, God's mercy will accompany God's discipline.

**SUGGESTION FOR PRAYER: Thank God for divine tenderness toward us, even when we fail.**

The day I left for college, my parents moved from the house in which I'd grown up. A van held countless items which, to me, represented "home." Our car bulged with clothing and creature comforts to adorn my generic dorm room. Pulling out of the driveway, I felt a strange mix of emotions: nervous excitement about this new world of college and fear-tinged nostalgia about the permanence of leaving. Would I ever really feel "at home" again?

Thanksgiving found me traveling to my new home for the first time. Upon arriving in the small west Texas town, I parked in front of a nondescript building, glanced at the slip of paper with my parents' apartment number, and grabbed my bags. I was soon knocking tentatively on a plain brown door, holding my breath in apprehension.

When the door opened, a quick glance revealed our comfortable couch, familiar pictures on the walls, and my father's handmade stereo speakers, now playing a longtime favorite. Feeling myself wrapped in hugs from Mom, then Dad, I inhaled for the first time, catching the scent of my favorite meal simmering. Suddenly, the sense of being home flooded over me—less on account of the well-known furnishings than because of my parents' warm presence, embodied in smiling hugs and loving preparations for my arrival.

Many read Psalm 90 as an imagined prayer of Moses who, with the Israelites, must have longed for home during that forty-year journey through the unwelcoming desert toward the Promised Land. Knowing of their profound loneliness makes the first line particularly poignant. In referring to God as the Israelites' "dwelling place," These words remind Moses' followers—and encourage us—that it is God's abiding presence, rather than physical surroundings, that allows us to be truly "at home."

**SUGGESTION FOR PRAYER: Thank God for being your dwelling place, despite the nature of your physical surroundings.**

# Taste and See

*October 27–November 2, 2008* • *Brother David Steindl-Rast[‡]*

## MONDAY, OCTOBER 27 • Read 1 John 3:1-3

Everything is gift. Living in a given world at a given time, we start this week's meditations by pondering the greatest gift of all: God's love for us—pure gift, not reward for some achievement on our part. We are runners in a strange race: we receive the grand prize before we ever start. This prize is the gift to be called "child of God," indeed to *be* child of God. This is why Paul says in 1 Corinthians 9: 24 that "only one receives the prize"—Jesus Christ, *the* child of God.

With this as our starting point, why do we have to run at all? John gives the answer: to purify ourselves; running the race reveals our true identity. Every human child is created in God's image and likeness. Our life stories, however, are apt to disfigure this likeness. Those who "purify themselves, just as he is pure," restore Christlikeness to the disfigured image.

Purification does not mean cleansing our faults one by one like stains from a rug after a messy party. The process demands something far more drastic: liberation from "the world" that does not know God. This world (not the world that "God so loved," but worldliness) has a firm grip on us; we are caught in its mind-maze as long as we confuse our competitive ego with our true Christ-identity. The race we run is no competition. Spiritual spot-cleaning only boosts our little ego, makes us feel a bit ahead of the spiritually unwashed. But there is no room for complacent comparison, since we are all one in the only One who wins the prize. The goal is to be able to say with Christ, "I have conquered the world" (John 16: 33).

SUGGESTION FOR REFLECTION: **What if I acted as God sees me—as Christ?**

---

[‡]A monk of Mt. Saviour Benedictine monastery, Pine City, New York; author, lecturer, and cofounder of www.gratefulness.org

Why does Jesus congratulate those who suffer persecution? Because they will inherit heaven as their reward? On one level this is so; on a deeper level, however, persecution for "righteousness' sake" proves that the kingdom of heaven is theirs already. The world does not know them because they "have conquered the world" (John 16:33). Why else would they be persecuted? When we can say, "It is no longer I who live, but it is Christ who lives in me," we take our seat with Christ in heaven (Eph. 2:6)— and are sure to be persecuted on earth.

"Indeed, all who want to live a godly life in Christ Jesus will be persecuted" (2 Tim. 3:12). Our world of war, oppression, and exploitation cannot tolerate people who live in Christ, the righteous one. Righteousness includes social justice, and those who stand up for justice take a prophetic stance.

Persecution takes many forms. Daily pinprick persecution may require more courage than heroism that makes headlines. In any social setting—family, church, politics—the moment comes when justice demands that we speak out. The temptation is to speak out and then quickly get out. Yet, "it is impossible for a prophet to be killed outside of Jerusalem," for then he or she is no longer a prophet but an outside critic. True prophets stay and speak out.

To meet this double challenge, we need to trust that our true life is "hidden with Christ in God." When we focus on this core of our being, we find a deep stillness within; we are anchored in joy. Our Christ identity is then revealed—even to ourselves— through persecution. Persecution is not only a test to be rewarded but a testimony proving that its reward, the kingdom of heaven, is within us.

**SUGGESTION FOR REFLECTION: What matters more to me, the story of my life involved with past and future, including persecution and suffering—or the great *now* of Christ's life within me?**

The theme of these psalm verses is a familiar one: Happy are those who take refuge in God, for God will rescue them. And the psalm depicts this deliverance in vivid detail: no more hunger but abundance of all good things; not one bone of those whom God protects shall be broken. But is this so? A quick reality check brings the answer: a resounding no! Our life stories demonstrate that God lets not only refreshing rain fall on the just and the unjust alike but atomic bombs as well.

And yet, our life stories are not our life. Our true life is Christ living in us. The moment we are no longer caught up in past and future and stop bewailing the past and worrying about the future, we live in the now of our true identity, our Christ identity. This is the true deliverance; any other is temporary at best, because in the end we all die. But we are "saved from every trouble" when we live in the now, the present moment, the presence of God. Then we deal with difficulties as they arise, instead of turning them into problems.

We have all heard accounts of parents showing almost superhuman strength and presence of mind, lifting cars or walking though fire to rescue a child. They act in the now without thinking. Thinking creates our problems. We can cultivate the art of tapping into a life greater than our life story, into a life force greater than our thinking by tasting again and again life in fullness—life in Christ. Thinking about it is not enough. We must taste and so see that the Lord does indeed deliver us—not simply from troubles themselves but from *fearing* troubles. Fear of God is the loving awe of Christ-in-us. Fear of God makes us fearless. This is true deliverance.

**SUGGESTION FOR REFLECTION: How can I make time for taste-and-see moments in my daily life?**

It is almost impossible for us to listen with fresh ears to the Beatitudes; we have heard them too often. Otherwise, it would sound like shocking irony to hear Jesus congratulate the poor, the hungry, and those who weep. If only we could recover some of this shock and ask, "What on earth does Jesus mean?"

Compared with Luke's version, Matthew has bolstered the shock. The poor here are no longer the poverty-stricken destitute; they are poor in a spiritual sense, relying completely on God's mercy. That God will reward them becomes predictable. But notice the contrast between the list of those who will be rewarded (in the future): the meek, the merciful, the pure of heart—and the two surprising beatitudes that bracket this list. To the poor and the persecuted Jesus does not promise a future reward; he does not promise at all. He wakens them to the realization that the kingdom of heaven is theirs right now. By this paradox Jesus challenges us to jump from the reward mentality into a new mode of thinking, which is, after all, what "conversion" means: to turn our conventional mind-set upside down.

The kingdom of God is not a reward for being poor. Poverty or riches don't matter. What matters is the kingdom. And, no matter how poor you are, congratulations! The kingdom is yours now and always; it is the breath within your breath, the Christ in whom you were created and who lives in you. Origen, an early Christian theologian, calls Christ himself the kingdom of God. Are you human? Then Christ—and so the kingdom—is the very core of your being. Live from this sacred heart of your heart, live as merciful, pure, and peacemaking—and the whole world will be blessed.

SUGGESTION FOR REFLECTION: **In what ways is Christ the innermost essence of every human being? How does that knowledge encourage me to act?**

"I will bless the Lord." In the Beatitudes Jesus proclaims all God's children blessed. In this psalm, we in turn bless God. The blessing that went out from God, making all creation blessed at its core, returns to God in a cosmic chorus of praise. This is why Rabbi Abraham Heschel can say, "Just to be is a blessing." God's life-breath is the original blessing; it made Adam a living being and shall be the life-breath of every human. With every in-breath, we receive God's blessing anew; with every out-breath, we are meant to praise God from whom all blessings flow. To stop the flow of blessing would be like stopping breathing.

A memorable image for the flow of blessing is the river Jordan. It cascades down from the Lebanon mountains and fills the lake of Galilee that teems with fish and whose banks abound with fruit of every kind—an image of Paradise, the perfect embodiment of blessing. From there the waters of the Jordan flow on into the Dead Sea—dead because no life can survive in it, and its shores are a desolate waste. What happened here? Is it not the same water that fills both the lake of Galilee and the Dead Sea? Yes, but the lake receives and gives; the Dead Sea only receives. To avoid stagnation, blessing has to keep flowing.

Give-and-take creates a mind-set of abundance. Awareness that the more we give, the more we receive makes us fearless. Fear in all its forms springs from a mind-set of scarcity. Fear leads to hoarding; yet, blessings hoarded turn into curses. The Lord delivers from fear those who bigheartedly share their blessings. Their eyes become radiant like those of our forebears in the faith of whom it was said that one could recognize them by their shining faces.

**SUGGESTION FOR REFLECTION: What are my greatest blessings? How do I pass them on?**

## ALL SAINTS DAY

The Feast of All Saints celebrates God's gift as it is realized in the lives of an innumerable multitude throughout the ages. As we saw in our first meditation, the gift, surpassing all other gifts of God, is "that we should be called children of God. And that is what we are," because the Christ life is at the core of every human being. All of us are "created in Christ" and called to give this timeless reality shape in time through our life stories.

Christ plays as the divine Wisdom, who delights in cosmic play (see Prov. 8:31); he plays an actor as it were behind the mask, the persona of every one of us, "created in him" (Eph. 2:10); he plays the harps "of harpists playing on their harps" (Rev. 14:2) in eternal worship of the Father. He plays because he is "the Lord of the dance." Having come forth from the Father, he returns to the Father as leader of a divine circle dance, as the early Greek theologians envisaged him.

Thus, Christ plays in the sense in which genuine liturgy is play. What the book of Revelation depicts in this passage is an eternal liturgy of thanksgiving. In a hymn framed by "Amen"— the expression of faith in God's faithfulness—all blessing flows back to its Source in thanksgiving. The Son has nothing that he has not received from the Father and gives it all back in thanksgiving through the Holy Spirit. And, through God's overflowing love, all creation is swept up into this surge of the triune life of Giver, Gift, and Thanksgiving.

SUGGESTION FOR REFLECTION: **What might the poet T. S. Eliot have meant when he wrote: "Except for the point, the still point, / There would be no dance, and there is only the dance"?**

How would you reply to the elder's question, "Who are these, robed in white?" One answer is suggested by the passage in First John with which we began this week. They are, like us, the "children of God," of whom John said, "We are God's children now; what we will be has not yet been revealed." Here, in this glimpse of a reality beyond time, the promise that "we will be like him" has been fulfilled: those clothed in white have become like the transfigured Christ, whose "clothes became dazzling white, such as no one on earth could bleach them" (Mark 9:3). The divine seed that made them human has burst into full bloom.

But is this broadly inclusive understanding of redemption justified? Let us see how the elder answers his own question, "Where have they come from?" He says, "They . . . have come out of the great ordeal." There "they have washed their robes and made them white in the blood of the Lamb." They purified themselves, "just as he is pure" (1 John 3:3). A narrow understanding would restrict "the great ordeal" to the early persecutions of Christians, which historically did indeed occasion this passage. But is not all of history a great ordeal for those who bear witness to "the Righteous One" by works of righteousness and hence face persecution?

They may have never heard Christ's name or may have misunderstood and rejected it. Yet, the kingdom belongs, without restricting clause, to all who "are persecuted for righteousness' sake," and *righteousness* is merely the Sunday word for justice. "If we endure, we will also reign with him" (2 Tim. 2:12). This promise holds for all who stand up for justice and suffer the consequences. Rejoice; no one can count this multitude.

SUGGESTION FOR REFLECTION: **What seems to matter more to the God of Jesus—doctrinal correctness or witness to the Christ in every human heart? Why?**

# Strengthened for the Challenge

*November 3–9, 2008* • *Tamara Elisabeth Lewis[‡]*

**MONDAY, NOVEMBER 3** • **Read Joshua 24:1-3***a***, 14-25**

"This is our river," my grandmother told me. I was four years old. She and I stood on the banks of the Arkansas River, which flowed right behind her house. We had taken a walk to survey its vast rolling currents and to reflect on our family's history. "Your grandfather built this house on the river over thirty years ago," she said, looking out over the muddy waters. "Our roots run deep in this river." My grandmother offered me, even at such a young age, a sense of belonging, a sense of identity.

So too Joshua, as leader of the people of Israel, gathers them together to recount their ancestral history. This history begins with Abraham who was called by God to begin a new life. It is from this new life that the now gathered tribes arose. Such history is told to remind the people of their identity, an identity that unifies and gives them purpose. Their identity centers on the very God who had called Abraham. This same God continues to call them, to love them, and to nurture them in faithfulness and compassion. They can serve the God of their father Abraham, or they can serve other gods. Joshua presents the options, and they decide resolutely that they will serve God!

Over time, the people of Israel would prove unfaithful to this agreement, yet God always remains faithful. Despite their sins, God always takes them back. Like the father in Jesus' parable of the prodigal son, God is there to receive the recalcitrant Israelites with love and forgiveness. No matter how far they run, God remains steadfast.

**PRAYER: Dear Lord, when we run far from you, remind us that you faithfully wait to take us back in love, forgiveness, and compassion. Amen.**

---

[‡]Doctoral student in church history, Vanderbilt University; elder in the Tennessee Conference of The United Methodist Church; living in Nashville, Tennessee.

I have always loved words. It all started with the magical stories my father read to me from big, colorful storybooks when I was a child. The words on the page seemed to contain great mysteries awaiting discovery and great knowledge awaiting learning. All a person needed was the tool, the ability to decipher words, and new worlds could be experienced. Words are instructive, powerful, and enjoyable.

The psalmist seems to share this same love of words. Not only does the psalmist want to get an important message across, but he conveys excitement in the telling of the story. The psalmist promises to delight listeners with a "parable" and to tickle appetites with ancient aphorisms. One can imagine young and old gathered in a circle around the storyteller with anticipation, straining to make out every syllable, every line. In all, the words offered cause much excitement and revelation. These stories are not told only once; they are told over and over again.

Just as in Genesis when God spoke words to form the universe and just as in the Gospels when Jesus spoke parables to create new paradigms, the psalmist speaks inspired meaning into the hearts, minds, and souls of the people. Remember, the psalmist says, the wonderful things God has done for you. Remember the laws of grace and mercy that stamp out oppression, injustice, and suffering. Hear the stories that speak again and again of God's goodness and power. Imprint these stories of faith in your mind. Keep the vision of God's goodness continually before you. Convey this faith to your children, so that one day they will rise up and pass on these stories with hope and joy.

PRAYER: Holy God, help us to renew our minds like the psalmist with words that speak of your love, mercy, and grace. Enable us to share these words of faith and hope with our communities and families. In Jesus' name. Amen.

Remembering our history can give us strength when we face challenges. The psalmist advocates that parents and elders recount Israel's history to their children. Younger generations, empowered by the strength of story, will then pass on this legacy. The faith and witness live on. The psalmist writes about Israel's history of the Lord's everlasting guidance to remind the people that just as God helped Israel before, God will do so again and again.

I recently attended the 2006 United Methodist Clergy-women's Conference in Chicago with my mother. As a probation-ary elder in the Tennessee Conference, I have served churches, worked as a hospital chaplain, and volunteered in prison ministry. My mother is also an elder in The United Methodist Church; through the years, I have witnessed her service to the church and community.

I found the experience of workshops, seminars, and worship at the conference with my mother extremely rich because it deepened the sense of family legacy in ministry. While we were there, I could sense the spirit of my maternal grandfather, who was also a Methodist minister. His legacy of faith and dedication has been passed on to us. I could also feel my paternal grand-mother, an extremely faithful and a deep lover of God's word, with us as well. Especially I remembered my maternal great-grandmother, who had introduced the family clan to Method-ism. Reflections on the generations who have gone before give me continued inspiration and motivation in ministry.

When I think about my mother, grandparents, and great-grandparents, I reflect on how they persevered in faith despite obstacles and roadblocks. This knowledge encourages me to cul-tivate my faith and to share it with others.

**PRAYER: Dear God, teach us the stories of your word as well as our personal and communal stories of faith. May these stories encourage and strengthen us. Enable us to pass on these sto-ries of witness and evangelism. In Jesus' name. Amen.**

It was a dark night. Driving down the road, I could make out two vehicles in the middle of the street. I parked my car and then gingerly stepped out onto the deserted street. One other woman had done the same, and together we approached the crashed cars with trepidation. The first car was empty. Its driver was lying motionless on the road. "I'll stay with this one," the woman said. "You go check out the other car."

Silently I walked in the direction of the second car. It was twisted and mangled beyond recognition. After looking intently inside for several moments, I finally made out an arm, then a man's body, amidst misshapen metal pieces.

"Sir," I called out softly, then louder. "Sir, can you hear me?" There was silence.

I felt the woman's hand on my shoulder. "How is he?" she asked, straining to look. "The man over there is not moving at all," she said sorrowfully. "Is this one alive?"

Suddenly we could hear a low, barely perceptible moan. "Sir, sir!" I cried. The man moaned again, trying to talk.

I noticed a cross hanging from the car's broken rearview mirror. "Sir, do you mind if I pray with you?" I asked. Hearing only another moan, I began to recite the Lord's Prayer. The woman joined me. As we prayed, the man began to moan and cry louder, as he seemed to be praying with us. Just then, bright blue lights of police cars and the stirring sounds of emergency vehicles filled the dark quiet of the empty street.

In the shock and tender flash of the movement between life and death, the presence and love of God was felt in the words of prayer. The hope of Christ in our faith assures, as Paul reminds us, that even as we face tragedy and pain, there is a promise of eternal life in Jesus.

**PRAYER: Dear God, help us remember the great promises of eternity you have offered those who trust in the death and resurrection of your son Jesus Christ. May this faith bless and keep us amidst all the demands of life. Amen.**

After witnessing the crashed cars on the road, I later heard that both men in the accident had died. As I prayed for the men and their families, my thoughts drifted to the question of life. Although we do not like to think much about it, all of us will die one day. This fact can be a cause of great concern and worry when we do not know what will happen to us after death.

Paul, as spiritual advisor to the Christian church of Thessalonica, had received word that the congregation was experiencing distress over this very issue. Therefore, Paul writes to console them about their fears of death. Although many of their loved ones have died, he says, that is no reason for the members to lose hope. The message of the Christian faith centers on life. Jesus Christ, our Savior, died, but then rose from the dead. And not only this, but this same Jesus promises resurrection to those who believe in him. Therefore, our deaths will not be the end—only a beginning. In Christ, we are offered eternal life.

So, despite the trials and tragedies of this life, the realization that such suffering will not last forever encourages us. Christ, armed with power as the living Word of God and Son of the Father, will come in heavenly glory for all God's children. So, even in times of pain, we are consoled. Even in death, we are comforted.

Paul is confident that we who are in Christ will be with God and our loved ones in eternal life forever. This is a joyous hope, offered to us by God in love. Reassuring one another of the promise in Jesus is therefore our task in Christian community.

**PRAYER: Dear God, as we face difficulties, strengthen us to encourage one another as did Paul about the assurance of everlasting life in Jesus Christ. This is our challenge of Christian witness. In Jesus' name we pray. Amen.**

"You've got to help," my friend stated desperately. She looked absolutely beautiful in her stunning white wedding gown and veil, holding her bouquet. However, her pretty face was lined with worry. "One of my bridesmaids has not shown up," she continued. "It's almost time for the wedding. You've got to step in."

Of course, I was surprised. Pleased with my role as hostess for the wedding, I certainly had not anticipated being a bridesmaid. But I found myself squeezing into the missing bridesmaid's dress and lining up with the others before the processional.

Jesus tells a parable about bridesmaids. In first-century Jewish culture, bridesmaids had the responsibility of going before the groom, not the bride. Since weddings often happened at night, their job was to go forward with lanterns in a joyous processional, leading the bridegroom to his bride. However, in Jesus' story, five of the bridesmaids do not prepare ahead of time by having enough oil for their lanterns. When the bridegroom comes later than expected, the five unprepared bridesmaids have run out of oil. Therefore, they cannot fulfill their responsibilities and are not admitted to the wedding. For me, an unprepared bridesmaid led to my inclusion in a special way; for the women in the parable, their unpreparedness brings exclusion.

If we interpret the parable as an allegory, the bridegroom is Christ. We, the believers, are bridesmaids. The wedding is the kingdom of God. Our job is to light the way to the kingdom by our faith, worship, and service. So we ask: how well are we doing our job? Are we prepared and ready? How will the bridegroom rate our work as Christians? Will we be accepted into the kingdom? These are the questions Christ calls us to answer.

**PRAYER: Help us, Lord, to prepare ourselves spiritually for the Christian life. Give us the strength to pray, study, work, give, and worship in order to serve the Bridegroom. May we show ourselves approved by Jesus Christ. Amen.**

"Good morning, class," the instructor stated calmly as students scrambled to their seats. "Put your books away, and pull out a sheet of paper. We are having a pop quiz."

Tonya groaned and looked over at her best friend, Lisa, who frowned. "I didn't read the book," Tonya mouthed and put her head down. Even though their teacher, Mr. Downs, had told them repeatedly all week to review the lessons in their history book, Tonya and Lisa had chosen to talk on the phone in the evenings instead of doing homework. Now they were stuck.

"Twenty questions," Mr. Downs was saying, "fill in the blank."

It's an awful feeling to be caught unprepared. And yet this is exactly the situation five foolish bridesmaids find themselves in according to Jesus' parable. Why are they foolish? Ancient Middle Eastern portable lamps burned oil quickly. Anyone carrying them would need extra oil. In fact, taking a lamp without extra oil would be like driving a car today without gas in the tank. The five bridesmaids are foolish because they had the opportunity to prepare but failed to do so.

This notion of preparedness can extend to the subject of spiritual disciplines. Many people sit in church pews Sunday after Sunday listening to sermons and singing praise hymns to God. Many share Christian community, tithe, and volunteer in Christian service. But how many of us continually commit ourselves to daily personal devotion, Bible study, and prayer? Although we acknowledge the necessity of spending regular time with God, we often fail to do so. Jesus reminds us in the parable of the ten bridesmaids to remain "awake" in personal piety. In this way, we maintain extra oil for our lamps so as to greet the presence of our precious bridegroom, Christ, throughout our daily lives.

**PRAYER: Dear Lord, help us to maintain regular spiritual disciplines of prayer, meditation, fasting, devotion, and Bible study. Enable us to return to our devotional practices whenever we stray. Teach us how to stay close to you. In Jesus' name. Amen.**

# Misplaced Priorities

*November 10–16, 2008* • *Gerald Kirksey*[‡]

## MONDAY, NOVEMBER 10 • Read Judges 4:1-3

A thief broke into a jewelry store. He didn't take anything; he just switched the price tags. I sometimes think about the thief. Was he waiting outside the jewelry store the following morning? Would the price changes be subtle and less susceptible to detection, or would the thief head for a fine diamond bracelet with the price tag from a costume jewelry bracelet? Would the store clerk be attentive and immediately note the deception, or would he enable the thief to "steal" the most valuable items?

But my thoughts of the jewelry store heist are often interrupted by a disquieting thought: I am the thief! I have misplaced my priorities by sometimes placing a high price tag on trivial, unimportant things while undervaluing the things most important in my life and in my spiritual journey. In the process, I have cheated others and myself out of the fullness of a life that might have been.

Like the thief in the jewelry store, the ancient Israelites in today's lectionary passage had, after eighty years of peace, lost sight of their true priorities and done "what was evil in the sight of the LORD." Because of their decisions, they found themselves enslaved for twenty years by an occupying foreign force.

Over and over again in the stories of ancient Israel, when the Israelites found themselves enslaved because of their evil deeds, a strong leader would usually rise from the suffering and refocus the Israelites on their covenantal relationship with God. We too can redirect our priorities by focusing on our covenantal relationship with our God. To assist us in breaking the bonds of misplaced priorities that enslave us, our prayers this week will remember words of a prayer adapted by John Wesley.

**PRAYER: I am no longer my own, but thine. Amen.**

---

[‡]Member, Belmont United Methodist Church, Nashville, Tennessee.

I have often wondered why women have had to work twice as hard as men to achieve recognition in our churches, many of which continue to deny women equal status. Why is a General Commission on the Status and Role of Women still necessary to ensure equality for women in The United Methodist Church? Shouldn't a person's status in the church and society be determined by ability, relationship with God, and response to God's call? Have the price tags been switched?

In ancient Israel, judges were military and civil leaders who had received "the spirit of the LORD." Deborah is one such judge. When she instructs Barak, a tribal chieftain, to take up battle against Israel's oppressor with the iron chariots, Barak says that he will go into battle only if Deborah accompanies him. Because the judges prophesy for the Lord, her reply must have made Barak's day: Deborah will risk her own safety to go with Barak into battle. But then comes the punchline: Barak will not receive the glory of the ensuing victory; rather, the oppressors will be beaten by a woman—Deborah.

Thousands of years later, many societies oppress women in the name of religion. Will a leader like Deborah be allowed to emerge, or will some societies prefer occupation to equality? Will today's generals accept a woman's leadership, as Barak ultimately did, or will they prefer defeat to fairness?

Will a modern-day Deborah or a Gandhi be denied a pulpit of leadership because of gender or color? Are justice, equality, and tolerance lifestyles that we pursue or just words that we utter? Do we need to change the price tags on the priorities of our lives?

**PRAYER: Put me to what thou wilt,**
      **rank me with whom thou wilt.**
      **Put me to doing, put me to suffering. Amen.**

As I took my regular pew in church this morning, I received my usual hug and smile from Ruby. Many Sundays, Ruby will stick a smiley-face on the shirt or blouse of everyone she meets although, alas, she seems to be partial to females. Ruby was born with Down syndrome and lives in Homeplace, a mission of my church. While Ruby may never enjoy the intellectual pursuits available to most of us, she has a love of life and a love of other people that many pew sitters may never know. Ruby has invested her talent wisely.

Jesus stongly supported the wise use of God's gifts. In the parable of the talents, the servants who work to increase the money entrusted to them receive reward, while the poor servant who buries his money for fear of losing it is admonished. Likewise, Jesus taught his disciples that a person should not put a candle under a bushel basket but let the candle shine to light the house. (See Matthew 5:15.) We are called to let the light of our lives shine so that others may see our good works and give thanks to God. Our limited talents are not the determining factor; it's what we do with the talents that's important.

If Christ came to my neighborhood, would he consider the huge houses—we've even got a name for them: McMansions—to be like bushels that hide the light of the lives housed therein? Would he reward our efforts to acquire and hoard more and more while others have less and less, or would he admonish us as he admonished the servant that hid his talent in the parable? Would my giving pale when compared to the sacrificial giving practiced by others? Are my priorities misplaced? Do I need to learn from Ruby and use my life and my smile to brighten the world?

**PRAYER: Let me be employed by thee or laid aside for thee, exalted for thee or brought low for thee. Amen.**

I'm in luck! The Lord may buy me that Mercedes Benz that Janis Joplin sang about! Isn't that what Jesus meant when he taught that those who have will be given more and have abundance? As a follower of Jesus, can't I expect to receive as many talents as the productive servants in the parable?

If my theology encouraged me to proof-text the scriptures, I would stop at the end of Matthew 25:30, which is, coincidentally, the end of the lectionary reading. But Jesus doesn't end his sermon after the parable of the talents—he had much more to say. His subsequent description of the Judgment tells us what we must do with the talents that we earn: feed the hungry, quench the thirst of the thirsty, clothe the naked, and visit the sick and imprisoned. It's sometimes difficult to see the hungry, thirsty, naked, sick, and imprisoned when we are surrounded with the luxury of the blessed. We've got to reset our priorities, get our hands dirty and our hearts troubled.

A recent movie *The Pursuit of Happyness* tells the story of Chris Gardner, a former homeless person in San Francisco who persevered and became a multimillionaire stockbroker. The story of Gardner, who ultimately used his ten talents very wisely, is also the story of Glide Memorial Church, a United Methodist church in the toughest part of San Francisco. When Gardner was at his lowest, Reverend Cecil Williams allowed Gardner and his son to stay at a new Glide Memorial shelter for homeless women. Now Gardner is a major supporter of Glide Memorial, which provides over one million free meals, serving people three times a day, seven days a week, three hundred sixty-five days a year, "in an atmosphere of respect, acceptance, and love."

Jesus taught us that as much as we help the least of his children, we help him. Might our unconditional love for the downtrodden include the servant who buried his one talent?

**PRAYER: Let me be full, let me be empty.**
**Let me have all things, let me have nothing. Amen.**

FRIDAY, NOVEMBER 14 • Read Psalm 123

In Psalm 123, the psalmist, writing on behalf of his community, laments the "contempt of the proud"—probably the contempt of an oppressor of Israel or a rival clan within Israel. At first blush, the psalm seems a little whiney. But then my gaze fell on an identification card from the Holocaust Memorial Museum in Washington that I use as a bookmark. It reminded me that I have never felt the hopelessness of oppression that many people in the world experience, even today. How would it feel to have no hope for tomorrow like so many of the Jews whose stories are contained within the identification cards given to each Holocaust Memorial Museum visitor? Would I then also write of the contempt of the proud?

A few months ago, I met a remarkable group of women, all of whom have felt the pain of the contempt of the proud. These are the women of Magdalene, a group of former prostitutes and drug addicts who are experiencing their own resurrection from a life of hopelessness and despair. Common threads bind their stories: acute poverty, low self-esteem, mental and physical abuse, and the false solace provided by drug use. With help, the women of Magdalene are encouraged to right their priorities and lift their eyes to the Lord and seek God's mercy.

The journey often begins when the director and others go to the places where the women of Magdalene live and ply their trades, walking the streets of unsavory neighborhoods. How many other Christians will drive by these women daily, simply shake their heads, and drive on?

We all have the "scorn of those who are at ease" in our hearts. May God help us assess our priorities and truly remember that as we help the least of God's children, we are doing the work of Jesus.

**PRAYER: I freely and heartily yield all things**
**To thy pleasure and disposal. Amen.**

I find some of this week's scripture readings difficult to understand. How can the God of the Israelites take part in some of the slaughters like the battles in Judges? How can the God of the Trinity condone such cruelty as the complete annihilation of a competing tribe when the Prince of Peace taught us to turn the other cheek? When Jesus teaches the parable of the talents, is he condoning the casting into darkness of the misguided servant who hides his talent? How can the Savior who taught us to love the poor, the prisoners, and the downtrodden unconditionally desire less for the poor servant?

As I reflect on the scriptures, particularly the Old Testament stories of the Jewish people, I allow myself to be guided by the four parts of John Wesley's theological test: scripture, tradition, reason, and experience. The writers of the Old Testament books had not experienced God as embodied in Jesus Christ, who would come to live among us thousands of years after Deborah.

My experience comes into play as I read today's scripture. When Paul writes about peace and security one day and sudden destruction the next, his writings hit a responsive chord. In fact I sometimes don't do very well with peace and security; I have an insatiable need to push the envelope and risk a bad result in the process.

Am I a child of the day or a child of the night? Like many other Christians, I am both a child of the day and of the night. While I often feel the peace and security of God's love, I also misplace my priorities and allow the trivial and unimportant to obscure the truly important things in my life. When will I finally be able to pray Wesley's Covenant Prayer and mean it?

A thief broke into a jewelry store—she didn't take anything; she just switched the price tags.

**PRAYER: And now, O glorious and blessed Lord,**
**Father, Son, and Holy Spirit,**
**Thou art mine and I am thine. So be it. Amen.**

Hear the good news: Jesus Christ died for our salvation so that, whether we wake as children of the day or sleep as children of the night, we may live with him. Because of the universal promise of salvation for both the vigilant and the backsliders, Paul admonishes the Thessalonians to build one another up. Although we may sometimes be children of the night with misplaced priorities, we are still God's children.

My pastor said it best: "What God creates, God never loses. . . . God will keep what God creates. Divine love is strong enough to love the world into God's vision!"

The good news often gets obscured under the weight of the world's problems. We have not been good stewards of our environment, and global warning now threatens our very existence. Our country is involved in a civil war in Iraq where brothers are killing brothers, both sides fighting in the name of Allah.

Because of the global economy, many more persons are now gaining the affluence long enjoyed by a few nations; but, at the same time, the disparity between the "haves" and the "have-nots" becomes greater and greater. Like the world I live in, my personal life is also conflicted. "I know better . . . " as my mother used to tell me, but living God's vision is a constant struggle. While we are both children of light and children of darkness, the warmth of God's universal love is strong enough to love this world and even me into God's vision. I am a child of God! Thanks be to God.

A thief broke into a jewelry store. He couldn't take anything because God had indelibly etched with love God's price tag on every item.

**PRAYER: And the covenant which I have made on earth,
Let it be ratified in heaven. Amen.**

# The God Who Cares

*November 17–23, 2008* • *J. Norfleete Day‡*

## MONDAY, NOVEMBER 17 • Read Ezekiel 34:11-16

The prophet Ezekiel ministered among his fellow Israelites during the darkest days of their history—the exile in Babylon. Ezekiel sees clearly that his people have no one to blame but themselves for their dire circumstances. They have been disobedient and now suffer the just consequences for their sins.

However, while all the people are responsible for their own sin, God considers some among them more responsible—the leaders. These kings provide leadership as God's personal representatives, caring for the people and protecting them from harm.

Unfortunately, as time went by, the kings of Judah became corrupt. They led the people not toward greater devotion and obedience to God but into idolatry, injustice, and social collapse. Therefore, God has Ezekiel pronounce God's judgment against the negligent leaders.

Ezekiel proclaims God's encouraging word of hope to the people. All is not lost. God personally will take over from the unreliable human leaders and restore the faithful covenant relationship that God intended. In spite of the people's sin, God remains their faithful shepherd. Their sin brings punishment, but God does not abandon them.

When have you experienced God's judgment in your life and wondered if things would ever be right again? Take heart; God, the faithful shepherd, never abandons the sheep. God is always in the business of forgiveness and restoration.

**PRAYER: Lord, remind me daily of your great love for me. May the imagery of shepherd and sheep keep me mindful that I am not alone and that I always belong to your flock wherever I may wander. Amen.**

---

‡Professor of New Testament and Spiritual Formation, Beeson Divinity School, Birmingham, Alabama; member, Vestavia Hills Baptist Church.

God promises to take over from the failed human rulers and to restore true divine governance. Specifically, God pledges to rescue and gather the scattered flock. To a people in exile, these are words of hope and anticipation. God will gather the people from all the places to which they had dispersed when Judah was overrun and plundered. Later, Jesus draws on this same imagery to describe his own mission "to seek out and to save the lost" (Luke 19:10)—"the lost sheep of the house of Israel" (Matt. 15:24).

The second phase of God's reclamation of the scattered sheep comes in provision for their needs: good pasture and loving care. The psalmist immortalized this metaphor in Psalm 23 as he describes elements of the shepherd's tender provision. The prophet Isaiah, in describing God's regard for the people, spoke of God as the nation's shepherd: "He tends his flock like a shepherd" (40:11, NIV). And of course, Jesus identifies himself as the good shepherd who provides safety and security for his sheep. (See John 10:1-6.)

While sheep tending is a foreign vocation to most of us in our technological age, we all can identify with the need for a sense of safety and security. Amid the threats of terrorism, nuclear war, and other fears of our time, we, like the exiled Hebrews, can draw hope and courage from the sure knowledge that our God watches over us and provides for us. We can depend on God to seek us when we stray, to bind up and heal our wounds, to strengthen us when we feel weak, and to govern our lives with justice.

**PRAYER: We give you thanks and praise, O Lord, that we need not be a slave to our fears since you, our shepherd God, watch over us to guard and protect us from all that threatens. Amen.**

This well-known discourse of Jesus comes at the end of a series of parables and instruction that he gives his disciples about the "end times." He tells these parables to teach his hearers what God expects from those who believe in his son, Jesus, and desire to live their lives as his followers.

The disciples have asked Jesus for insider information about the timing of God's final judgment and what signs they might observe that will give warning of that day. Jesus responds by telling them that even he does not know of God's timing for that monumental event and warns them not to heed false prophets who will appear and claim to know.

Then Jesus tells his disciples that they are asking the wrong question. Rather than inquiring to know when that final day of judgment will come, they need to be searching themselves to know if they will be ready whenever it comes. In this narrative about the sheep and the goats, Jesus tells them how to be ready— by faithfully doing God's work on earth.

Many of us long to do deeds for God that are great and praiseworthy in the estimation of others, but Jesus says the deeds that please God are the seemingly small and relatively insignificant deeds we do for other human beings. Indeed, God entrusts us with a part of God's work on earth, and we will ultimately be judged by how faithfully we carry it out.

Are you looking for something great and memorable to do for God today? Then locate a human being in need and, where possible, do for that person what you would ask God in prayer to do for him or her. You can become part of the answer to your own prayer; nothing will please God more.

**SUGGESTION FOR MEDITATION: Whom do I know that I can do some service for today, remembering that as I serve God's people I am actually serving God?**

God's evaluation of the kind and caring acts we do for others is to consider them as done for God's own self. If we consider this text in concert with the earlier meditations based on Ezekiel, we see unmistakable parallels.

In the Ezekiel passage we saw that God has entrusted the care of the people to the kings and the priests who have been unfaithful to that trust. God has appointed them to shepherd, to watch over, to protect, and to provide for the people. These unfaithful shepherds have focused on themselves and their own comfort instead of responding wisely to God's assignment.

When Jesus tells the parable of the sheep and the goats, he addresses this same matter in God's new covenant. With the Incarnation, God has sent God's own shepherd to demonstrate the role of the good and faithful shepherd. Then, as Jesus prepares to leave his followers on earth, he passes on to them the task of being his "under-shepherds." In specific instructions to Simon Peter, he said if you truly love me, show it by feeding my sheep— by caring for my people (John 21:15–17). The writer of First Peter later reminds the early church that as followers of Christ they are now God's priests, appointed to be caretakers over his flock (2:9).

We often think about our trust in God, but how often do we think about God's trust in us? Into each of our lives God brings sheep that need the tender care and protection of godly shepherds. In what ways are you a faithful shepherd to those whom God has entrusted to you? How does knowing of God's trust enable you to be more trusting of God?

**PRAYER: God, forgive me for those times when I have failed you by neglecting the needy persons you have brought into my path. Give me new eyes to see the hurting people in my life, and give me your heart to love and minister to them. Amen.**

## FRIDAY, NOVEMBER 21 • Read Ephesians 1:15–19*a*

In the first chapter of Ephesians, Paul, the attributed writer of this letter, expresses thanksgiving for these faithful believers. He is thankful because what he has heard about them makes him confident in their genuine faith, which is evidenced by their love for others. As a way to express his gratitude, Paul prays regularly for the Ephesian Christians that they continue to grow and develop in their Christian walk.

Paul first prays that they will grow in their understanding of all that they have gained by their salvation, especially the quality of the hope that is theirs as believers. The Christian's hope is not the world's sort of wishful thinking but is based on the certainty that God will do what God has promised.

Paul's second petition for the Ephesians is that they would understand how precious they are to God. They, along with all the saints, are God's inheritance—an inheritance glorious in God's eyes. It may seem strange to think of God having an inheritance; we are more accustomed to think of "our" inheritance, which is referred to in 1:14. But here the reference is to "his" [God's] inheritance. The Old Testament frequently uses God's inheritance/heritage as a synonym for God's people. The idea here is that of God's possession of God's people. God considers the people who make up this inheritance so valuable that God purchases them with the blood of God's own son.

Paul's third and climactic petition is that these Christians might understand and experience the amazing power of God working on their behalf and on the behalf of all who believe in Christ. This prayer naturally grows out of Paul's appreciation for what God has done and is doing in the lives of these Christians.

In your life, whose faithfulness in serving God causes thanksgiving to swell up in your heart? How and when have these persons encouraged you? Pray that God will continue to deepen their faith and strengthen their ministry.

**PRAYER: Thank you, Lord, for the great cloud of witnesses who bless my life. Amen.**

Paul's prayer includes his desire that the Ephesians understand the incomparable power of God that is available to them as they await God's consummation. To emphasize the importance of this truth, Paul uses four different terms to describe God's power.

Unpacking these four Greek words, we learn that God's power includes the ability to take action, involves the active exercise of supernatural power, manifests its dominion or mastery over something, and is a strength or power that can be possessed. Using these varied terms does not emphasize their distinctiveness but conveys the idea of God's power as surpassing any other power, known or imagined.

As a skillful teacher, Paul follows this assertion with an example, indeed, the supreme example: God's power demonstrated in raising Christ from the dead and exalting him to a place of great honor in heaven. As if that weren't enough, God's power is bolstered and reinforced by the subjection of all other powers to Christ. So we learn that God's power is life-giving and can defeat any hostile power we as Christians may encounter.

Paul intends his prayer to offer encouragement and assurance to the Ephesian believers as they try to live for Christ in the face of great opposition. It can offer encouragement to us as well when we realize that God's power, present in its fullness in Christ, is available to us as Christians. We need not be afraid—of terrorists, of natural disasters, of injury or disease, even of death. The power of God is at work on our behalf all the time and is available in every moment if we but call upon it.

**PRAYER: O God, may we take courage as we face the hostile forces of our world, knowing that your power exceeds any that would oppose us. May we be bold to claim your power in our times of need. Amen.**

In this psalm, we recapture the imagery of Ezekiel in depicting God as Israel's shepherd. In Ezekiel, God expressed judgment upon those who proved themselves unworthy shepherds. Here, the psalmist calls upon the people of Israel to express their thanksgiving for God's faithful care over them by offering praise.

The Hebrew language has no word that means "to thank." When thanksgiving was offered to God, the means of expressing it was praise—declarative praise, referring to what God had done; or descriptive praise, referring to what God characteristically does. This psalm includes both types of praise: declarative, affirming God's creation of this people; descriptive, extolling God's goodness, steadfast love, and faithfulness.

The setting for this particular hymn was probably just outside the gates of the sanctuary as the worshipers prepare to enter. The psalmist instructs the people to initiate their praise by making a joyful noise to the Lord, worshiping God with gladness, and coming into God's presence with singing. What could be more appropriate considering all they had to be thankful for?

The people's praise also contained a confession that acknowledges that Yahweh alone is God and rightfully receives the praises of this people because God made them—they owe their very existence to God. And they eagerly extend this praise because God does not treat them as some occasionally remembered novelty of creation but tenderly cares for them as the sheep of the Creator's pasture. No wonder they are moved gladly and joyfully to praise the Almighty. God has proven to be good and faithful, with no end to God's steadfast love.

How joyful is your worship? Do you need to be reminded of what God has done for you, including creating your life? Perhaps a mental rehearsal of God's faithful provision will renew a sense of gratitude and revive your praise.

**PRAYER: God, help us to live lives of gratitude and praise that reflect our joy in being your people, the sheep of your pasture. Amen.**

# Come, Lord Jesus!

*November 24–30, 2008 • Don Saliers[‡]*

## MONDAY, NOVEMBER 24 • Read Isaiah 64:1-9

At times in our lives we cry out to God to come in power and do something dramatic. Perhaps you have seen too much hunger and homelessness, seen and heard too many stories of war and death. Maybe you weary of carrying within you contradictions. Whatever the cause, you find yourself crying out: "God! Do something! Come with power and transform this situation!"

If you have experienced this, you qualify for Advent—that strong stretch of days in the Christian year toward which we move. Here we approach a season of urgency and yearning. The prophet Isaiah already cries out a prayer to God to "tear open the heavens and come down." He wants the mountains to tremble at the divine presence and action. Israel has turned from God for too long, and the prophet desires that God be once again the God of old: strong, terrifying, decisive, active in human affairs.

But soon we recognize in moments when we crave an almighty power to break in that we also must stand before God. In our impatience with the way the world is, we so often overlook our own complicities in the suffering of others. This is a turn that Isaiah takes in today's scripture. It is not easy to hear that God is hidden from us because of our *own* participation in the sins of the world. Could the very things that make us rage reflect who we have become?

Such a tangle of motives within us! But Isaiah shows us a way. We appeal also to the God who is the potter; we, fragile and from the earth, are the clay. So we ask God to remember that we are still God's people.

**PRAYER: Have mercy, O most holy God, for we are still the work of your hands. Amen.**

[‡]William R. Cannon Distinguished Professor of Theology and Worship, Candler School of Theology at Emory University, Atlanta, Georgia.

I once knew an elderly man who restored neglected and damaged furniture. His dusty shop was filled with all kinds of discarded wood. On the walls hung amazing racks of tools. I found it more amazing to see what he could do with broken tables and chairs, with old discarded desks and cedar chests. He seemed too feeble for all the hard work with those tools and the hours spent with finishing stains and waxes. I always gaped in astonishment at his ability to restore such damaged goods. He would take compliments graciously and always say, "Savin' these things is a joy to me. I just try to restore the beauty that should be there!"

Ah, restoring the beauty that should always have been there. This comes close to a strand in the psalmist's plea, "Restore us, O God; let thy face shine, that we may be saved!" Restoring furniture is a wonderful craft. I remember that my friend the woodworker's face would shine with sweat at the end of the final polishing. Now I wonder about the shining face of God who labors over our restoration. The handiwork of God is wondrous.

So many things about human beings need restoration. The tender first line in our psalm refers to God as the "Shepherd of Israel," the one "enthroned upon the cherubim." God the shepherd is also the one who repairs and polishes us toward perfection. No matter how badly human beings have been damaged or neglected, God the restorer of humanity never stops lavishing care over us. How the divine countenance must shine when a human life is restored to the beauty God intends for us!

**PRAYER: God, you are both Shepherd and Savior. Take what is broken in me and mend; take what is damaged and dull in my soul, and restore the lost image of Christ in me and in our community. Amen.**

Again today the prayer for deliverance: "Restore us, O God; let your face shine, that we may be saved!" We can pray the Psalms in many ways. We can pray with the tribes of Israel mentioned in verse 2 of this psalm. In this case we join the cry of the tribes of Ephraim, Benjamin, and Manasseh for deliverance from the destruction their enemies have done. It is the lament of a whole people who have been given tears to drink. In this way the psalm offers a discipline of solidarity with all those suffering people who cry out from oppression and war. The ancient destruction and occupation of Jerusalem becomes a metaphor for all such human suffering in our own time.

But we can also pray this psalm as our own need when we know we have turned away from God, or when God seems far away from us. "Restore us, O God; let your face shine, that we may be saved!" This comes from a truthful lament over what we might call the "enemies within us." C. S. Lewis, in *Reflections on the Psalms*, speaks of praying strongly against those forces within us that seek to tear down and taunt us, sometimes angry, shrill voices in our own tendency to prefer vengeance over the longer road to justice and righteousness. These spiritual forces line up against us, not so much from "outside" as from "inside" our lives.

The sense of God's absence often signals alien forces occupying our most inner life, as well as our way of life in the world. "Restore us . . . that we may be saved!" Give us the life that the Son of man brings. We lean already toward the yearning of the Advent hymn, "O Come, O Come, Emmanuel."

**PRAYER: Teach us to speak truthful words to you, O God— words of lament and words of our hope for deliverance from all that destroys life with you and with others. Amen.**

Suddenly it is Thanksgiving Day again. As we grow older, this day takes on more meaning. We remember as children telling the story of the Pilgrims, of dressing up in school, or looking at pictures of a peaceful time between the Native Americans who brought gifts of planting and friendship to the struggling community of European immigrants. And we thankfully reflect on all the accumulating years of celebrating this feast in different homes with different folks; or the time we served a community meal to strangers and persons off the streets. All the loved ones with whom we have shared such a meal have become our communion of saints at this table. This day gains so much meaning because we gather to bless God and to feast on the abundance we have received.

In the midst of our struggles against things that keep us from loving God and neighbor freely, this ritual meal comes 'round again. Listen to the psalm, and picture again that strong image of God's shining face. For one brief shining moment we say that the earth yields its increase and that God is gracious beyond our deserving. So we pray this psalm, joining all the nations in praise.

This is not empty praise or self-congratulatory giving of thanks. This is praise and thanks that carry the hope that the very face of God will shine upon us, that God's way may be known on earth, and God's "saving power among all nations." Isn't it wondrous that a meal could carry so much meaning and joy? It reminds us that God has given us another meal in Jesus' name that brings even greater hope and joy—a meal in which the great communion of saints gathers about us.

**PRAYER: In food and sharing and love, O God, you give yourself to us and to all your people on earth. We bless and praise you. Amen.**

Much has been written about the problem of low self-esteem. Persons who have been told since childhood that they "aren't worth a thing" suffer from this malady. So do those who find themselves in difficult relationships or who have overwhelming responsibilities in life and feel, for whatever reason, that they simply can't do the job. Some of us may be in quiet desperation about this issue. When we reach a low point, something has to happen to provide a new sense of ability, a fresh sense of who we are that can sustain us.

While Paul's letter to the church at Corinth is not oriented to modern psychological views, these opening lines relay a message that is absolutely central to the gospel. A short version of this message might be: Christ is sufficient. While true, this passage involves something much deeper. It reminds us that we are "waiting" for something we haven't seen or known. Because of the Incarnation we find ourselves between the world as it actually is and the world as it may yet become. We await a completion and fulfillment of what God has promised.

While we may lack physical and psychological capacities we wish we had, we are here reminded that Christ has already given gifts and grace. In our very desire to follow Jesus, we find no lack of spiritual gifts as we "wait for the revealing of our Lord Jesus Christ" who will "strengthen [us] to the end." Desire for the revealing of Christ's reign already brings courage and hope, a community of grace, and God's esteem of humankind—no matter what the circumstances.

**PRAYER: Most faithful God, we hold our poverty up to the riches of Christ's grace, knowing that you have promised to sustain us as we await the fullness of the kingdom. Amen.**

These are confusing times. Many believe the world is heading for the end and that we are living in the "last days." Apocalyptic images fill movie and television screens. Some popular Christian writers have specialized in depicting the final battle between good and evil and a domestic American version of the book of Revelation. Often the trailers we see of forthcoming films show the principal characters being hurled toward us with a terrible explosion and fireball behind them. More seriously, our recent knowledge of global warming has caused some to think we are entering a time when there is little to be done—while others think we must act now to head off a final disaster.

This is the last day of the Christian year, and we encounter a portion of text from Mark called the "little apocalypse." In the midst of Christ's ministry is this question of the end of things. Judgment of the earth there will certainly be. And the end of history as we understand it there will certainly be. But Jesus will have no cheap apocalyptic teaching. Rather, he gives his hearers the teaching of the fig tree, with its startling notion that the "end times" will come in his own generation. Could it be that the current world crisis exists because he has come? Let us ponder this: wherever Christ's words and deeds and promises are taken seriously, we experience the tension between the "is" and the "ought to be" of this world.

The signs of life from the fig tree will forever remind us of this fact. Heaven and earth may pass away, "but my words [and my actions] will not pass away." There resides *our* hope and the hope of this weary, worried world.

**PRAYER: Teach us, dear Christ, to read the signs of the times but always to rely on your words and deeds and the hope for all to be fulfilled in the love of God. Amen.**

## FIRST SUNDAY OF ADVENT

In many of our churches today we will sing "O Come, O Come Emmanuel," or perhaps "Savior of the Nations, Come." These hymns speak the language of Advent. We now have arrived at a tension-filled season of the church year. We begin to experience the timpani beat of the Messiah's coming. We join ancient Israel in the cry for God to save us, for the restoration of justice and right relationships, for the fulfillment of God's promises.

At the same time we must learn a new patience with God and with ourselves. The definite word from Mark's little apocalypse is not: "Be afraid, God's going to wipe us all out in final judgment!" Rather it is: "Take heed, watch; for you do not know when the time will come" (13:33, RSV). The point is not fear or despair, but to be awake, alert to the ways in which God will come to us. In a fearful time that exposes us to so much that says "the end is near," we are to watch with Christ.

*How* are we to watch? We look daily for small signs of how God has already come into our midst—the hidden acts of love, the great acts of faith done by people we don't even know, the daily graces that sustain us. *How* are we to watch? With hope, with yearning, with expectation that God's promise is ultimately faithful and true.

So we are invited to number the great yearning days of Advent for the Emmanuel to come. The great good news is that, whatever form his coming takes, we know that it will be the same Jesus Christ who came to set the prisoners free, to bind up the brokenhearted, to heal the lame, and to give sight to those who cannot see. Because he has already come to us with such mercy, we can sing the Advent song, "Come, Lord Jesus!"

**PRAYER: In this stillness, God of all hopefulness, give us grace to watch and wait for you. Amen.**

# A Constant Advent

*December 1–7, 2008 • Leticia Guardiola-Sáenz[‡]*

### MONDAY, DECEMBER 1 • Read Psalm 85:1-2, 8-13

As we move into a new Christian year, Psalm 85 helps us keep in mind that Advent is not only the first season of the liturgical year but is the mode in which we are invited to live our daily lives as Christians. This psalm reminds us of the constant advent of God into our lives and offers the possibility that we might consider the season of Advent to be a triple celebration.

First, we celebrate that God has come to us in the past. In the communal prayer of Psalm 85 we hear the voices of the people of Israel in the post-exilic era, acknowledging how God has come to them in former times, shown favor to their land, forgiven their sins, and restored their well-being. Second, we rejoice in knowing that God's Spirit is always willing and ready to come to us in our daily life when we are open to the divine. Verses 10 and 11 speak of the daily encounter that takes place when the loyal love of God comes to meet the faithful ones, bringing them deliverance and peace. Third, in faith we prepare for the future advent of God. Verses 9 and 12 promise that God's loyal followers will receive deliverance and will again enjoy God's blessings.

As we meditate on God's word during this second week of Advent, let us live with this triple celebratory spirit every day. Let us *celebrate* that Jesus has come to show us the way to the divine; let us *rejoice* in our daily encounter with God's spirit, our guiding light; and let us *honor* God's promise of coming to us at the end of time by living every day in the light of God's splendor.

**PRAYER: Loving God, thank you for reminding us of your constant advent in our lives. Help us to live everyday with this awareness so that others may experience your presence through us. Amen.**

---

[‡]Assistant Professor of New Testament, Drew University, Madison, New Jersey.

After what must have felt like an eternity, more than seventy years of suffering, estrangement, destitution, and hardship in exile, surely these reassuring words bring joy to the people: "Comfort, comfort my people, says your God." In a split second the feelings of rejection and abandonment melt away as the people begin to experience the warmth of God's love anew. Not only do these words provide comfort, but God restores the familial relationship. The use of phrases such as "my people" and "your God" reestablishes the characteristic intimacy of the relationship.

Moreover, this loving relationship is not only for the nation but for individuals. In verse 2, God extends a personal call. We can hear the tender tone of God's voice: "Speak tenderly to Jerusalem, and cry to her that she has served her term, that her penalty is paid." Symbolically, in the singular name of Jerusalem we hear every single name of all God's people.

Verse 3 makes it evident that God's advent is not simply for God's nation or for Jerusalem but for *all* the people. A voice cries out, giving the command to construct a road for God, to prepare all terrains for the spectacular advent of God's splendor which, once revealed, will be seen by all people at the same time.

As we ponder the exilic experience of Israel, let us embrace God's words of comfort. Listen! God kindly calls us by name out of our personal exiles. The hardship and estrangement are over; God invites a renewal of our intimate relationship with the divine.

**PRAYER: Gracious God, thank you for calling us out of exile. May we clear the way for you so that all may come to see your splendor. Amen.**

The popular belief of a catastrophic end of the world, which will occur soon, has been one of the most successful genres of Hollywood movies. In the last four decades, there has been at least one of these fatalistic movies per year. However, in the past few years, movies about deadly plagues, worldwide famines, terrible droughts, and nuclear wars have proliferated even more.

These fantastic apocalyptic films are not a complete invention of Hollywood. Film makers have simply exploited a biblical vision that sells well in our culture. Unfortunately, they do not tell the story accurately, biblically speaking. They have highlighted the cataclysmic images of the heavens disappearing and the collapsing of the celestial bodies, similar to the record of 2 Peter 3:10-12. But Hollywood has erased the hopeful ending of 2 Peter 3:13, the arrival of the new heavens and new earth where righteousness truly resides.

Belief in a cataclysmic ending of the world prior to the advent of the Lord was popularized during times of national crisis, when God's people suffered persecution and oppression at the hand of evil rulers and unjust empires of the world. Such is the case of Second Peter, an epistle written during the oppressive rule of the Roman Empire.

As much as the people might have been hoping and praying for God's intervention in history to vindicate them and destroy the evil rulers, they willingly waited. They knew that the Lord's advent was delayed because of God's patience and love for those who do not believe rather than abandonment of those who were waiting for the Lord.

As we play our own movie of the end of the world in our mind, let us not forget the most important scene: the one in which our patient God lovingly waits for us to ready ourselves for the divine meeting.

**PRAYER: Timeless God of time and eternity, thank you for your patience. As we meditate on your constant advents, keep us open to the surprising grace of your love. Amen.**

We often think of Advent and highlight the coming of the divine into the world. Yet this manifestation is never a unilateral experience in the Bible. As we reflect on Jesus' entering the world, his becoming flesh to live with us and be one of us, we acknowledge that this event happened as a result of human-divine interdependency. Mary accepts the invitation of the divine, willingly carrying the savior in her womb. As a result, Jesus came to be.

In like manner, the prayer of Psalm 85 links the everyday coming of the Lord to the believers' response. The metaphors in verse 10 reveal God's advent as an interdependent experience: God's loyal love comes to encounter the faithfulness of the believers. God's deliverance then greets with a kiss the peace produced in the believers. Verses 11 and 12 reaffirm this divine-human reciprocity: the faithfulness that grows from the ground meets the deliverance that looks down from the sky, which in turn bestows the blessings that fertilize the land.

This psalm issues an invitation for human beings to repent and be faithful to God, believing that what prevents God from acting in the world is *our* unfaithfulness, not the world's evil nature. This invitation to faithfulness offers the greatest hope as we wait for and continue to experience God's constant advents. God *can* work and transform us and the structures of this world when we live faithfully, when we live God's advent as an experience of interdependency.

In just a few words Psalm 85 reveals a key message for life. Our lives on earth reflect our relationship of mutuality with God. As we live our daily encounter with the divine and await the future coming of God, we are reminded that all creation must live interdependently with the Creator.

**PRAYER: Loyal Love, help us to live in faithfulness to you, so that we may kiss your deliverance with peace and remember that we can only be fruitful and see your splendor when we live in mutuality with you. Amen.**

The film *An Inconvenient Truth*, a documentary on the facts of global warming, confirmed for me that interdependency is not just a nice theory about universal interconnectedness but rather a concrete reality that demands our attention. From the beginning of time the children of God were charged with the care of nature, to be faithful stewards of God's creation

Today's selected verses highlight the belief that the well-being of the land, the promise of God's splendor, the bestowal of blessing on our land to make it a fruitful, as well as the promise of new heavens and a new earth all connect to the present and future advent of the Lord. More importantly, fruition depends on faithfulness to the Creator.

The words of Psalm 85:9 invite us to live in accordance with God's deliverance. When we seek to live as faithful followers of God, as Psalm 85 invites us, we are compelled to take responsibility for our actions, examining ourselves and turning to God who can help us change our ways and show us our duty as cocreators of this world.

Looking at the changes humanity has caused in the environment due to our pollution and waste, we see clearly the interconnectedness of all things. The earth itself longs for the advent of the Lord, longs for transformation. Let us consider how our actions affect our environment and explore ways to collaborate with God in restoring the well-being of our land. As we reflect on the interdependency of creation, let us examine how our decisions related to care of the environment express our embrace of God's constant advent in our midst.

**PRAYER: Loving Creator, help us assume our role as faithful stewards of your creation, knowing that we are part of one another and of you. Amen.**

The word *Advent* comes from the Latin *adventus*, which means "coming." While the church has accentuated the dual meaning of this "coming"—the ancient waiting for the Messiah and the current waiting for his second coming—we usually associate Advent more with the celebration of Jesus' birth rather than the Second Coming.

The most common word used to refer to the Second Coming of Jesus Christ is the exact equivalent of *adventus* in Greek, *parousia*. Regardless of which word we use, both speak equally of how God comes into our history and transforms our world.

In the Bible we find two basic ways of understanding how God works in the world. The first perspective is called prophetic, the second apocalyptic. Both perspectives are considered eschatological because they expect a future, at the end of time, when God will be revealed and will vindicate the faithful. But these two perspectives fundamentally differ in how each visualizes the unfolding of history and God's role in it. This week's readings have presented both views.

Isaiah, Mark and Psalm 85 highlight the prophetic hope that if we repent and are faithful, God will forgive our sins, pardon our wrongdoings, and restore our land. On the other hand, Second Peter stresses the apocalyptic view that the world's corruption and evil make it unredeemable. The world needs to be destroyed and replaced with a new one; nothing we can do will save it.

These opposing views, which emerged from different contexts, fulfilled their particular purposes and have influenced our theology in dramatic ways. As we meditate in the spirit of Advent, let us ponder on *our* view of God's acting in history. How do we see God coming into our midst? What are the implications of such a view for our acting in the world today?

**PRAYER: God of history, we seek to follow the way of Jesus. He proclaimed your love and redemption to a world in need. May our lives reflect these teachings of Jesus today. Amen.**

## Second Sunday of Advent

$A$ll of this week's scripture passages have invited us to repent, to turn to God, to receive forgiveness for sin, to enjoy the salvation of our Lord, and to be mindful of the interdependency of our personal and communal responses to God's constant advents. But more particularly, we have received the privilege and the call of preparing the way for the Lord.

First, Isaiah called us to prepare the way of the Lord. Now in Mark 1:2-8 we receive the training and example from John the baptizer on *how* to prepare the way of the Lord. If we choose to enjoy God's presence in our midst and God's favor in our land, then it becomes our responsibility and privilege to prepare the way for the divine. Only then can we fully assume our role as cocreators in the transformation of our world. John the baptizer once again reminds us of the need to clear a way in the wilderness, to elevate the valleys and level the mountains and hills—and even the rough terrain and rugged landscape—so that the Lord's splendor will be revealed to all people.

Each of us prepares the way of the Lord in a unique fashion but note that in Isaiah we are called first to clear a way in the wilderness before moving on to level other terrain. The wilderness as a place of purification and divine encounter or revelation offers the possibility that we will experience firsthand God's advents in our life. Once we have walked the way of the desert and experienced the advents of God, other opportunities for preparing the way will present themselves. These opportunities might be through ministry, through secular jobs and positions, through special events in the community. Let us be open to God's constant advents as we find creative ways to bridge the gap between God and people.

**PRAYER: Loving God, thank you for your love and the privilege we have to prepare your way so that we and others can encounter you every day. Guide us as we walk your way and seek to transform this world with you. Amen.**

# Mind the Light

*December 8–14, 2008  •  Lauren F. Winner[‡]*

## MONDAY, DECEMBER 8  •  Read Isaiah 61:1-4

Much as my pastor is trying to help it feel like Advent, most of us are already acting like it's Christmas. With this season comes real celebration, of course. We're attending parties, singing hymns, visiting with family. At the same time, Christmas is, for many of us, a time of great sorrow and hardship. We think of dead friends and family and wish they were here to celebrate with us. Or some aspect of our life feels crushingly difficult and sad, and the cheery seasonal script we feel we're supposed to be following only magnifies the sorrow.

We need the adult version of the Christmas story—the story that recognizes that even though it's December, not everything and everyone feels cheery. What genuinely good news, then, to know that Advent is the season when we await not just a cute baby in a manger. During Advent we await the one who comes to bind up the brokenhearted.

And how much better to remember with Mary that binding up the brokenhearted is not something God promises to do in the distant, far-off future. No, as Mary proclaims in her famous prayer of praise, the Magnificat, God is already at work filling up the hungry with good things and exalting the weak. God is already suturing our wounds and succoring us in our loneliness. God is binding up our broken hearts, even now.

**PRAYER: Gracious God, comfort those who, during this season when we feel pressure to be joyful, are in fact, mourning. Succor those who feel bleak and who lead lives of suffering and hardship. Make yourself known to them as the one who binds up their wounds and frees them from their shackles. Amen.**

[‡]Author and member of Christ Episcopal Church, Charlottesville, Virginia.

Last summer, I encountered a picture of suffering that we don't see often in our culture. I saw a grown man sobbing and weeping freely, uncontrollably.

I was working at a hospital and knew that getting paged late at night rarely meant something good. In this case, a man's three-week-old daughter was going to die by morning.

I don't remember any words I spoke to the weeping man. I hope I didn't offer some useless platitude, the kind that makes the speaker feel better but gives little help to the listener.

But I remember how often I thought about that grieving father in the ensuing weeks. Whenever I saw a dad with his daughter, I thought of that heartbroken man and reflected on how suffering seems an inevitable companion of even the most faithful lives.

During Advent, as we contemplate both Christ's birth as a human baby and his eventual return in glory, our verse from the Psalter reads as a powerful eschatological promise. When, oh when, will our weeping be turned to songs of joy? Maybe tomorrow, maybe next year, and maybe not until the consummation of all things.

But we can rest assured that God *will* turn our weeping to joy. That eschatological promise can feel far off. It may not always bring immediate comfort. And so we have another promise.

We can rest assured that when we weep, we do not weep alone. God the Father, who knows what it is like to watch a child die, is with us in our weeping. And Jesus, who wept, also joins us.

**PRAYER: Lord, keep us in our suffering and strengthen our faith in the One who will come again, turning our sorrow into laughter. Amen.**

A crucial phrase in Quaker spirituality is the instruction to "mind the light." It means to see deeply—to notice the light, which usually just illumines other things, for itself.

"Mind the light"—and then, as John did, testify to the light. Sometimes I admit that I get a little overwhelmed by the seemingly simple task of living as a Christian. Occasionally, I find myself in a situation where I can't discern what "the Christian thing to do" is. And sometimes I'm simply too broken, too mired down by sin and selfishness and pride, to act in a Christian way.

But the Gospel of John may be telling us that Christian witness boils down to one straightforward instruction: testify to the light. There is something freeing about John's instructions to offer testimony. When I feel overwhelmed about the perfect Christian response to a given situation, I can remember that the Christian response is one of testimony, of doxological praise and witness. Testimony about God is never, ever finished; it is inexhaustible. There will always be more praise, more testimony for me to give.

If we can mind the light and testify to it throughout the day, surely we will have gone a long way toward living faithfully.

**PRAYER: Dear Lord, at this dark time of year, when the sun sets early and the night seems to last forever, shine brightly in the corner of your kingdom that I inhabit. Interrupt my winter darkness with your light, and give me the grace to mind the light and to testify to the light in all that I do. In Jesus' name. Amen.**

Recently, I went to visit a woman (M.) who lives at a retirement community a few miles from my house. M.'s life has narrowed in recent years: she's survived her husband and her only child—and most of her friends. She lives on a tight budget. Her body is frail, and the last twenty years have been riddled with medical problems.

When I first started visiting M., I mistakenly thought that I was doing her a nice favor—you know, using some of my precious time to cheer up an elderly woman with few companions. In fact, the opposite has proved true. It is really M. who is doing me a favor by giving me a picture—an icon, even—of life on the narrow path well lived.

One day M. said to me, "Hon, I think you feel just the tiniest bit sorry for me." I had to admit that I did. "Well, hon," she said, "don't waste time pitying me. Of course sometimes I miss my family and my health, and I look forward to being reunited with my beloved son and husband in my resurrected body in heaven! But my Lord is keeping me company even now, and that gives me plenty of joy. Of course," she added politely, "I appreciate your visits too."

During this season, when many are delighting in giving and receiving presents, in holiday travel, in the completion of fall projects at work or school, it has been a blessing for me to see M. She has no family left, and she won't be traveling this Christmas; she hasn't worked in decades; the presents she will exchange will be modest. By worldly standards she doesn't have much to rejoice in. Yet "GOD will cause righteousness and praise to spring up." She has found true joy and delight in the Lord.

**PRAYER: Lord, grant that I may find my true joy, not in those earthly things that pass away but in you. Amen.**

The other night at a party, I was introduced to a couple I hadn't met before. The couple asked me, first, what I did for a living. Then they asked where I was from. Then they asked how long I had lived there. Then they asked whether my husband was at the party with me.

In the course of the conversation, the couple did get to know me a bit—certainly my family and my work, not to mention my hometown, are all important pieces of my identity. But I left the exchange wondering if I'd managed to introduce myself without actually giving any hint of my most essential identity: my identity in Christ.

When pressed by his interlocutors, who demand that John identify himself to them, John replies only that he is fulfilling the prophet Isaiah's command. He is going into the desert crying, "Make straight the way of the Lord."

How remarkable it would be if we could identify ourselves chiefly, even solely, by what we did for God, by the ways in which our lives conform to God's will for us. If, when asked about ourselves, we responded not first with our job title or with our family connections or by explaining what neighborhood we live in or where we attended college. What a delight to say instead, "I am a person who is trying to make straight the way of the Lord and who is trying to help others follow on that road."

**PRAYER: Dear God, give us grace to find our true identity in you and to proclaim our relationship with you in all that we do. Amen.**

I often think these instructions to the Thessalonians are easier said than done. Can I really be joyful all the time? And pray constantly? And give thanks even in the bleakest circumstances? Well, no. Some days, thanksgiving and joy are distant aspirations.

But then I realize that this instruction is not about feeling a certain way: feeling happy or feeling thankful. It is about *practicing* joy and thanksgiving and prayer, even when—maybe especially when—I don't feel like it.

I am reminded of the prayer that Jewish mourners are commanded to say—the mourner's kaddish. The prayer is recited daily for thirty days. It's not, in fact, a prayer about mourning or a prayer of bitter lament. It is rather a prayer of praise that begins with these words: "Magnified and sanctified be God's great name in the world which He has created according to his will." Why are mourners commanded to say such a prayer? Because even when they are in the pit, even when they are in the valley, God remains deserving of praise. And that very prayer, which the mourner repeats day in and day out, may in fact be one tool that God uses to heal the mourner's heart.

Just as God uses the mourner's kaddish and time to heal the hearts of the bereaved, so God slowly grows us into joyful disciples who can be people of constant prayer. God uses countless tools: my neighbors, my husband, my students, the sacraments, my prayer book, the novels I read, the simple act of cooking, even the tree outside my window to turn me into a Christian who is truly eucharistic, truly thankful.

**SUGGESTION FOR MEDITATION: Devote a few minutes to offering thanks for particular blessings in your life.**

**PRAYER: Dear God, who is at all times worthy of praise, transform my hard heart into a heart that is always joyful. Amen.**

### THIRD SUNDAY OF ADVENT

"I'm really not sure I can do this." That was what one of my entering seminary students said to me this fall. "I have a deep sense that I'm called to ordained ministry—but, really, I'm a very ordinary, flawed person. I'm not sure I can live up to the charge of being a minister!"

"When Rebecca was put into my arms, I was overwhelmed with both love and fear. How was I going to be able to take care of this precious little person?" That was a neighbor, describing the day her daughter was born.

"Marriage is a lot harder than I thought! It requires so much change and compromise! Some days I just don't think I am cut out for it." That was a college friend, shortly after her fifth wedding anniversary.

Indeed, we're not usually called to simple tasks. Our vocations, our callings from God, require sacrifice and renunciation; few persons ever describe their life's work—in ministry or in their family—as "easy as pie." None of us is good enough to do what we're called to do by ourselves. (Indeed, even scripture is rife with stories of messed-up people who manage, through God's grace, to live into their callings.) And so we do not quench the Spirit but hold fast to what is good.

The epistle's words offer another helpful reminder: God is faithful to those whom God calls. A sermon I once heard put it well: "God doesn't call those who are equipped," said the preacher. "God equips those whom God calls."

**SUGGESTION FOR PRAYER: Spend a few moments asking yourself what work God has called you into; then reflect, giving thanks, on the ways God has equipped you for that call. Petition God for strength and skill where you feel a lack, and be assured that the one who calls you is faithful and will do it!**

# Doorway to Divine Intimacy

*December 15–21, 2008* • *Susan Muto*[‡]

## MONDAY, DECEMBER 15 • Read 2 Samuel 7:1-11, 16

The initiative for covenant love comes from God. This lesson has to be learned not only by the prophet David but by all of us. We make plans—even ones we assume will be pleasing to God like building the Almighty a house according to our designs. But God's plans, impossible as they may seem, always supercede our puny efforts.

Before David can so much as hammer the first nail, God turns his intentions in an unintended direction more stupendous than David could have imagined. David envisions an earthly temple to give glory to God when all along God wants to build a house for David—not one of bricks and mortar but a veritable dynasty wherein the Holy One shall rule forever (v. 13).

This house of the Lord has no temporal limits. Satan himself will not be able to crush its gates. Neither flood nor fire can destroy it. What God promises David is that the Messiah to come, Jesus Christ, shall be of the house of David. David's son Solomon will build a temple to honor the Almighty, but the Lord will give divine endorsement to the kingship of David. The covenant initiated by God with the chosen one will extend for all generations; it will teach us never to doubt the power of the divine initiative in our own lives.

**PRAYER: Loving Creator, grant us the grace to accept the full truth of your covenant promise. May the peace and joy it brings to our wayward hearts give us the courage to do what we can to transform the world into your dwelling place. Amen.**

---

[‡]Roman Catholic author, teacher, and scholar of the literature of spirituality; executive director of the Epiphany Association, a nonprofit ecumenical center dedicated to spiritual formation; and cofounder and dean of its Epiphany Academy of Formative Spirituality, Pittsburgh, Pennsylvania.

In narrating the dispositions, decisions, and deeds that transformed a scattered population of warring tribes into the people of God, the psalmist identifies two keys of divine kingship that converge to form a covenant with David's descendants—among whom we are numbered. They are God's steadfast love for us and God's fidelity to us. Such love saves us despite our sins. Such fidelity goes in search of us despite our faithless hearts. The question is this: what lessons about steadfastness and faithfulness can we learn from these revelations?

The first is that steadfastness and faithfulness form the bridge between our lonely existence and God's call to a covenant relationship. In a climate where promise keeping can no longer be counted upon, we have the assurance that God's word is utterly trustworthy. God's loving plan for our lives is so stupendous that its unfolding over time goes far beyond our understanding. The worldly wise cannot grasp it, but to the poor and lowly it is increasingly clear.

The second lesson is that the bridge built by love and fidelity stands firm amidst the storms of life. In our worst hours we can still count on the fact that the covenant bond between us and God is unbreakable. However defeated we may feel due to life's vicissitudes, we can still catch a glimpse of the promised land that lies on the other side of this bridge and begin our crossing.

**PRAYER: Lord, so great is the consolation you give us, so profound is its blessed assurance that we have no choice but to sing of your love and faithfulness in hymns of praise and thanksgiving. Thank you, Most Holy One, for numbering us among the descendants of the house of David and for calling us your disciples. May the witness of our lives offer those living in doubt and despair proof of the promise that you will be with us always. Teach us to rely on your word and your wisdom from the rising to the setting of the sun. Amen.**

To acknowledge the steadfast love God has for us does not mean that our troubles will fade like morning mist and that perfect peace will instantly come upon us. Knowing how easily outwitted we are by the enemy, we must beg God to be our strength moment by moment. Being humbled by the wicked who get the best of us makes us give up any illusion of self-salvation. We are always in danger of being crushed by our foes, of being struck a deadly blow dealt by those who hate us. Our only hope lies in the fact that God chooses to exalt the lowly and scatter the proud in their conceit. (See Luke 1:48-51.)

The anointed of Israel, among whom we are numbered, may bear the woes all people endure but not be defeated by them. Because the hand of the Father remains upon us, we find our strength not in ourselves but in the might of God's holy arm. No enemy will be able to outwit us as long as our wisdom comes from God. The shields of divine faithfulness and steadfast love surround our soul and guarantee our protection.

SUGGESTION FOR MEDITATION: **Pick up the daily newspaper and write on an index card a list of whatever disasters the headlines feature of the evils that lurk in every corner of life. Choose a few items from your list to bring to prayer. Converse with God about them and don't be afraid to ask: "If you are steadfast and faithful, why do you allow tragedy to strike so often and so furiously?" In prayer follow the movement in your soul from anger at God to awe for the divine majesty that entered this broken world at the moment of Christ's birth. Jesus saw around him worse crimes than we can imagine, but he never lost his conviction of the Father's saving plan. Reread these verses from Psalm 89, and compose your own thank-you prayer.**

Giving praise to the glory of God flows naturally from the lips of a man like Paul. From the moment of his conversion until his martyr's death, he was a living witness to the Father's fidelity. While he was still a sinner, Christ died for him. (See Romans 5:8.) The lessons Paul teaches are living tributes to the steadfast love of God that changed his life from its bellicose beginnings to its faithful ending.

Paul never calls attention to himself or takes credit for others' conversions. His humility emulates that of the Lord's, which is why he sees himself only as a messenger of the mystery. Everything he teaches points away from himself to Christ's saving glory. His testimony reveals that there can be no understanding of salvation history until the coming of Christ, in whom the mystery of redemption is fully revealed. Jesus of Nazareth is the culmination of the prophetic promises made by God to the chosen people. His death and resurrection reveal the full meaning of covenant love.

Paul reaffirms to the Romans that at the appointed time the Word became God-with-us. The Eternal made Godself accessible in time. The Infinite took on the sinful burden of our finitude. What Paul asks of anyone with ears to listen is obedience to these truths in a posture of pure faith that finds it perfectly reasonable to proclaim God's presence with us from the beginning to the end of time.

**Prayer: God of power and might, your mercy overshadowed our misery. You gave us the courage to proclaim your plan of redemption in a world desperate to hear the good news. Pour forth into our stubborn minds and unreceptive hearts the grace to say, "I believe" and "I will obey." Despite our unworthiness, grant us a taste of your wisdom. Use us to make your truths known to those ready to receive them in love and fidelity. Amen.**

In this epiphanic announcement of the birth of our Savior, we see at one and the same time the continuity of his coming in Bethlehem with the whole of Hebrew history. The King of kings ascends the throne of his ancestor David. He who is the radical revelation of God's saving plan for all people reigns forever over the house of Jacob.

Previous revelations of covenant love pale in comparison to this one. The young woman to whom the angel Gabriel is sent does not live in Jerusalem—the center of Jewish life and worship—but in Galilee, a lowly province considered an outpost of Judaism. It startles us that such a proclamation would be made to a humble woman in a town of no consequence whatsoever; yet Mary finds favor with the Most High. She will be the mother of God's only begotten Son.

Persons as poor as Mary can hardly believe they are great in God's sight, but so be it. Mary will remain a virgin and give birth to a son through purely supernatural means. Perplexed as she is about the full meaning of this angelic greeting, there is no doubt as to what her response will be.

SUGGESTION FOR PRAYER: **Pause for a moment and enter into Mary's perplexity. Rather than trying to master the mystery of this birth, ponder with her the amazing way in which God chooses to show us steadfast love and fidelity. God is not content to save us from a distance. God chooses to become one of us in all things but sin. Christ, fully human and born of Mary, is fully divine. Pray for the grace to accept this central mystery of our faith. Pray for the courage manifested in Mary's consent to this perplexing disclosure. Pray for the trust never to doubt God's power to forgive our sins and lead us to everlasting life.**

Mary's understandable amazement about how she, a virgin, can conceive a son does not block her consent to the message of an angel. What makes no sense at all, humanly speaking, becomes an opening that binds heaven to earth and seals her place in the divine plan. Nothing can be more unimaginable than the Holy Spirit's coming upon her and the Most High overshadowing her, yet who is she to doubt the power of this divine initiative that will ordain the child of her womb to be the Son of God?

Before the angel leaves, he tells Mary that her cousin Elizabeth, once thought to be barren, is already in the sixth month of her pregnancy. Her child, to be called John, will be a prophet who beckons Israel to return to God and repent of every transgression. Mary's child, to be called Jesus, will be the everlasting king of Israel, a promise made possible by the power of God who decrees that she would be the immaculate vessel to bear God's son.

All that Mary hears from the angel's message confirms the disclosure reserved for the humble of the awesome role the new Eve will play in salvation history. The sense of her own unworthiness compels Mary to ask, "How can this be?" But the courage of her consent flows forth with no hesitation.

**PRAYER: Dearest God, bring me into the company of Mary and let me too ponder the paradoxical meaning of Christ's birth and death, his passion on the cross, and his resurrection in glory. Give me a taste of the grace granted to this gentle woman, never forgetting your steadfast love and fidelity. In the face of my own weak faith, give me strength to cling to the divine promises that rescued me in my humanity. Let me consent to your will, as Mary did, not because I understand its consequences but because I believe in your word. Amen.**

## FOURTH SUNDAY OF ADVENT

Mary's "Here am I" offers us in three little words the model of Christian discipleship. She identifies herself not as a special specimen of the human race but simply as a servant of the Lord. Before the angel departs from her, she gives her consent to this overwhelming proposal even though she may freely withhold her yes.

Mary does not resist the call for a moment, and neither should we. Her "Here am I" and her "Let it be . . . according to your word" enabled her to bear in her womb the God-man whom we adore, the Savior who will set us free.

Mary is so full of grace that she becomes blessed among women. Her obedience to the angel's disclosure makes her the first disciple, the foremost messenger of the word of God. She ponders the meaning of this graced encounter for the rest of her life, and so must we: Are we willing to allow the Word to come to birth in our soul? What must we do to emulate the one person who absorbed body and soul the full power of God's steadfast love?

Mary offers the purest proof of the end to which divine fidelity will go to save us. Is it any wonder that her soul magnifies the Lord and her spirit rejoices in God her Savior?

SUGGESTION FOR MEDITATION: **Picture yourself in the room where Mary received the visitation of the angel Gabriel. Study the expressions on her face as they move from perplexity to appreciative abandonment to the mystery of full consent. Picture this fairest of creatures before the face of the Father and thank her for saying yes to the one request that seals the covenant and completes the course of salvation history. Name what seems most impossible in your life at the moment, and then remember that nothing is impossible for God if you dare to utter with Mary your own, "Let it be."**

# The Light of Christmas

*December 22–28, 2008 • Wm. Loyd Allen[‡]*

## MONDAY, DECEMBER 22 • Read Isaiah 61:10-11

Third Isaiah (chapters 56–66) addresses the former Babylonian exiles rebuilding war-ravaged Jerusalem. Chapters 60–62 encourage a downhearted people wavering between their hope for a better tomorrow and the harsh reality of life amidst ruins (61:4). Isaiah 61:1-9 announces the prophet's mission, along with a promise from God for a bright future.

Today's passage is a confident thanksgiving psalm in response to these happy proposals. In verse 10, devastated Zion gaily sings a little song of anticipatory joy while getting dressed to the nines, like a bride and groom putting on Semitic high fashion. John's Revelation chooses a similar image in its closing vision of the New Jerusalem as the dazzling, bejeweled bride of the Lamb of God (21:9-10). Any child familiar with fairy tales can see Isaiah's point: this city is about to live happily ever after.

Rejoicing Zion is clothed by God in salvation and righteousness. In Hebrew these terms used together in parallel lines indicate exoneration by a liberator. At Christmas, Zion's ultimate liberating savior (and ours) appears. For his Nazareth sermon, Jesus reads the mission of Isaiah 61's prophet and claims himself as its fulfillment (Luke 4:17-18). In light of Christmas we need not fear any darkness. Like the survivors in the old wrecked city, we see Christmas most clearly through the eyes of prophets and children. Isaiah's little song of Zion ends with confident words about a liberating God sure to raise Judah from ruin as the spring is to bring fresh life from buried seed. Believers, let us prepare for the week's festivities.

**PRAYER: Giver of joy, prepare our hearts this Christmas to receive Christ and to join him in liberation and celebration. Amen.**

---

[‡]Member and Bible study leader, Parkway Baptist Church, Duluth, Georgia.

Third Isaiah presents visions of light for those "who mourn in Zion." I imagine the city's mood as a kind of collective seasonal affective disorder, which most doctors believe is caused by deprivation of light. In today's passage, the prophet of Third Isaiah vows neither to rest nor keep silent until a restored Jerusalem shines brightly in the hands of God. Through the prophet's vision, the first hearers of this text could see a future Jerusalem lit from within, its circular walls rebuilt and resting in God's hand like a sparkling jeweled crown, its inner and outer transfiguration so complete it required a new name.

This passage clarifies the main purpose of a renewed Jerusalem, and it is not to make its citizens' life easy. If their physical comfort were the goal, a better solution might be to move back to the suburbs of Babylon. God promises Zion a bright future in order to create a witness to far-off lands and their leaders.

God's brilliant vindication is not in doubt. The prophet's question is this: Who will see it? God is willing to go outside the law to get help to finish construction jobs. After all, God made Persian King Cyrus supervisor of the first phase of temple rebuilding: getting the laborers to the work site. (Read Isaiah 4:28.)

Relighting hope in cities is still God's work. Christ came to save cities as well as souls. Jerusalem lay in ruins in the prophet's time, suffered under a violent megalomanic ruler at Jesus' birth, and remains bitterly divided today. Christmas's promise is not given us to hoard in little circles aglow with sentimentality. In light of Christmas, the silent night should ring with cries of peace on earth, goodwill to all, until the job is finished.

SUGGESTION FOR PRAYER: **Pray for the peace of Jerusalem, for your city, and for the cities of all nations.**

## CHRISTMAS EVE

In light of Christmas we are all one family. Paul wrote Galatians in response to the question: Can Gentiles become part of the Christian family without converting to Judaism? Today's passage explains God's equal access provision for full Christian liberty. Judging the time right, God sent his son to earth as Mary's child to join the people of the Judaic covenant; God in Jesus freely merged with the limitations of human existence and divinely ordained religious obligations. Jesus transfigured all human restrictions, both of natural circumstance and spiritual requirement, into the perfect liberty of God. Through the babe in the manger— the Joseph-adopted Jesus Christ—anyone born of woman became eligible without qualification for adoption by God. The Spirit of God's son confirms this claim by calling out to God from within us, "Abba! Daddy!" Our part is to heed this reality, which early Quaker Christians called the Indwelling Light, from John 1:9's phrase, the "true light that enlightens everyone."

My adopted daughter, Clare, crafted a family tree in high school. In part, it includes her birth mother, birth mother's other children, birth mother's adoptive parents, birth mother's biological parents, Clare's birth father, his children, and his parents—not to mention my wife and me and our parents. In this kaleidoscopic kinship network, no one knows the majority of the others by name or sight, but everyone named above is Clare's parent, grandparent, brother, or sister. In Clare we are family.

The Christ child created kinship among Jew and Greek, slave and free, male and female, heaven and earth. Christmas calls everyone from the servant's quarters to the family table to feast alongside our brother Jesus and all our siblings in the family of God. Christmas Eve is a family night like no other.

**PRAYER: Abba, show me Christ's likeness in every face I see. Amen.**

## CHRISTMAS DAY

Christmas is here! That fact makes all the difference between daylight and dark. Throughout Advent we long for better light. On Christmas Day we celebrate its arrival. The light Mary births is primordial, life-giving, unquenchable, universal, and ever with us. For those with eyes to see, like the disciples at the Transfiguration (Luke 9:29), the babe is God's visible glory lying in a manger.

In this light all things reveal their true form, as a rose is made visible by the light falling on it. We do not see the light; we see by the light. Sometimes we see things in the wrong light. Shortly after my wife's bout with breast cancer, the death of her mother, and my parents' forced withdrawal from their ancestral home, our rebellious teenaged daughter Clare brought a kitten into our house while I was out of town. By my light, Clare, whom I correctly guessed would require help with pet care, had selfishly made a stressful time worse. Several weeks later I was telling my spiritual guide about the frequent laughter the kitten incited among us, especially my wife. He said maybe my daughter saw in the kitten something she couldn't name but knew we needed. That put a new light on the situation for me.

In the fifth century, as Rome's glory sputtered and dimmed, Bishop Augustine of Hippo lay dying. Barbarians assailed his city in their march across North Africa. The old man must surely have been tempted to see his life's work as a waste in light of the inexorable destruction of the Christian world as he knew it. Fortunately for us, Augustine lived, wrote, and died in a different light. One of my seminary professors called it the searchlight of eternity. John called it the Word made flesh. Mary and Joseph named him Jesus.

**SUGGESTION FOR REFLECTION: How might this Christmas Day cast a new light on the difficult parts of your life?**

The root, *Hallel*, "to shine," is common to the Hebrew words translated "light," "glory," and "praise." At Jesus' birth, glory blazed forth in heaven's angelic heights and in lowly shepherds' praises. Psalm 148's fourteen verses contain the word *praise* thirteen times.

The psalm's division into praise from the heavens above (vv. 1-6) and the earth beneath (vv. 7-12) link all creation in one basic purpose. While humanity rightly glories in God's salvation (signified in the "horn" idiom of v. 14), we are a small and often off-key section of the universal hallelujah chorus. Christmas glory radiates from all creation—angels to earthworms. Anne Lamott once said that if you do the math, you'll realize it's only about one-seven-billionths about me or you. And that's only counting our part of the choir, the global human population.

Everything reflects God's glory. The praise of stars, hail, wind, whales, and creepy-crawlies is not mere anthropomorphism in Psalm 148; these realities voicelessly praise God simply by remaining true to what they are, thus fulfilling God's command. If mortals vanished, the earth and heavens would continue to praise God. Listen for it.

God is near to us. "If you would know the creator, study the creation," states an ancient Irish saying. When we destroy the earth and air as if it were disposable personal property, we dim creation's praise of God and blind our souls to the glory of Christmas. God's universe is not here for us to consume but to love and serve alongside. According to Celtic legend, as Saint Kevin raised his arms in prayer, a bird laid her eggs in his hand. For Christ's sake, he remained motionless until the eggs hatched and the fledglings flew away singing.

**SUGGESTION FOR MEDITATION: See nature, lift your hands, and join the universal song of praise with the words of "Joy to the World."**

Christmas may be last week's news, but its hopes and consequences remain. Mary and Joseph go about their religious duties as Jewish parents. The completed law then meets prophecy fulfilled in Simeon and Anna. Simeon is righteous and devout. The Greek terms suggest a plain man who can be trusted to do the right thing because, like Zechariah (1:6) or Joseph (Matt. 1:19), he "gets it" spiritually. The Spirit has led Simeon, a hopeful man living during Roman oppression, to believe he will survive to see the Messiah, Israel's consolation. When the old man takes the baby Jesus into his arms, believing becomes seeing. Simeon lifts a hymn about personal destiny realized, ancient hopes fulfilled, and a future wideness in God's mercy.

This canticle, called the *Nunc Dimittis*, has now been prayed daily for sixteen hundred years at evening prayers and beside deathbeds. It proclaims liberation—from fear of death, anxiety about the future, regret about the past, and estrangement between people. In Christ, Simeon is free to die in peace with hope for the future. Christmas illumines Isaiah's ancient promise of Israel's glory as a revelation to all nations and the present promise of future peace on earth, goodwill among all.

Simeon also sees judgment brought in Christ. Christ is "destined" or "set" (ASV), like a building stone, on which everyone's life will rise or fall. One either builds on the universal truth seen in the face of Christ or is tripped up by contradicting it. Even Mary will find these opposing choices cutting into her own soul as she faces God revealed in the sign of the cross. Christmas has come and gone, but the world will never be the same again.

SUGGESTION FOR MEDITATION: **Reflect on the events of the last twenty-four hours with the prayer, "My eyes have seen your salvation."**

If we desire to live in the light of Christmas, we must become poor. Anna the prophet says so without words. Anna is one of the *anawim*, a social class and a voluntary spirituality named after the Hebrew translated "oppressed," "lowly," or "poor." Anna is old, widowed, living on the Temple grounds. She is the social equivalent of today's voiceless homeless. Her vulnerability fires her prophetic vision, for she and "all the others looking for redemption" can look only to God for help.

Is this bond of poverty and piety only metaphorical, or do wealth and poverty truly shape the soul? Even sincere Christians materially blessed usually reverse or sever the connection between poverty and spiritual humility. We connect low wages or no wages with low morals. (Which side do you call the "bad side" of your town?) We believe wealth and humble yearning for Christ are independent of each other. (Is a wealthy suburban congregation or an impoverished inner-city church more likely to yearn for Jesus to return and replace the present inequitable economic system?)

Material poverty does not equal spiritual blessing, but the light of Christmas always shines brightest on the poor. Not all the poor are humble, but all humble Christians choose voluntarily to have less stuff than they would otherwise. Christmas isn't about a poor man God made rich, but a rich God choosing to become poor for the Annas of this world. Not by accident was Jesus born in a stable or killed by the rich and powerful.

Widows received a place in the New Testament church. (See 1 Timothy 5:13-17.) Later, Emperor Julian complained Christians took care of pagan poor as well as their own. This Christmas, the marginalized, vulnerable, and voiceless remain in our precincts. For our souls' sakes, may we see and serve Jesus among them.

**SUGGESTION FOR REFLECTION: Who are the *anawim* near you? How many do you know by name?**

# This Little Light of Mine

*December 29–31, 2008 • Janet Wolf* [‡]

## MONDAY, DECEMBER 29 • Read Psalms 8; 72:1-7, 10-14

We are in between times this week, moving from Christmas into Epiphany, from 2008 into 2009. Our scripture passages press us to feel the pull, exploring the movement between times and texts as we journey into the manifestation of God's glory.

Psalm 8 sings, "O Lord, our Lord, how wonderful, awesome, is your name in all the earth! Who are we that you have given us dominion and marked us with you glory?" (AP)

Psalm 72 defines this dominion: to "judge . . . your poor with justice" [note the poor belong to God]; to defend the cause of the poor, give deliverance, crush all oppression; redeem the poor from violence and oppression, for "precious is their blood in his sight."

God requires that the poor, the oppressed, all victims of violence and brutality, be precious in our sight, minds, hearts, *and* public policies. We are to challenge and change the systems of oppression at the same time we are binding up the injured and washing wounds in the waters of grace. It is a haunting requirement in a world in which two-thirds of the world's population lives in poverty and so many communities struggle daily with violence and hostility.

SUGGESTION FOR PRAYER: **What does it mean to exercise dominion in ways that are marked by God's justice and tenderness? Whose blood is precious in our sight?**

---

[‡]Community organizer, college professor, and elder in the Tennessee Annual Conference; living in Nashville, Tennessee.

What does it mean to look for God's glory in this messy, troubled, and troubling world? "Arise, shine; for your light has come, and the glory of the LORD has risen upon you."

Bernice Johnson Reagan tells a story about the 1960s civil rights movement. Folks were gathered inside a church, singing, praying, testifying—getting ready to go out and face the dogs and hoses, the hostile crowds and escalating violence. Someone suggested that the group sing one more song before walking out the door into all that awaited. There was a momentary debate over which song, and then they settled on "This Little Light of Mine." Wanting to emphasize the importance of unity, of collective witness, one person proposed that they sing "this little light of ours." Murmurs of assent moved through the room until an older woman rose and declared: no, we need to sing "this little light of mine" because it's only when each of you decides that you will let your light shine, that I begin to know I can let God's light shine through me.

The woman went on to say, "We gonna shine so bright, they'll have to put on shades just to walk by!"

We are called to be, individually and collectively, a source of God's light in the world, so that all might see and give God glory. May it be so.

**SUGGESTION FOR MEDITATION: Where do we see and how might we be sources of God's light in the world?**

This judgment of nations, not simply individuals, continues to define God's requirements for dominion, the plumbline of justice and compassion. It is both challenge and comfort, a reminder of God's priorities and an invitation to be partners with God in *tikkun olam*, repairing the world.

In the Wesleyan tradition, watchnight is the renewal of our covenant with God, a remembering of all that has been and all that is yet to be. In the Black church tradition, one specific moment defines the night.

On December 31, 1862, lines formed outside many churches as people gathered to pray through the ending of the old age and the welcoming of the new. They were waiting, hoping, yearning for confirmation that the Emancipation Proclamation had been signed, that slavery had officially been ended, that freedom was more than a dream. They gathered in churches across the countryside, sinking into the spirituals that had brought them this far on the journey, wrapping themselves in the prayers of the elders, the yearning of the mothers of the church, the impossible hopes of the young. And they remembered the God who had sustained, nurtured, defended, embraced, propped up on every leaning side. Fires were lit, candles burned, as congregations waited.

Finally the word came. Liberation would be a long journey, but the Emancipation Proclamation had been signed.

**SUGGESTION FOR MEDITATION: For what do we wait? How might God's glory be spilling into this new year? What liberating word has God sent among us?**

# The Revised Common Lectionary[‡] for 2008
## Year A – Advent / Christmas Year B
### *(Disciplines Edition)*

**January 1–6**
**New Year's Day**
Ecclesiastes 3:1-13
Psalm 8
Revelation 21:1-6a
Matthew 25:31-46

**EPIPHANY, January 6**
Isaiah 60:1-6
Psalm 72:1-7, 10-14
Ephesians 3:1-12
Matthew 2:1-12

**January 7–13**
**BAPTISM OF THE LORD**
Isaiah 42:1-9
Psalm 29
Acts 10:34-43
Matthew 3:13-17

**January 14–20**
Isaiah 49:1-7
Psalm 40:1-11
1 Corinthians 1:1-9
John 1:29-42

**January 21–27**
Isaiah 9:1-4
Psalm 27:1, 4-9
1 Corinthians 1:10-18
Matthew 4:12-23

**January 28–February 3**
**THE TRANSFIGURATION**
Exodus 24:12-18
Psalm 99
2 Peter 1:16-21
Matthew 17:1-9

**February 6**
**ASH WEDNESDAY**
Joel 2:1-2, 12-17
Psalm 51:1-17
2 Corinthians 5:20b–6:10
Matthew 6:1-6, 16-21

**February 4–10**
**FIRST SUNDAY IN LENT**
Genesis 2:15-17; 3:1-7
Psalm 32
Romans 5:12-19
Matthew 4:1-11

**February 11–17**
**SECOND SUNDAY IN LENT**
Genesis 12:1-4a
Psalm 121
Romans 4:1-5, 13-17
John 3:1-17

**February 18–24**
**THIRD SUNDAY IN LENT**
Exodus 17:1-7
Psalm 95
Romans 5:1-11
John 4:5-42

**February 25–March 2**
**FOURTH SUNDAY IN LENT**
1 Samuel 16:1-13
Psalm 23
Ephesians 5:8-14
John 9:1-41

**March 3–9**
**FIFTH SUNDAY IN LENT**
Ezekiel 37:1-14
Psalm 130
Romans 8:6-11
John 11:1-45

## March 10–16
### PASSION/PALM SUNDAY

*Liturgy of the Palms*
Matthew 21:1-11
Psalm 118:1-2, 19-29

*Liturgy of the Passion*
Isaiah 50:4-9*a*
Psalm 31:9-16
Philippians 2:5-11
Matthew 26:14–27:66
   (*or* Matthew 27:11-54)

## March 17–23
### HOLY WEEK

#### Monday, March 17
Isaiah 42:1-9
Psalm 36:5-11
Hebrews 9:11-15
John 12:1-11

#### Tuesday, March 18
Isaiah 49:1-7
Psalm 71:1-14
1 Corinthians 1:18-31
John 12:20-36

#### Wednesday, March 19
Isaiah 50:4-9*a*
Psalm 70
Hebrews 12:1-3
John 13:21-32

#### Maundy Thursday, March 20
Exodus 12:1-14
Psalm 116:1-4, 12-19
1 Corinthians 11:23-26
John 13:1-17, 31*b*-35

#### Good Friday, March 21
Isaiah 52:13–53:12
Psalm 22
Hebrews 10:16-25
John 18:1–19:42

#### Easter Vigil, March 22
Exodus 14:10-31
Psalm 136:1-9, 23-26
Isaiah 55:1-11
Romans 6:3-11
Matthew 28:1-10

### March 23
#### EASTER DAY
Psalm 118:1-2, 14-24
Acts 10:34-43
Colossians 3:1-4
John 20:1-18
   (*or* Matthew 28:1-10)

### March 24–30
Acts 2:14*a*, 22-32
Psalm 16
1 Peter 1:3-9
John 20:19-31

### March 31–April 6
Acts 2:14*a*, 36-41
Psalm 116:1-4, 12-19
1 Peter 1:17-23
Luke 24:13-35

### April 7–13
Acts 2:42-47
Psalm 23
1 Peter 2:19-25
John 10:1-10

### April 14–20
Acts 7:55-60
Psalm 31:1-5, 15-16
1 Peter 2:2-10
John 14:1-14

### April 21–27
Acts 17:22-31
Psalm 66:8-20
1 Peter 3:13-22
John 14:15-21

#### Ascension Day—May 1
*(These readings may be used for Sunday, May 4.)*
Acts 1:1-11
Psalm 47 (*or* Psalm 93)
Ephesians 1:15-23
Luke 24:44-53

**April 28–May 4**
Acts 1:6-14
Psalm 68:1-10, 32-35
1 Peter 4:12-14; 5:6-11
John 17:1-11

**May 5–11**
PENTECOST
Psalm 104:24-34, 35b
Acts 2:1-21
1 Corinthians 12:3b-13
John 7:37–39

**May 12–18**
TRINITY SUNDAY
Genesis 1:1–2:4a
Psalm 8
2 Corinthians 13:11-13
Matthew 28:16-20

**May 19–25**
Isaiah 49:8-16a
Psalm 131 or
1 Corinthians 4:1-5
Matthew 6:24-34

**May 26–June 1**
Genesis 6:11-22; 7:24;
 8:14-19
Psalm 46
Romans 1:16-17; 3:22b-31
Matthew 7:21-29

**June 2–8**
Genesis 12:1-9
Psalm 33:1-12
Romans 4:13-25
Matthew 9:9-13, 18-26

**June 9–15**
Genesis 18:1-15; (21:1-7)
Psalm 116:1-2, 12-19
Romans 5:1-8
Matthew 9:35–10:23

**June 16–22**
Genesis 21:8-21
Psalm 86:1-10, 16-17 (or Psalm 17)
Romans 6:1b-11
Matthew 10:24-39

**June 23–29**
Genesis 22:1-14
Psalm 13
Romans 6:12-23
Matthew 10:40-42

**June 30–July 6**
Genesis 24:34-38, 42-49,
 58-67
Psalm 45:10-17 (or Psalm 72)
Romans 7:15-25a
Matthew 11:16-19, 25-30

**July 7–13**
Genesis 25:19-34
Psalm 119:105-112 (or Psalm 25)
Romans 8:1-11
Matthew 13:1-9, 18-23

**July 14–20**
Genesis 28:10-19a
Psalm 139:1-12, 23-24
Romans 8:12-25
Matthew 13:24-30, 36-43

**July 21–27**
Genesis 29:15-28
Psalm 105:1-11, 45b
Romans 8:26-39
Matthew 13:31-33, 44-52

**July 28–August 3**
Genesis 32:22-31
Psalm 17:1-7, 15
Romans 9:1-5
Matthew 14:13-21

**August 4–10**
Genesis 37:1-4, 12-28
Psalm 105:1-6, 16-22, 45b
Romans 10:5-15
Matthew 14:22-33

**August 11–17**
Genesis 45:1-15
Psalm 133
Romans 11:1-2a, 29-32
Matthew 15:10-28

**August 18–24**
Exodus 1:8–2:10
Psalm 124
Romans 12:1-8
Matthew 16:13-20

**August 25–31**
Exodus 3:1-15
Psalm 105:1-6, 23–26, 45c
Romans 12:9-21
Matthew 16:21-28

**September 1–7**
Exodus 12:1-14
Psalm 149 (or Psalm 148)
Romans 13:8-14
Matthew 18:15-20

**September 8–14**
Exodus 14:19-31
Psalm 114 (or Exodus
   15:1b-11, 20-21)
Romans 14:1-12
Matthew 18:21-35

**September 15–21**
Exodus 16:2-15
Psalm 105:1-6, 37–45 (or Psalm 78)
Philippians 1:21-30
Matthew 20:1-16

**September 22–28**
Exodus 17:1-7
Psalm 78:1-4, 12-16
Philippians 2:1-13
Matthew 21:23-32

**September 29–October 5**
Exodus 20:1-4, 7-9, 12-20
Psalm 19
Philippians 3:4b-14
Matthew 21:33-46

**October 6–12**
Exodus 32:1-14
Psalm 106:1-6, 19-23
Philippians 4:1-9
Matthew 22:1-14

**October 13–19**
Exodus 33:12-23

Psalm 99
1 Thessalonians 1:1-10
Matthew 22:15-22

> **Thanksgiving Day
> (Canada)—October 13**
> Deuteronomy 8:7-18
> Psalm 65
> 2 Corinthians 9:6-15
> Luke 17:11-19

**October 20–26**
Deuteronomy 34:1-12
Psalm 90:1-6, 13-17
1 Thessalonians 2:1-8
Matthew 22:34-46

> **All Saints Day—
> November 1**
> *(Use for Sunday, November 2.)*
> Revelation 7:9-17
> Psalm 34:1-10, 22
> 1 John 3:1-3
> Matthew 5:1-12

**October 27–November 2**
*(Use All Saints Day lections above.)*

**November 3–9**
Joshua 24:1-3a, 14-25
Psalm 78:1-7
1 Thessalonians 4:13-18
Matthew 25:1-13

**November 10–16**
Judges 4:1-7
Psalm 123 (or Psalm 76)
1 Thessalonians 5:1-11
Matthew 25:14-30

**November 17–23**
REIGN OF CHRIST SUNDAY
Ezekiel 34:11-16, 20-24
Psalm 100
Ephesians 1:15-23
Matthew 25:31-46

## November 24–30
**FIRST SUNDAY OF ADVENT**
Isaiah 64:1-9
Psalm 80:1-7, 17-19
1 Corinthians 1:3-9
Mark 13:24-37

### Thanksgiving Day (USA)— November 27
Deuteronomy 8:7-18
Psalm 65
2 Corinthians 9:6-15
Luke 17:11-19

## December 1–7
**SECOND SUNDAY OF ADVENT**
Isaiah 40:1-11
Psalm 85:1-2, 8-13
2 Peter 3:8-15a
Mark 1:1-8

## December 8–14
**THIRD SUNDAY OF ADVENT**
Isaiah 61:1-4, 8-11
Psalm 126
1 Thessalonians 5:16-24
John 1:6-8, 19-28

## December 15–21
**FOURTH SUNDAY OF ADVENT**
2 Samuel 7:1-11, 16
Psalm 89:1-4, 19-26
Romans 16:25-27
Luke 1:26-38

## December 24
### CHRISTMAS EVE
Isaiah 9:2-7
Psalm 96
Titus 2:11-14
Luke 2:1-20

### December 25
#### Christmas Day
Isaiah 52:7-10
Psalm 98
Hebrews 1:1-12
John 1:1-14

## December 22–28
**FIRST SUNDAY AFTER CHRISTMAS DAY**
Isaiah 61:10–62:3
Psalm 148
Galatians 4:4-7
Luke 2:22-40

## December 29–January 4

### New Year's Day, January 1
Ecclesiastes 3:1-13
Psalm 8
Revelation 21:1-6a
Matthew 25:31-46

### EPIPHANY, January 6
*(or use for January 4)*
Isaiah 60:1-6
Psalm 72:1-7, 10-14
Ephesians 3:1-12
Matthew 2:1-12